SOFTWARE METRICS FOR PRODUCT ASSESSMENT

THE McGRAW-HILL INTERNATIONAL
SOFTWARE QUALITY ASSURANCE SERIES

Consulting Editor

Professor D. Ince
The Open University

Other titles in this series

Practical Implementation of Software Metrics	Goodman
Software Testing	Roper
Software Quality Assurance and its Implementation	Ince

Related titles on software engineering are published in an accompanying series: *The International Software Engineering Series*, also edited by Professor Darrel Ince.

SOFTWARE METRICS FOR PRODUCT ASSESSMENT

Richard Bache
Infometrix Software

Gualtiero Bazzana
Etnoteam

Mcgraw-HILL BOOK COMPANY

London · New York · St Louis · San Francisco · Auckland · Bogotá · Caracas
Lisbon · Madrid · Mexico · Milan · Montreal · New Delhi · Panama · Paris
San Juan · São Paulo · Singapore · Sydney · Tokyo · Toronto

Published by
McGRAW-HILL Book Company Europe
SHOPPENHANGERS ROAD · MAIDENHEAD · BERKSHIRE · SL6 2QL · ENGLAND
TELEPHONE 0628 23432
FAX 0628 770224

British Library Cataloguing in Publication Data

Bache, Richard
  Software Metrics for Product Assessment.
  – (McGraw-Hill International Software
  Quality Assurance Series)
  I. Title II. Bazzana, Gualtiero
  III. Series
  005.1

  ISBN 0-07-707923-X

Library of Congress Cataloging-in-Publication Data

Bache, Richard
  Software metrics for product assessment/Richard Bache, Gualtiero
  Bazzana.
    p. cm. — (International software quality assurance series)
  Includes bibliographical references and index.
  ISBN 0-07-707923-X
  1. Computer software — quality control. 2. Computer software — Testing.
  I. Bazzana, Gualtiero. II. Title. III. Series.
  QA76.76.Q35B33 1993   93-29406
  005.1'4–dc20   CIP

1234 CUP 97654

Typeset by TecSet Ltd, Wallington, Surrey
and printed and bound in Great Britain at the University Press, Cambridge

To our parents and to Cathy, Stephanie,
Elisa and Federico

CONTENTS

Foreword   xi
Acknowledgements   xiii
List of trademarks   xv
Quality Assurance Forum   xvii

1 Introduction   1
  1.1 Reasons for assessing software   1
  1.2 What is software quality?   3
  1.3 Problems of data collection   4
  1.4 The SCOPE project   7
  1.5 Structure of the book   9
       Summary   10

2 Approaches to Software Assessment   11
  2.1 Assessment, evaluation and certification   11
  2.2 Metrics collection in context   12
  2.3 The SCOPE approach   13
  2.4 General process certification   15
  2.5 Specific process assessment   16
  2.6 Specific product assessment   17
  2.7 Specific characteristic assessment   18
  2.8 Benchmarking   21
  2.9 Black-box product assessment   22
  2.10 Management by metrics   24
       Summary   26

3 A Quality Model for General Product Assessment   27
3.1 The ISO 9126 model   27
3.2 Software quality characteristics   29
3.3 The evaluation process model   33
3.4 Usage of the 9126 model   34
     Summary   35

4 Underlying Principles of Measurement   36
4.1 Consistent metrics collection   36
4.2 Motivation for a framework   37
4.3 Product and process models   39
4.4 Measurement theory   45
4.5 Assessment and prediction   50
     Summary   53

5 Assessment Techniques   54
5.1 Classifying the assessment techniques   54
5.2 Anomaly checking   60
5.3 Textual measurement   63
5.4 Structural analysis   66
5.5 Test cross-referencing   71
5.6 Black-box testing   75
5.7 Failure data collection   76
5.8 Test coverage   79
5.9 Inspection via checklists   82
5.10 Modelling   85
5.11 Mixing techniques   86
5.12 Process data collection   86
     Summary   87

6 Metrics Analysis   88
6.1 Using statistics for product assessment   89
6.2 Problems with metrics data   90
6.3 Aggregating metrics   94
6.4 The common pool of data   96
6.5 Outlier analysis   97
6.6 Establishing thresholds and norms   99
6.7 Comparison across projects   100
6.8 Relations between metrics   102
6.9 Reliability estimation   105
6.10 Limits to reliability prediction   108
     Summary   111

7 Tools for Data Collection   **112**
7.1 Requirements for data collection tools   112
7.2 Session data collection systems   114
7.3 Checklist manager   121
7.4 A filter for lint   123
7.5 Extensions to program analysers   129
7.6 Running analysers in batch mode   133
Summary   134

8 A Metrics Database   **135**
8.1 Why a database?   136
8.2 Requirements for the database system   137
8.3 Architecture of the database system   138
8.4 The database proper   139
8.5 Data transfer   142
8.6 Naming conventions   145
8.7 Data standardization   147
Summary   148

9 Case-Study Experiences   **149**
9.1 Overview of the case studies   149
9.2 Static analysis of case studies   150
9.3 Reproducibility of checklists   160
9.4 Collection and analysis of failure data   166
9.5 Test coverage and structure   171
9.6 Results from the case studies   173
9.7 Software product assessment in the industrial domain   175
Summary   182

10 A Workbench for Software Assessment   **183**
10.1 Requirements for an assessor's workbench   183
10.2 Functions of an assessor's workbench   184
10.3 Design of an assessor's workbench   186
10.4 Database technology   191
10.5 Experiences in the derivation of the assessment   192
10.6 Examples based on state-of-the-art technology   194
Summary   200

11 Management Issues   **201**
11.1 Managing software assessment   201
11.2 Cost of the evaluation procedure   202
11.3 Needs and expectations of product assessment and certification   207

11.4 The politics of data collection   214
11.5 From assessment to certification   216
      Summary   230

12 Conclusions   **231**
12.1 Meeting our objectives   231
12.2 What a metrics scheme should look like   233
12.3 How to proceed from here   234
12.4 Product and process   236
12.5 Future directions   236

Glossary   **238**
Bibliography   **241**
Index   **248**

FOREWORD

It is only in recent years that there has been an awareness of the important role of measurement in software engineering. Prior to this everybody knew that there was a problem with poor software quality and productivity, but few people bothered to quantify the situation. Most people believed in at least some of the revolutionary new methods of software development, but few bothered to quantify their efficacy. It is a pleasure to be able to recommend this book as one of the small, but growing set of texts explicitly devoted to the problem of quantitative assessment.

The book has evolved out of the important CEC-funded project SCOPE which is concerned with software assessment for certification. Prior to the project's start in 1989, existing software certification procedures were based entirely on qualitative assessments of the software development *processes*. This situation stemmed from a (still widely held) belief that if we could get these processes under proper control then high-quality software would inevitably result. Although intuitively appealing this viewpoint is not as yet substantiated by hard empirical evidence. Moreover we are nowhere near to understanding just which development processes are most likely to assure product quality. For a user seeking a certified *product*, assurances about the way the product was developed fall far short of the normal expectations of certification. As a reaction against such limited notions of software assessment, the SCOPE project attempted to define a certification procedure that was based on quantitative assessment of the product, thereby providing users with information of direct relevance to the 'certified' product which they might purchase. Think of the analogy of buying a car. Just knowing that the manufacturers applied the best development techniques would not convince you of its fitness for its purpose; you would be much keener to know something about its reliability record, its fuel efficiency, and its dimensions. These are the kinds of basic measurable product attributes which enable you to make your purchase decision.

Thus this book provides a comprehensive, yet practical, approach to product-based assessment. The authors speak from genuine experience of software measurement programmes. The techniques which they describe are not just theory; they have been tried and tested in real projects. The emphasis on automated data-collection methods reflects this experience. Anybody embarking on any kind of software measurement programme would be well advised to read this book so that they can learn from the authors' experience and avoid the many pitfalls that the authors have already discovered. The approach to measurement is admirably rigorous and is tied to a consistent data-collection strategy. The book is written in a simple, direct style which makes it accessible to any software engineer. It could prove to be an important milestone in the quest to make software a true 'engineering' discipline.

Norman Fenton, Centre for Software Reliability

ACKNOWLEDGEMENTS

We would firstly like to thank AEA Technology, City University, Etnoteam and Institut für Sicherheitstechnologie for sponsoring the writing of the book and Strathclyde University for providing computing facilities.

We would like to thank Uwe Anders, Ole Andersen, Jørgen Boegh, Martin Brewer, Riccardo Brigliadori, Norman Fenton, Richard Flor, Hans Kyster, Martin Neil, Daniela Pina and Paolo Salvaneschi who contributed to the book (their contributions are acknowledged in the text).

We would also like to thank all those who were part of or associated with the SCOPE project, in particular Graham Adams, Giovanna Agostoni, Adriana Bicego, Alexander Bors, Sarah Brocklehurst, Ndombe Cacutalua, Paola Caliman, Josep Dexeus, Paul Doyle, Stephane Geyres, Alfredo Guida, Hans Ludwig Hausen, Robin Hunter, Timo Jokela, Elmar Kaiser, Manfred Kersken, Kenneth Kirkwood, Roberto Lancellotti, Bev Littlewood, Ian Lloyd, Kenny MacDonald, Marco Maiocchi, Peter Mellor, Horst Miedl, Tony Moynihan, Bernard de Neumann, T. Paul Park, Roberto Pollilo, Andrew Rae, Philippe Robert, Giovambattista Rumi, Françoise Seigneur, Robert Troy, Dieter Welzel, Brian Wichmann, Alan Wingrove and Giannino Zontini. We would also like to thank those who drove the setting up of the certification scheme in Italy: Giancarlo Zappa and Angelo Belloni. We also thank Giuseppe Ariano, Laura Gaida and Francessca Vanzetta for helping with the illustrations.

The writing of the book arose out of the ESPRIT II project SCOPE (P2151). We are therefore indebted to the Commission of the European Communities—Directorate-General XIII and in particular the project officers, David Callahan and Brice Lepape. We acknowledge also the constructive comments from the reviewers: Antonio Cicu (Bull, Italy),

Folkert Rienstra (Kema, The Netherlands) and Kees Stuurman (University of Amsterdam).

The SCOPE consortium was composed of: AEA Technology, Cabinet Alain Bensoussan, Commissariat de l'Energie Atomique, City University, Dublin City University, ElektronikCentralen, Etnoteam, Glasgow Polytechnic, GMD, GRS, ICT, Strathclyde University, Veridatas, Verilog (prime contractor), VTT and TüV Bayern.

Please note that the opinions expressed in this book are those of the authors and not necessarily those of all the SCOPE partners.

Part of Chapter 5 was taken from 'Metrics Tools for Measuring Quality' by Richard Bache and Kenneth Kirkwood delivered at the Third Software Quality Workshop, 5–6 July 1993, Napier University, Edinburgh.

Finally Gualtiero would like to thank his wife, Elisa, for being so patient while he was spending so much of his free time on the book.

LIST OF TRADEMARKS

Ada	is a trademark of US Department of Defense
Aegis	is a trademark of Hewlett-Packard Company
Apollo	is a trademark of Hewlett-Packard Company
dBase	is a trademark of Ashton-Tate
DYNIX	is a trademark of Sequent Computer Systems
Logiscope	is a trademark of Verilog
HP-UX	is a trademark of Hewlett-Packard Company
MALPAS	is a trademark of Rex, Thompson and Partners Software
Metropol	is a trademark of Control et Prevention
NUOVO TEFAX	is a trademark of Etnoteam
OCCAM II	is a trademark of Inmos
Prometrix	is a trademark of Infometrix Software
RULER	is a trademark of Phimac
SPADE	is a trademark of Program Validation
SUNOS	is a trademark of Sun Microsystems
Sunview	is a trademark of Sun Microsystems
TEFAX	is a trademark of Etnoteam
Testbed	is a trademark of Liverpool Data Research Associates
Unix	is a trademark of AT&T Bell Laboratories
VAX	is a trademark of Digital Equipment Corporation
VMS	is a trademark of Digital Corporation

QUALITY ASSURANCE FORUM

The Quality Assurance Forum is pleased to publish jointly with McGraw-Hill this book which covers topics pertinent to software quality assurance.
The aim of the organization is 'to help the member organizations improve the quality of their computer services through the exchange of information between members and with other organizations with similar interests'.
The QA Forum has over 200 members, including organizations from all sectors of industry and commerce, as well as local and national government. While these organizations are predominantly based in the UK, this includes a growing number from other countries in Europe.
This series of books aims to provide an opportunity for authors to publish works which are both practical and state-of-the-art. In this way QA Forum members and other organizations will benefit from the exchange of information and the development of new ideas which will further the cause of quality in Information Technology.
The QA Forum publishes these books with the aim of stimulating discussion in the software community so that the industry as a whole will move forward to improved products and services. It is proud to be associated with the series while not endorsing every single point of view in every book.
If you would like to know more about the QA Forum, please contact:

Quality Assurance Forum
17 St Catherine's Rd
Ruislip
Middlesex HA4 7RX
UK
Tel: +44 (0) 895 635222
Fax: +44 (0) 895 679178

1

INTRODUCTION

1.1 REASONS FOR ASSESSING SOFTWARE

Computer systems have increasing importance throughout society. We are all reliant on them more than ever and there is good reason to believe that our dependence will grow. If these systems do not behave in the way that we expect, then it will cost time and money. In a safety-critical domain, the cost can be much higher, resulting in serious injury, death and damage to property. The quality of these systems should therefore be of concern to everyone. In any computer system the software (programs and their documentation) is a major part. The time and money used to develop the software is often greater than for the hardware component. So the quality of the software is itself a matter of growing importance.

There are innumerable cases of software failing to perform as expected, of crashing unexpectedly, or of just being difficult to use. You may have your own personal experiences. These are examples of the most obvious manifestations of poor quality. Less dramatic, but still important, is where software has been difficult to alter because it was badly constructed. It is not difficult to imagine the money that would be wasted if a large software system were abandoned and replaced because it could not easily be changed.

All these examples are symptoms of poor software quality. We define our terms later, but it should be clear to anyone who works with computer systems that poor software quality is an identifiable problem. Not surprisingly, software engineers over the last 25 years have proposed numerous methods which attempt to improve the quality of software. There have been methods of specification and design, new languages, CASE (computer-aided software engineering) tools, validated compilers, testing strategies, development models, management techniques and so on. Any software developer can choose one or a combination of these methods, but there is no guarantee that the necessary level of quality needed for a given application will be met. The inventors and vendors of the various methods with their associated tools, books and training courses will of course claim that quality will be improved if their particular methods are applied. Although we would not want to question their sincerity, this does not give us a clear indication as to whether the quality is 'high enough'. We have no way of being sure that the right level of quality has been attained, without some independent evaluation.

A Europe-wide survey on the needs and demands for software assessment and certification has clearly shown the following perceptions by software producers and users:

- Software process certification is not enough to guarantee the quality of software products but product certification is also necessary.
- Customers are looking for better quality of software products up to the point that they are willing to pay up to 20 per cent more in order to have it.
- The assessment of a software product is of paramount importance in making decisions about its evolution strategy.

We propose in this book a practical method of assessing software quality based on the measurement of product quality attributes. Such assessment is intended for certification by a recognized independent body. This was the motivation for developing the ideas and methods proposed here. Nevertheless all the methods proposed are relevant for many forms of software quality assurance (QA). This includes QA carried out by the software developers themselves or by a third party as independent verification and validation.

There are already numerous product-based assessment techniques in existence. Many of these, such as black-box testing techniques and static analysis, are used in software development at the present time. But such techniques are often seen as free-standing; a particular technique such as inspection or test coverage is used at a particular point in the life cycle. They are not seen as part of a general scheme for assessing the software quality as a whole. We propose here a way of integrating the diverse techniques into a coherent scheme so that information in the form of metrics can be collected from the products and used to give an assessment of their quality. To do this we have first to solve a number of technical problems.

The primary purpose of the work described in this book is to produce a means of assessing software for certification. The techniques can clearly be used for internal QA as well and these uses would in themselves justify the work. But there are other applications. Software metrics may be collected for a variety of purposes, of which software certification is just one. Metrics may be used for cost estimation, for management, or for the evaluation of different development processes. The ideas proposed here are also applicable to researchers in the software engineering field who wish to determine the effectiveness of a proposed new technique, language, etc. Thus many of the ideas proposed here have applications well beyond software certification.

1.2   WHAT IS SOFTWARE QUALITY?

Until now we have been vague about what we mean by software quality. We certainly do not need a precise definition to recognize that there is a quality problem in the first place. Nevertheless if we wish to find methods of assessing the software then it is necessary to know what criteria we are assessing it against.

ISO 9000 (also known as BS 5750)[35] provides the definition of quality as 'the totality of features and characteristics of a product or service that bear on its ability to satisfy stated or implied need'.

The two key parts of this definition are 'totality of features' and 'stated or implied need'. The totality of features means that we can split the notion of quality into a number of *characteristics*. These are also known as *quality factors, capabilities* or just *ilities* because they are described by words such as reliability, maintainability and testability. This idea of breaking down the global notion of quality into quality factors was first proposed by McCall *et al.*[119] There have been many attempts to decompose quality into particular characteristics, and then to break these characteristics down further into named metrics. We can cite the work of Arthur,[8,9] Boehm *et al.*,[31] Bowen *et al.*,[33] Deutsch and Willis,[57] Forse,[68] Gillies,[70] Grady and Caswell[71] and von Maryhauser.[117] We could have chosen any one of these quality models, which are in many respects very similar to one another and differ mainly in terminology. However, we have decided to adopt the characteristics which have been standardized in the ISO 9126 standard.[89] This standard has drawn on the various quality models to produce a small set of six consistent characteristics which give coverage of the main concepts of interest. In any case, most of the techniques described for data collection, storage and analysis are independent of the quality model chosen. A certification body or QA department might choose a different quality model, but a large part of the work described here would still be relevant.

The term 'implied need' in the definition of quality means that we cannot assume a product's own specification is absolutely complete and correct.*

---

* Certification should be carried out according to an assessment specification which is prepared as the first stage in certifying a product.

Non-functional features such as maintainability are rarely specified, yet these are often of great importance to the customer. Also a product specification may contain omissions or errors. It may thus describe a system quite at variance with what the customer wants or needs. For example, an omission in the specification might mean that the software can cause a dangerous state. A computer-controlled washing machine may go into a hazardous state. For example, it might overflow under a set of unthought-of yet feasible circumstances. Such a product would be considered by most to be of inadequate quality although at the same time it conforms to its specification.

When we discuss the quality of the software, we do not mean only the source code even though many of the assessment techniques are geared to assessing the code. This emphasis is due, in no small part, to the fact that we do not yet have a full battery of techniques to assess products earlier in the life cycle. For the purposes of assessment we will consider methods of assessing products such as specifications and designs. In the early days of programming (before software engineering really began) the software was often little more than the code. We accept that this is no longer the case, but some researchers have taken the opposite extreme position. They take the view that coding is an insignificant part of the software development: once the specification and designs are right the coding is a trivial activity. This is not a view supported here. Maintenance, which is often the largest part of life-cycle cost, is strongly influenced by the quality of the code. There are still a number of software products around that consist entirely of code, other documentation having become hopelessly out of date or not having been produced in the first place.

1.3 PROBLEMS OF DATA COLLECTION

Any assessment or certification based on product assessment will require that the metrics are actually collected. Without collection of data there can clearly be no assessment; this is a point explicitly made by the EN 45000 standards.[38] The best organizational framework and the highest quality models in the world would be absolutely useless without a means of obtaining the appropriate metrics data. We would maintain that it is these technical problems that have until now been the main obstacle to using software metrics for assessment or indeed other purposes.

The data collected during assessment needs to be stored, since for any kind of formal assessment or certification previous results will need to be archived. Furthermore, historic data is useful for establishing norms, determining typical values of metrics and setting pass/fail criteria. Finally there need to be methods of analysing the data. The quantity of data from even a fairly small software product can run into many pages of numbers.

Any assessment scheme requires methods of extracting the relevant information from this mass of data. The activities of collecting, storing and analysing the data will be referred to as a *metrics scheme*. It is an essential part of any certification scheme based on product assessment. As we stated earlier, a metrics scheme may also be used for quite different purposes such as methods evaluation or cost management. The metrics collected may be different but many of the principles and techniques will be very similar.

Several metrics schemes have been defined, implemented and used in the past for any number of purposes such as management, QA, or the validation of some proposed model of software. Numerous research projects such as REQUEST and SWDL have all set up such metrics schemes with various degrees of success. Many larger companies have their own metrics schemes used to assess their own products and processes. One of the first and best-publicized examples is the experience described in *Hewlett-Packard: Establishing a Company-Wide Program*[71] where the company established a programme to collect metrics and store them at a central site with a view to improving productivity. This is really quite different from the kind of scheme we need for assessment. Our scheme will need to collect many more metrics and obtain a much greater quantity of data.

In any subject area there are two levels of ignorance: first, not knowing something and, second, not knowing you do not know it. It is perhaps because people are often at this second level that they have believed that data collection was a simple and trivial matter. Many metrics projects have been beset by specific problems. The purpose of this book is to show how such problems have been solved. First, what are the problems?

1. Data collection often starts without a clear idea of the data requirements and how the data will be analysed. Projects often try to 'collect everything'. This leads to a large and complex mass of data. As time passes it is realized that not everything was collected at all, and the metrics of real use have been omitted or not collected in a proper way. Basically, if you do not have a clear purpose for the data in mind, then do not bother collecting it.
2. The definitions of the metrics are often not clear. This means that different sites will collect the metrics in inconsistent ways. If managers at different sites are given any scope to change definitions, human nature dictates that they will try and put their own personal stamp on them. The data will thus not be comparable. This is the classic problem of trying to compare apples with pears.
3. Metrics projects will often not survey the literature, or else reject existing work on spurious grounds, wanting something bigger and better than that which is obtainable. This is the classic NIH (not invented here) syndrome. They often then invent their own metrics.

These may be subjective, and not form part of any validated theory. One project collected 'metrics' on the design of the office where the programmers worked. It is difficult to understand how this would be useful.

4. A consequence from point 3 is that metrics with no tools support may be applied. This leads to expensive and error-prone data collection.

5. Metrics projects collect only a very simple set of metrics at a very high level (e.g. lines of code over entire projects). In this case they are falling well short of the current state of the art since there are many better-defined metrics which capture particular attributes of interest.

6. Metrics are collected on paper forms. This will work if you are collecting only a small set of simple metrics but not for more extensive collection. Paper forms can be produced cheaply and rapidly. Nevertheless they are expensive in the long run. Forms have to be typed in to a computer eventually. Inevitably, transcription errors will be made, particularly when the work is done by clerical staff who have no understanding of software. It is worth noting that one metrics project still had 15 000 forms which had not yet been entered into its database two years after the project ended. They probably never will be entered.

7. Any reasonably sized metrics scheme will have to cope with diverse hardware and different versions of operating systems. This may lead to problems in transferring data between machines if it is in an electronic form.

8. Data is often collected at the wrong level for the purposes it is needed for. For example, if the number of faults is collected at the level of a whole project, the information cannot then be used to identify which parts of the product are more fault-prone.

9. Often the data is considered sensitive by the provider. The data has to be sanitized without being rendered useless.

10. The onus of data collection is often placed on the programmers. They may forget to record things or else resent the extra and apparently pointless task and not give it sufficient attention.

11. Programmers are often asked to make evaluations of their own or even a colleague's work. They will try and give the best possible impression so as not to betray their colleagues.

12. The Hawthorne effect should also be considered. The very fact that people are being monitored means that they subconsciously tend to work in a different way, in order to show their best.

13. If data is collected in different ways, by different people, or at different times, the data must be cross-referenced so that it can be related when it is stored.

14. Inappropriate statistical techniques are often applied to software metrics data without due consideration to the assumptions, aims and technical constraints.
15. The central repository for storing the data is often not appropriate for the complexity and quantity of data.

It may still seem to some that the problems mentioned above are obvious and that solutions are easy. Yet from our experience many metrics projects are still making the same mistakes. For example, before a case study began, one provider had already established a fault log. This is a good start but the provider believed it was a full metrics programme. Another provider wanted SCOPE to develop an (automatic) way of assessing the completeness and consistency of specifications written in informal English. They did not appeciate that there were deep theoretical and practical problems involved in this.

The most significant step to solving these problems is to use tools. Tools will reduce the effort of data collection and to a large extent enforce consistency of the metrics collected. But using tools, particularly when they have been produced outwith the metrics scheme, brings its own problems.

1.4   THE SCOPE PROJECT

This book draws on the experience of several research projects, but mainly of SCOPE. Many of the researchers of SCOPE had worked on previous projects and brought with them a wealth of experience. We have learnt from the successes and mistakes of these previous projects.

SCOPE (Software CertificatiOn Programme in Europe) was a four-year collaborative ESPRIT II project funded by the Commission of the European Community (CEC). There were twelve partners and four associated partners in a total of eight countries. Its purpose, according to the technical annexe of the project[144] was to 'define, experiment, and validate European software assessment procedures allowing certification'.

The SCOPE certification scheme is intended to cover all low- and medium-criticality products, since there are already schemes for certifying high-criticality systems such as nuclear reactors and civil aircraft. The latter were explicitly excluded from the scheme but the results of SCOPE are still of interest to these certification bodies who may wish to incorporate part or all of the SCOPE scheme into their own programmes. For further information the reader is referred elsewhere.[129,139]

The project was divided into a number of tasks which can be split into three main themes:

1. A top-down definition of an assessment and certification scheme with organizational details of certification and the various models to underpin it.
2. A bottom-up experimental application based on attempting to assess actual software products as case studies. These case studies were supported by the construction of a database and a set of tools to collect and transfer data to it.
3. A legal study to assess the legal basis for certification in the various countries of the EC.

The bottom-up experimentation was seen as a way of validating the certification scheme. However, the tools, database and case study tasks produced many interesting results in their own right, solving many of the problems that had until then plagued data collection. This book arose out of the SCOPE project and describes primarily these *indirect* results of the project that came from the tools, database and case studies. Indeed, these results are applicable beyond certification, to quality assurance and informal third-party assessments.

More detailed information about the proposed certification procedures can be found in various public-domain deliverables which describe the proposed certification model and descriptions of the various assessment modules (known as 'bricks').

There were about 25 case studies in SCOPE, each run by one of the SCOPE partners (known as the 'case study partners'). Usually the software under examination was provided by a third party (known as the 'provider'). In return for allowing us to examine their software the provider obtained feedback on the product in the form of a product evaluation and exposure to the various techniques. SCOPE was in two phases. In the first phase of SCOPE the case studies were experimental and speculative since an assessment procedure had not yet been established. They tried out different assessment techniques to determine if they could be incorporated into the SCOPE scheme. Nevertheless there was coordination between the partners, ensuring that common data was collected for purposes of comparison.

By the beginning of the second phase the other parts of the project had already produced a certification model and a set of assessment procedures. These procedures were defined in self-contained descriptions known as bricks. They were periodically updated and enhanced until the end of the project. The bricks were an attempt to modularize each assessment technique. A set of bricks would then be chosen to assess a given product. As a result the case studies were more focused and the types of metrics produced were known in advance.

The tools and database tasks were intended as service activities to support the case studies. The tools assisted in applying specific techniques and were to be driven by the requirements of specific case studies. The database stored all the metrics data and allowed comparisons across and between case studies. This was used both to assess individual products and to sharpen the assessment methods by establishing norms for the different metrics.

The tools task did not produce any completely new sets of tools but modified and enhanced existing tools by extending their range of applicability and allowing them to be integrated into the scheme. In this sense SCOPE was similar to many organizations that wish to start using metrics. It is rarely feasible to construct a complete tools set, so usually they must integrate existing tools into their own scheme.

Collaborative projects usually build on the results of previous projects. SCOPE is no exception, particularly as many of the researchers had worked on collaborative projects before. Much of the work concerning data collection and storage followed on from the work of REQUEST (REliability QUality for European Software Technology), an ESPRIT I project, and SWDL (SoftWare Data Library), a UK-funded project. Other projects such as Structure Based Software Metrication, another UK-funded project, can be seen to have influenced SCOPE by providing a rigorous approach to product measurement.

1.5 STRUCTURE OF THE BOOK

The book takes a pragmatic and bottom-up approach in that any assessment scheme has to be assembled from existing components. We will show how various techniques can be used to assess characteristics of the software products. The information (metrics) collected can then be stored in a central repository. This means that we can make comparisons with previous software and thus improve the assessment criteria. In order to make inferences about the quality of particular software we then need the right statistical techniques to analyse the large amount of data available. Finally we will need an integrated set of tools to allow this assessment to be done easily, cheaply and in a routine and repeatable way.

We do not claim that this is the only way to assess software or indeed that it is the only way to collect metrics data but we do have one recommendation for this approach. It has been shown to work.

Chapters 1–4 provide the foundations for product assessment. Chapter 2 explains how metrics for product assessment relate to other uses of metrics such as process assessment and metrics-for-managers. We review existing approaches to assessment and see that many aspects of these schemes can be used in product assessment.

Chapter 3 describes the ISO 9126 quality model and uses this as a justification for collecting the product metrics. ISO 9126 has six quality characteristics: functionality, reliability, usability, efficiency, maintainability and portability; later chapters show how these can be measured.

Chapter 4 sets out the theoretical fundamentals of product metrics. We distinguish between the characteristics which are of interest to the purchasers and users of the software, and the internal attributes of the software product which we can measure, and explain how these are linked. Finally we look at the limits of what is possible, given the current level of technology and understanding.

Chapters 5–8 describe the SCOPE approach; these are really the *guts* of the book. Chapter 5 details the techniques which have so far been used for assessment as well as explaining the strengths and weaknesses of each approach.

Chapter 6 explains how the data collected by the methods of Chapter 5 may be analysed. This ranges from simple descriptive statistics to more elaborate multivariate techniques and reliability models.

Chapters 7 and 8 describe the nuts and bolts of the metrics scheme. This is one of the major contributions of the SCOPE project in that we developed a painless way of transferring the data from its original site to the central database. Chapter 7 deals with tools and Chapter 8 with the database and data transfer mechanisms.

The metrics scheme has been used both in and outwith SCOPE and will eventually lead to commercial exploitation. Chapters 9–12 explore how the scheme was used and is likely to be used in the future. Chapter 9 recounts some of the interesting results which emerged from the analysis of the data from the case studies.

SCOPE was a research and development project. The tools constructed were prototypes that were sufficient for the purposes of the project. A commercial scheme would require more elaborate tools and need to be more tightly integrated; Chapter 10 addresses these issues.

Chapter 11 addresses the managerial issues of assessment and certification. We discuss how this will impact on the needs of producers and customers and include considerations of cost.

Chapter 12 provides conclusions and indicates future directions for the work.

The Glossary at the end defines the key terms used throughout the text.

SUMMARY

As software becomes increasingly important in all fields, there is a growing need to assess software quality. Any software product assessment, whether for certification or QA, will require a metrics scheme to collect, store and analyse software data. Constructing such a scheme is not trivial and is fraught with difficulties. Nevertheless SCOPE and other projects have built and used such a scheme. They have done so by using existing techniques which are supported by tools.

2

APPROACHES TO SOFTWARE ASSESSMENT

The essence of our approach to software assessment is that we are measuring quality characteristics by means of product metrics. There are numerous other assessment schemes based on measuring both the product and process so it is important to understand how our own approach fits in with these. Software metrics can be used for many purposes of which product assessment is just one. We therefore need to understand how our use of metrics differs from other uses such as 'metrics for management'. We should also bear in mind that many of the data collection and storage techniques discussed in later chapters may be usable for these other purposes, such as cost estimation, management information, research, etc.

2.1 ASSESSMENT, EVALUATION AND CERTIFICATION

In the experience of the authors, a lot of confusion has arisen concerning the terms *certification* and *assessment*. The purpose of the SCOPE project was to propose a certification scheme based on analysis of software products. *Certification* is the issuing of a seal or certificate. It is essentially an administrative activity. Of course any certificate would be valueless unless it was based on some type of *evaluation* carried out in a fair and objective way. The *evaluation* is the process of identifying quality targets, selecting product parts, choosing appropriate techniques and tools, performing the measurements and reporting the results. The actual application of techniques and collection of metrics is referred to as *assessment*. The *assessment* is thus a technical activity. It may be used to arrive at the decision whether or not to certify a particular product, process, or organization. Assessment may be used for many purposes other than certification, as we indicated in Chapter 1; examples are QA and third-party evaluation.

2.2   METRICS COLLECTION IN CONTEXT

As Lord Kelvin recognized in the nineteenth century:

> When you can measure what you are speaking about and express it in numbers, you know something about it; but when you cannot measure it, when you cannot express it in numbers, your knowledge is of a meagre and unsatisfactory kind.

There are at least three areas in software engineering where metrics and assessment can be usefully employed. We will try to single them out in order to position clearly the topics addressed in this book and show how metrics-related topics are interrelated.

Measurement of software is essential to determine the level of quality at any particular stage in the life cycle, to motivate improvements and to determine whether these have been successfully achieved. Therefore, metrics and assessment can be used in the following areas:

Process assessment This is intended to analyse the software development process and to highlight areas for improvement. The assessment can be conducted towards either international standards or maturity models (see also Sec. 2.4). Research is moving to combine them into a unifying approach.

Management by metrics This is intended to devise high-level quantitative indicators, used by managers to control software projects and products. Indicators are derived from the corporate needs in a top-down approach, usually by either GQM (goal–question–metric)[15] or function-deployment matrices, and address factors like cost-effectiveness, timeliness and fault rates. Analysis is generally performed over a large number of projects, to improve the development process by means of the adoption of those techniques which have proven to work best.

Product assessment This is intended to address a single software product to judge its quality level. Analysis is done towards a predefined set of characteristics by means of several low-level metrics applied to various product parts: specifications, technical documents, source code, user manuals, etc.

There are several areas of overlap between product assessment and the other two areas. For instance, process assessment might be needed when we want to certify a software product to a high level of confidence. Furthermore, for the indicators used in the management-by-metrics approach, we are simply applying, at multi-project level, a subset of metrics that are used for product assessment.

All these topics are of great importance for the progress of software engineering. Any attempt to rank them in order of priority would be inappropriate and meaningless. Rather, it is important that we understand what purpose the metrics we collect will be used for.

2.3 THE SCOPE APPROACH

The SCOPE project was specifically directed to the problem of *product assessment* and *evaluation*, and its implications at technical, organizational and legal levels. Our aim was also to take the first steps towards *software product certification*.

Our approach to software assessment can be best described as *general software product assessment*. It has four features that distinguish it from other types of software assessment. These are:

1. The assessment is based on the artefacts produced by the software process (i.e. the *products*) and not the process itself.
2. The assessment is not restricted to any one class of application but covers, in principle, all software except that which is very safety-critical.
3. There is no restriction on the development style, methods, or languages used in development.
4. The assessment covers a wide range of quality characteristics, and different methods are used to assess those characteristics.

2.3.1 What is the SCOPE method for?

The assessment and certification method[29] that we propose describes a software evaluation procedure which takes software characteristics, product information, development-process information and acceptance criteria as input and produces an output stating whether a product can be certified according to given requirements and conditions. The procedure was refined many times thanks to the experiences gained in case studies and to the evolution of related standards. At the time of writing, the method had recently been tabled to the International Standards Organization as a guideline for the application of ISO 9126 to product evaluation.

Our approach is to assume that the technology of software quality developed by the research community is ready to use for software assessment and certification. In consequence, our strategy is to use existing techniques to build a consistent framework and to rationalize their application.

The aim of the overall scheme is to be of value for software producers, resellers, users and the community at large. What general characteristics must the scheme exhibit in order to reach this goal? First of all, it must be stable, unbiased and trusted by all. It follows that the scheme should therefore be regulated, consistent, understandable, cost-effective and respected. Moreover, it must be flexible, evolutionary and capable of rapid response to changes. In particular, the scheme needs to be harmonized and kept up to date with respect to any changes in law, standards or regulations which impinge on software products and their use. Furthermore, assessment must be able to deal with any kind of software products. This means that it must be equally applicable to products ranging from off-the-shelf packages, to turn-key systems, to embedded software. There was one limitation in SCOPE; the project agreed that it would not address two special classes of software: military applications and software which is used in highly safety-critical systems. These systems are already subject to scrutiny and approval by existing regulatory authorities. In any case our belief is that the method is in principle applicable in these circumstances also.

2.3.2 The assessment approach

The basis of the assessment process is to verify that the actual service exhibited by a software product is a trusted representation of its specified service. In other words: 'Has the product been made correctly?'

On the other hand, product assessment cannot deal with the correspondence between expected service from the user's perception and actual service; this means that we are not addressing the question: 'Is it the right product?'

This view presents problems for users who may be expecting that an assessment or certification by a third party would be an assurance that a product meets its specifications. But this can only be true when the product fully meets its specifications and these correspond precisely to the expectations. Unfortunately, users' expectations are usually informal, subjective and well beyond the written specifications of the product. It follows that the key relationships are the following:

• It must be the user's responsibility to ensure that the choice of the product corresponds to their needs.
• It must be the producer's responsibility to ensure that a product corresponds to its description.

There can be an exception to the principle that the assessment should only look into the correspondence between actual and specified service. This is the case of systems that can lead to a hazard. It might be expected that it was the responsibility of the assessor to find out safety-related anomalies during the evaluation of the product.

There are a number of other types of software assessment in existence which may well complement our own approach. Before we develop the SCOPE approach, we shall look at other types of assessment.

2.4   GENERAL PROCESS CERTIFICATION

This means assessing the methods that are used to produce the software. It is usually an assessment of the organization that develops the software rather than any product that comes from it. The fundamental assumption is that high-quality software requires a consistent and rigorous process with well-defined activities and responsibilities. The ISO 9000 approach (BS 5750)[35] is based on having detailed descriptions of all the activities that make up the process—a so-called quality system. The guarantee of quality of a product comes from the fact that it was produced from such a process. The ISO 9000 standard is not specific to software but applies to any product or service. However, ISO 9000-3[88] is an interpretation of the standard specifically for software development. In the UK, the Tick-IT scheme has been based on such an approach and is having considerable success. Some of the best-known IT certification bodies in Europe have set up, under the name of ITQS,[149] an agreement group recognized by EOTC (European Organization for Testing and Certification) that guarantees the mutual recognition of ISO 9000 certificates throughout Europe, provided that the evaluation has been done in accordance with agreed rules.

The process maturity model,[80] proposed by the SEI (Software Engineering Institute) in the USA, is a form of process assessment specific to software production and promoted by the US Department of Defense. It consists of asking a series of detailed questions about the process concentrating on topics such as:

General management
Project planning
Configuration management
Quality assurance
Standards
Inspections
Testing
Development processes
Data gathering and analysis
Software quality management
Defect prevention
Process automation
Subcontracting

The approach is 'general' in that it is not tied to any one specific technique or language.

The SEI approach[132] is also perceived as one way to set up a total quality management[146] in software-producing units. Even though the capability model does not cover completely the TQM requirements (Silver makes an interesting comparison[148]) its dynamic optimization view is much more constructive than the static approach of ISO 9000-3.

The European project Bootstrap[37,73,155] has set up a scheme which combines the ISO 9000-3 and SEI approaches. It is based on two steps: investigating the definition of the quality system at the software-producing-unit level and then checking for its practical adoption within major development or maintenance projects. After more than 50 successful experiences throughout Europe, a software assessment service has been set up in most European countries and is extending also beyond Europe.

An interesting approach has also been developed under the name of Trillium.[42] This merges most types of process assessment: i.e. SEI maturity models, ISO 9000-3, IEEE standards for software products, IEC 300 for reliability and availability management, some Bellcore standards and a significant part of the Malcolm Baldridge examination.[153] It is specially tailored for the telecommunications domain.

There is currently a debate in the software community as to what is the real value of process assessment,[32,81] even though many organizations are now committed to this kind of assessment for their own QA. It seems obvious that a good process is precisely one which produces a good product. Our view is that it is also wise to assess directly the product itself. The proof of the pudding is in the eating, not in the recipe. The problem we have is that assessing products is difficult. Even though the work proposed here shows that product assessment is feasible, there is no complete and foolproof way to assess everything about the quality of software from its components. Process assessment is more readily established and provides a means of assessment at the present time. As product assessment becomes more accepted and more widely used it should take some of the burden from the process. However, it is likely that process standards will require the collection and analysis of the very metrics on which product assessment is based. One could indeed argue that product assessment is just one part of the process.

2.5 SPECIFIC PROCESS ASSESSMENT

A quality system such as that described by ISO 9000 can encompass a large number of different development models. Specific process assessment would mean that only one type of development method were prescribed. For example, the assessment may require the software to be specified in VDM, written in Standard Pascal, not in any other way. If this approach were to have any rational basis there should be some evidence that these methods are better than the alternatives. In any case, such an approach would agitate against change and improvements in the development methods. Furthermore, were such a scheme ever implemented for certification it would almost certainly be challenged by the software producers as a restriction on trade. Of course, customers are free to impose as they see fit any restrictions on the development methods used by their suppliers. Many large procurers of software such as government departments have done exactly this. The US Department of Defense requires that software be written in Ada, and by implication insists on a validated compiler (any compiler that calls itself an Ada compiler must have been validated). The UK Ministry of Defence now seeks all safety-critical software to be specified using a formal (i.e. mathematical) technique in accordance with its own interim standard 00-55.[91]

2.6   SPECIFIC PRODUCT ASSESSMENT

A few classes of software products can be assessed in a way specific to that product class. Several of these certification schemes have been set up in Europe under the Conformance Testing Services (CTS) programme. The advantages of this approach are the relatively limited costs of the assessment and its acceptance and understanding by both producers and customers.

However, it lacks generality. To set up such an assessment, there is a need for an a priori standard definition of the certifiable characteristics of the product; since those are a rarity in the IT world for the time being, it is possible to perform specific assessment and certification for very few products.

Perhaps the best example of specific product assessment is *compiler validation* which is used to test the functionality of compilers.* Compilers have a clearly understood functionality since this is determined by the definition of the language. There are well-established methods of defining programming languages and these definitions are often supported by a standard. Furthermore, we have a number of products each of which purports to do exactly the same thing. This means that test suites, consisting of programs written in the appropriate language, can be devised and these can form a basis for assessment for any compiler supporting that language.

As of December 1992, in Europe it is possible to have products certified under the auspices of ECITC-EOTC (European Committee for IT&T

---

* Using a validated compiler should affect the reliability of the compiled code, but this is a process issue.

Testing and Certification—European Organ for Testing and Certification) only in the following areas:

Open systems (OSTC (Open System Testing Consortium) consortium represented in nine countries), in particular

–Message-handling systems
–File transfer, access and management, transport

Compilers

–Pascal
–FORTRAN 77
–COBOL 85
–ANSI C

Graphic libraries (GKS—graphics kernel system)
Communication components

–DTE X.25
–MHS X.400

It is likely that in the near future it will be possible to extend the coverage of certifiable products (good candidates are, for instance, SQL interpreters), but in any case this approach cannot be extended to the majority of software products, due to their diversity and the cost of developing specific test suites. Moreover, only functionality is addressed: no other quality characteristics, such as efficiency or maintainability, can be assessed.

There is no reason why general product assessment as advocated here cannot be applied to software even if a specific product assessment technique exists since they will assess different aspects of quality.

2.7 SPECIFIC CHARACTERISTIC ASSESSMENT

The assessment of software products towards specific characteristics other than functionality does already exist. Such schemes could eventually be subsumed within a general product certification scheme. This approach is feasible when one of the following conditions hold:

A well-defined standard (or pre-standard) exists
An industrial *de facto* standard is widely accepted
A (big and powerful) company develops many software products under rather stable conditions
A (big and powerful) company has to deal with several subcontractors

In the following, some examples are given for each of the situations identified above.

2.7.1 Existence of a standard (or pre-standard)

In the case of the sub-characteristic 'security', both the evaluation criteria[44] and the evaluation manual[45] exist as pre-standards. These criteria, largely influenced by the so-called 'Orange Book'[52] (published and used for product evaluation by the US Department of Defense), were derived by harmonizing the best features of security standards from France, Germany, the United Kingdom and The Netherlands. Their aim is to provide a compatible basis for certification by the national bodies, with an eventual objective of allowing international mutual recognition of evaluation results. In this context, security has a meaning very close to the one assigned in general product assessment (see later the synonymous sub-characteristic in ISO 9126). Security consists of:

Confidentiality—prevention of the unauthorized disclosure of information
Integrity—prevention of the unauthorized modification of information
Availability—prevention of the unauthorized withholding of information or resources

In order to make assessment and certification possible, the following guidelines are provided:

The definition and description of security requirements, including classes of assessment
The evaluation criteria, broken down into: requirements for content and presentation of the documentation that must be provided by the sponsor, requirements for evidence inside the documentation and evaluator actions to be performed
The evaluation process
The evaluation methodology
Deliverables that have to be produced
Detailed content of the evaluation report
Tools and techniques that can be used
Re-evaluation criteria
Re-use of evaluation results

As we will see later, all these things are needed in order to perform a general product assessment; therefore the evaluation towards security certainly constitutes a good example of a specific instance.

Something similar is likely to happen also in the field of usability, with the progress of work related to the ISO 9241 standard.[90]

2.7.2 Existence of an industrial *de facto* standard

This situation is evident, for instance, in the field of graphical user interfaces (GUIs), where we have a number of competing but rather similar interaction systems (Presentation Manager, Motif, Open Look, CUA, etc.). When a software product is built with a user interface based on one of these GUIs, it is possible to assess several aspects of usability by checking the full adherence to the appropriate style guide. From this point of view, the assessment of usability has been shown to be very successful with respect to the IBM CUA (common user access) standard,[82] owing to the fact that such a standard provides details of the following features:

The guidelines for different levels of interfaces: not only the advanced one but also an entry model (with interface elements based on alphanumeric characters) and a 'text subset of the graphical model' (that is, similar to most existing user interfaces).

The presentation style, the interaction rules and the look-and-feel of the various components of the interface (i.e. panel elements, entry and selections, prompt, action bars and pull-downs, special areas, scrolling, pop-ups, help, messages, controls, windowing, etc.).

A checklist summarizing all the aspects to which conformance is mandatory, recommended, or suggested.

2.7.3 A company with many software products

Large companies that develop large projects with teams distributed over many sites often produce an assessment handbook to ensure consistency and guarantee a minimum level of quality. These handbooks, usually based on checklists, are oriented to those software-product characteristics relevant to the specific application domain. For instance, the United States Air Force has set up evaluation schemes for both usability[54] and maintainability,[53] specifying the check-points (very detailed questions supplied with examples and explanations) and the procedures to be used in assessment. These kinds of assessment schemes are very relevant to general product assessment, because from the analysis of the check-points it is possible to derive guidelines for the assessment of several characteristics at a basic level.

2.7.4 A company with several subcontractors

This is the case, for instance for Bell, concerning telecommunication exchange centres. In order to control the countless releases of systems from different suppliers, Bell has defined a set of indicators[26] checking the reliability at operating plants. Measures are specified at different levels (system, software, hardware) and for various components (e.g. network switching elements, transport systems, operations systems). Measures are service-driven rather than product-driven and are therefore similar to the *management-by-metrics* approach addressed later. Examples are: outage performance, release application problems, feature conformance, problem reports, fault/fix history, and faults and prediction. In any case, it represents a good example of transferring a generic assessment scheme to one specific application domain of great importance, namely telecommunications.

2.8 BENCHMARKING

Benchmarks are typically a way to measure the efficiency of a software system. They are often used to compare products to determine which is the 'best' as well as to determine if a particular product has reached the required level of efficiency.

In order to be valid, a benchmark must be executed in a controlled environment, under stated conditions. Benchmarks exist for different application domains and under different environments and this can cause some problems. It is not uncommon to find brochures of a software system with a declaration of its performance in MIPS or TPS (transactions per second) without any indication of the benchmark used to derive such data. If you are selecting between competing platforms and ask about benchmarks, be prepared for endless bloody battles among the commercial agents of the hardware and software distributors! For this reason the definition of benchmarks is normally done by a council including representatives of major hardware manufacturers and relevant software producers. As an example, we give a high-level description of the TPC/B benchmark as defined by the Transaction Processing Council.

TPC/B is one of the most widespread benchmarks for relational databases. It accesses distributed systems by making several insert/delete/modify queries invoked by a large number of concurrent users, with think time equal to zero. Efficiency is measured in terms of response time and transactions per second during low, normal and very intensive operation. Even if we avoided the technical details of such a benchmark (number of rows in the database, record size, etc.) it is clear that the definition, execution and evaluation of a benchmark is a far-from-trivial matter. Moreover, these benchmarks are applicable to only a limited number of application domains. For these reasons, it is unlikely that this kind of efficiency benchmarking could be used in a general product assessment scheme.

A different and much more straightforward kind of benchmark is the one applied for information dissemination or commercial purposes. It consists of ranking several products (usually in the same application domain) against a pre-specified set of specific check-points that cover several quality characteristics. An example in the USA is represented by the activities of ISTL (ITT Center Software Testing Laboratory) and ABA LTAC (American Bar Association's Legal Technology Advisory Council) where benchmarking was applied to software for use by lawyers and law offices.

This initiative was designed to help small and medium-sized law firms choosing software suited for their needs. Testing adopted a black-box approach using scenarios similar to those in an actual law office, against appropriate guidelines. Guidelines were of two kinds: general guidelines[1] which listed the basic requirements that all systems must meet and additional system-specific guidelines[2] for particular types of software such as: time and billing, word processing, litigation support, docket control, real property, employee benefits, general ledger, individual income tax, planning, probate and trust. These guidelines require that software satisfy vendor claims, be adequately documented, exhibit no unexplained program failures, and produce usable and accurate reports. Over 50 systems have been tested and 'certified'. As time went on the initiative shifted from the check of conformance to ABA's standards to providing lawyers with information to make knowledgeable buying decisions.

Product-oriented assessment towards commercial purposes is nowadays made by a huge number of specialized IT periodicals, each of which claims to be the depository of the ultimate *silver bullet* for software evaluation.

This kind of assessment, clearly oriented to specific product classes, is indeed interesting even for a generic assessment scheme, since it can provide guidelines for the assessment of functionality for specific products (usually at a low level of stringency), keeping the cost of definition of the test suite acceptable.

2.9   BLACK-BOX PRODUCT ASSESSMENT

By black-box product assessment we mean an assessment based solely on actual execution of the product without any reference to its internal workings. The approach is based on:

The software product description (which must clearly define what the product should and should not do)
The software product itself (limited to the executable code and its documentation), which must satisfy the description

This approach has been implemented by two national certification schemes:

In Germany by Gütergemeinschaft Software (GGS)
In the United Kingdom by the British Standards Institution (BSI)

We shall briefly describe both of them.

2.9.1   The GGS scheme

This scheme can be applied to software packages where there is no issue of safety. The test procedure[100] is defined by a standard[59] giving the requirements for product description and specifying the use of black-box testing techniques to ensure the consistency of the product with respect to its description.

About 20 products are qualified per year on the basis of a report from a test laboratory; test labs can be of two types:

* Test labs entitled to verify third-party software products (typically TÜVs —German government test houses)
* Test labs entitled to verify their own software products (typically large companies)

If the product is successfully qualified, a quality seal is granted; the quality seal states that the software product conforms to its product description.

This approach is very relevant to the topics dealt with in this book, since it addresses a wide range of application domains and uses the product-based approach. Indeed, as we see in later chapters, we have tried to incorporate parts of the GGS scheme into SCOPE.

The GGS scheme has had the following results:

* Creation of a public quality standard for software
* Provision of verification guidelines
* Making qualified software clearly visible

However, some limitations also exist:

* Assessment is limited to suitability
* Evaluation is largely based on checklists about documentation quality
* Embedded software is not addressed

To cope with some of these drawbacks and to extend the validity of the quality seal, discussion is undergoing at international standardization level about:

* The possibility of issuing the quality seal on the basis of operating experience
* The extension of the standard to requirements about the user interface
* The question of the quality seal on new versions of already qualified software
* The issuing of the quality seal for specific user groups

2.9.2 The BSI scheme

BSI QA has set up a scheme, called PAS (Product Approval Scheme), through which a software supplier can obtain a licence to use a PAS mark with a particular product. It is not a guarantee of adequacy but is intended to assure the user that certain requirements have been fulfilled, including testing of all functions of the software. The aspects addressed are: quality, stability, support and maintenance.

Here we list some of the requirements for 'quality': the quality management system of the supplier must conform to ISO 9000; requirement specifications should follow the ANSI/IEEE 830-1984 standard; the product release plan must be agreed between BSI QA and the supplier; product testing must be assessed; regression testing must be checked. Stability assesses issues like: number of releases produced each year, number of outstanding complaints raised, lifetime of the product, complexity of the tasks performed. Support and maintenance are concerned with the following aspects: provision and agreement of a release plan, mechanisms for feedback and management of problems from users, time to fix faults, correction of major faults before issuing a new version.

The scheme is wider than the GGS one, since it addresses not only the documentation and the tests, but also the quality system, the complaint-logging system and the product release plan. However, only stable products (with a minimum of one year's operation with complaint logging) are eligible for the PAS mark. Moreover, the approach does not quantify any measure; for example, for support and maintenance, the object of the assessment is to be able to say that the software is supported and maintained, rather than to measure maintainability.

2.10   MANAGEMENT BY METRICS

By 'management by metrics' we mean the approach to measurement in which indicators are collected as part of the process of managing software development. Metrics are seen as a standard way of measuring attributes of the software development process, such as: size, cost, defects, timeliness, difficulty, and so on.

The best-known model for management by metrics is probably the one used at Hewlett-Packard.[71,72,121] We can draw from it the following lessons:

1. Metrics must be related to the company's strategy and business
2. The success of such initiatives is heavily dependent on managers' commitment and human factors (metrics councils, metrics selling, training, success stories, etc.)
3. Metrics are focused on subjects like: costs, timeliness, errors
4. Data is collected at a very high level
5. Metrics must be used to monitor and drive process improvement
6. Metrics can be used for justifying changes in a quantitative way

A good example of a European application of such a scheme is the Pyramid approach.[136,137] It provides a metrics programme implementation strategy and shows evidence of successful experiences and examples of current best practice. In this approach the following features are considered desirable for metrics collection:

1. A limited number of metrics that are easily calculated
2. Tools support
3. Metrics related to software process and project management
4. Acceptance by the organization where the scheme is applied

It is then straightforward to combine these theoretical foundations of management by metrics into a unifying framework. For example, the cyclic schema that comes out of the AMI (application of metrics in industry) project[7] consists of the following steps:

1. Process assessment (SEI-based[132]) to derive business objectives and current practices, i.e. primary goals for measurement
2. Derivation of metrics from goals by means of the well-known GQM (Goals–Questions–Metric)[15] approach
3. Metrics collection and analysis with a management-by-metrics attitude
4. Feedback of results and process improvement

This last step completes the loop.

The management-by-metrics approach can also be combined efficiently with product assessment, as shown again by Grady.[72] If we think of using these techniques to organize customers' needs and deciding which attributes are most important for a particular product, then we are defining the requirements for our assessment. Indeed, a quality model, combined with quality function deployment[43] techniques, has been shown to be very useful both in product assessment and management by metrics.

The reader may also find useful a comprehensive study[10] of the derivation of indicators specifically intended for ISO 9126. A user's viewpoint is adopted, resulting in metrics somewhat similar to those adopted in a management-by-metrics approach.

As far as data handling is concerned, the management-by-metrics approach is quite naïve, and includes the following:

• Commercial spreadsheets used for data gathering
• Data analysis mainly concerned with presentation of graphs
• Very simple tools often based on forms

We should remember that whereas the management-by-metrics approach is excellent for the introduction and usage of software metrics in industry, it does not solve the problem of software product assessment, which usually requires the collection and storage of huge amounts of data and the use of advanced data-analysis techniques. Even in collecting very few indicators, the Hewlett-Packard experience has encountered some problems concerning data:

- Difficulty in integrating with metrics-collection tools
- Lack of a well-defined data model
- Problems in updating and distributing copies of the data other than by manual means and with quite a long turn-round time (no less than one week)
- Limitations in the amount of data that it is possible to collect
- Confidentiality and security issues about private data

Therefore, even if a spreadsheet is good at the start[36] (the scheme is easy to modify, graphics are created easily, software is ready to use, totals are automatically generated, usability is promoted), we normally need something more sophisticated as soon as data is collected. Hewlett-Packard itself decided to shift to a relational database (with programmed interface for tool integration) and to develop tools to support data collection.

SUMMARY

Although there are many instances of software assessment and certification currently available, they do not fit the description of *general product assessment*. They do, however, impact on our proposed scheme in two ways. First, many of the initiatives should be seen as complementary. For example, process assessment and specific product assessment can be carried out in tandem with general product assessment. Secondly, many aspects of these schemes can be either incorporated or built upon. For example, the GGS scheme gives us an approach to black-box testing which we can use. The Hewlett-Packard experience of data collection and analysis shows us that paper forms and spreadsheets are not powerful enough for our purposes.

3

A QUALITY MODEL FOR GENERAL
PRODUCT ASSESSMENT

Before we can concentrate on the collection and analysis of product metrics, which is the main theme of the book, we must first identify and justify the characteristics to which the metrics collection is directed. We do this with reference to the international standard ISO 9126.

3.1   THE ISO 9126 MODEL

The standard ISO 9126 divides quality into six characteristics: functionality, reliability, usability, efficiency, maintainability and portability. We will attempt to map these characteristics to specific methods and metrics in Chapter 5. But first we give the ISO 9126 definitions and justify why the attributes are of interest. We also briefly mention the breakdown of characteristics into sub-characteristics. It is important to underline that this decomposition is not part of the standard, since it is thought that, though 'there are a number of such quality models in the literature and applied in practice, the maturity of the models, terms and definitions does not yet allow them to be included in a standard'.[89] Therefore, the sub-characteristics are not part of the standard; rather, they have been proposed in an appendix, as informative and non-prescriptive guidelines. The key point is that, in accordance with the ISO model, the breakdown of characteristics is a necessary step towards quality measurement; there should be a quality model to at least the level of sub-characteristics, whether or not of the precise form described in the annexe to the ISO 9126 model.

Characteristics   Sub-characteristics

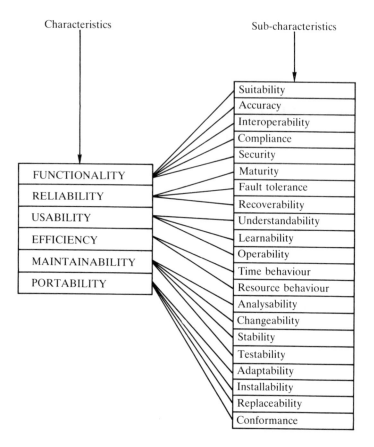

Figure 3.1 The ISO 9126 model.

This introduces the difference between internal and external attributes, which will be dealt with in Chapter 4.

Another important aspect of the standard is the proposal of a quality evaluation process model. Such a model is also briefly explained, so that it will be possible to show that our general assessment method complies with it.

A quality model can be seen from quite different points of view: a user's point of view, a developer's point of view, a manager's point of view and an evaluator's point of view. Of course the view presented in this book is the evaluator's one. Figure 3.1 shows the ISO 9126 model.

3.2   SOFTWARE QUALITY CHARACTERISTICS

3.2.1   Functionality

This is defined as 'a set of attributes that bear on the existence of a set of functions and their specified properties. The functions are those that satisfy stated or implied needs.' Clearly such an attribute will be of importance in all software.

In accordance with the ISO 9126 guidelines, functionality can be broken down into sub-characteristics as follows.

Suitability defined as the 'attribute of software that bears on the presence and appropriateness of a set of functions for specified tasks', covers *fitness for purpose* and represents one of the most controversial and tricky attributes to assess.

Accuracy checks the degree of precision of calculated values defined as 'attributes of software that bear on the provision of right or agreed results or effects'.

Interoperability means 'attributes of software that bear on its ability to interact with specified systems'.

Compliance covers the adherence 'to application-related standards or conventions or regulations in laws and similar prescriptions'.

Security is intended as 'attributes of software that bear on its ability to prevent unauthorized access, whether accidental or deliberate, to programs and data'.

Quite surprisingly, there is no mention of *safety*, one of the key features of many systems subjected to assessment, which has therefore been used within the SCOPE project.

3.2.2   Reliability

This is defined as 'a set of attributes that bear on the capability of software to maintain its level of performance under stated conditions for a stated period of time'.

Reliability is decomposed into the sub-characteristics maturity, fault tolerance and recoverability.

Maturity means 'the frequency of failure by faults in the software'. Many people consider this a description of reliability itself. This is the most important quality attribute for high-criticality systems where low reliability can cause death, injury, or damage to the environment. Any assessment of

Figure 3.2 Human error causes software failure.

maturity can only be meaningful for a given operational usàge. Figure 3.2 conveys the fact that software failures are of course due to design faults caused by human error.

Fault tolerance is directed towards the robustness of software and is defined as 'attributes of software that bear on its ability to maintain a specified level of performance in cases of software faults or of infringement of its specified interface'.

Recoverability means the 'capability to re-establish its level of performance and recover the data directly affected in case of failure and on the time and effort needed for it'.

As the reader will notice, the decomposition of reliability into sub-characteristics introduces a dichotomy between failure occurrences (captured by *maturity*) and technical aspects trying to cope with them (*fault tolerance* and *recoverability*). From an evaluator's point of view it is therefore likely that the maturity aspect will be the most important to assess.

3.2.3 Usability

This is defined as a 'set of attributes that bear on the effort needed for use and on the individual assessment of such use by a stated or implied set of users'.

The degree of usability will depend on who exactly the users are. Software intended to be used by a system's administrator may justifiably be less user-friendly than a home-accounts package. The problem with usability is that it depends on people's perceptions of what is easy to use. It is thus the least objective quality factor and probably the most difficult to measure.

Usability can be split into understandability ('users' effort for recognizing the logical concept and its applicability'), learnability ('users' effort for learning software application') and operability ('users' effort for operation and operation control').

3.2.4 Efficiency

This is defined as 'a set of attributes that bear on the relationship between the level of performance of the software and the amount of resources used, under stated conditions'.

There will of course be applications, such as real-time software, where there will be time and possibly space constraints. If the software ignores these, then it may simply not be fit for its purpose. Even in application software and data processing, slow software will cause inconvenience and delay, leading to costs borne by the users or customers.

Guidelines by ISO propose a decomposition of efficiency into time behaviour and resource behaviour. The former, time behaviour, bears on 'response and processing times and on throughput rates', whereas the latter, resource behaviour, looks into 'the amount of resources used and the duration of such use'.

3.2.5 Maintainability

This is defined as 'a set of attributes that bear on the effort needed to make specified modifications'.

The modifications may be due to enhancements or adaptations and not just be fault fixes. Many software systems are bespoke products developed either within an organization or for a single customer. These systems often undergo enormous change during their lifetime. The classic example is the payroll program which has to accommodate changes that could have not been foreseen at the time of development such as if taxation laws were to change dramatically. If the software is difficult to change, making alterations will incur extra costs or worse still will require the software to be rewritten. Many contracts for software are on a *cost-plus* basis so the customer ends up paying for poor maintainability of the product. Even for off-the-shelf products, maintainability will still affect the user. For products which are quite specialist and have a small user base, a producer may respond to a software failure by supplying a new version to a customer immediately (rather than releasing periodic new versions). The elapsed time to a new version will be dependent on, among other things, the time taken to correct the fault and this will itself depend on the maintainability.

Maintenance requires analysing the software to find the fault, making a change, ensuring that the change does not have side-effects and then testing the new version. Maintainability includes factors that affect all these activities: analysability ('effort needed for diagnosis of deficiencies or causes of failures, or for identification of parts to be modified'); changeability ('effort needed for modification, fault removal or environmental change'); stability ('risk of unexpected effect of modifications'); testability ('effort needed for validating the modified software').

We think of software as being maintainable when it can adapt to new situations throughout the life cycle like skin and we do not need to periodically start from scratch as we would with shoes.

3.2.6 Portability

This is defined as 'a set of attributes that bear on the ability of the software to be transferred from one environment to another'.

The term *environment* can of course refer to operating system, machine, etc. Many software products will outlive the hardware for which they were first developed and will need to be ported to new hardware. Others may be intended to run on many platforms. In either case the portability will be an important quality attribute. There will of course be some software products where portability does not matter, where the software will only ever be intended for one particular environment.

Portability can be broken down, in accordance to the ISO 9126 annexe, into the following sub-characteristics: adaptability (to different specified environments), installability, conformance (to specific standards or conventions), replaceability.

3.2.7   Relative importance of the characteristics

The attributes functionality and reliability will be relevant to all software. Their inclusion in any set of attributes is obvious. Usability will usually be important, the exception being software that is only invoked by other software and not by a human user. Efficiency will nearly always be important, although for a large number of applications it will be a slack constraint in that it is well within an acceptable range. Maintainability and portability will depend on how the software will be developed and serviced in the future.

It is worth noting how software producers and users perceive the importance of these attributes as recorded in a survey by the SCOPE project. They were asked to grade on a scale of 0–10 their willingness to seek assessment for the products they develop or use (0 means not interested; 10 means assessment is very important). They judged all six characteristics to be relevant. Reliability and functionality scored highest with a median of 9, followed by maintainability and usability (8). Less importance is assigned to efficiency (7) and portability (5). More detailed results of this survey are given in Chapter 11.

3.3   THE EVALUATION PROCESS MODEL

The evaluation process model proposed by ISO 9126 has been designed so that it may in principle be applied at any phase of the development life cycle for each component of the software product. It consists of three main stages:

- Quality requirement definition
- Evaluation preparation
- Evaluation procedure

It is to be noted that the process is high-level and relies on the existence of a set of (undeclared) techniques and metrics. As a consequence, a number of detailed activities are not present. In particular, analysis and validation of metrics are considered as contributing to this set of techniques, and thus not being part of the main process. In the following, a short explanation of the three stages of the evaluation process is given.

The purpose of the initial stage (*quality requirement definition*) is to specify requirements in terms of quality characteristics (and possibly sub-characteristics). Since a software product is composed of different components, the requirements may differ for the various components.

The purpose of the second stage (*evaluation preparation*) is to set up an evaluation and to prepare its basis. It is refined into three steps:

1. Quality metrics selection: here metrics that correlate with the characteristics of the software product and allow direct measurement are established. Possible metrics are limitless: every quantifiable feature of software or interaction with its environment is a candidate metric.
2. Rating level definition: the purpose of this activity is to define the scales on to which measured values will be mapped. Moreover, scale values must be divided into ranges corresponding to the levels of satisfaction of the requirements. No general values are allowed; rather, they must be defined for each specific evaluation.
3. Assessment criteria definition: this activity must prepare a procedure for summarizing the results of the evaluation of the different characteristics. For instance, decision tables or weighted averages might be used. Managerial aspects such as time and costs may also be included in the procedure.

The last stage, *evaluation procedure*, is where the evaluation is actually performed in terms of:

Measurement the selected metrics are applied to the software product, obtaining as results values distributed on the defined scales.
Rating for each measured level, the rating level (i.e. satisfaction) is determined.
Assessment the final step of the software evaluation process implies the summary of rated levels. By using the assessment criteria defined, a global result on the quality of the product is derived and then compared with managerial aspects (time, costs and so on) in order to take a decision.

3.4 USAGE OF THE 9126 MODEL

We do not preclude the addition of new quality attributes if a need is found and assessment methods are available. The advantage with our flexible approach to quality modelling is that new attributes can be added if they are deemed important. Many of the previous quality models have proposed different and often larger sets of characteristics. Many of these are in fact subsumed within the set which we already have. For example, testability is a sub-characteristic of maintainability whereas in other quality models it was a characteristic in its own right.

The phrase 'set of attributes' used in the definitions indicates that these characteristics can be further broken down into lower-level attributes. These are then measured by metrics defined on the various software components. However, no mapping of characteristics to metrics can be seen as definitive. The techniques and metrics are advancing all the time. We propose this quality model based on ISO 9126 because it provides a framework and justification for collecting and analysing the lower-level metrics. We expect the quality model will change with time.

There is far more to analysing software products than proposing a quality model, and indeed we could no doubt find similar models which would serve our purposes just as well.

SUMMARY

The ISO model provides a useful framework for defining the quality characteristics (functionality, reliability, usability, efficiency, maintainability and portability) and then seeking metrics which can assess them. We do not see it as the ultimate model and accept that, in time, modifications may be made to this model. Furthermore, the techniques for collecting, storing and analysing metrics which are discussed in later chapters are in no way dependent on this particular model. They do require some model, for otherwise data collection would be *ad hoc* and directionless. This model, in our opinion, serves the purpose well.

4

UNDERLYING PRINCIPLES OF
MEASUREMENT

A prerequisite for any metric scheme used for assessment or QA is that it must collect the same metrics consistently in a number of different situations so that the conclusions can be trusted and reproducible. Only if the metrics from different projects are comparable can there be any meaningful assessment against standard criteria. This in turn requires that the metrics be collected in a standard and repeatable way. To this end we propose to set up a conceptual framework for defining and collecting those metrics of interest to ensure that they can be standardized.

In this chapter we describe such a conceptual framework for metrics collection and analysis. We appeal to measurement theory, a body of knowledge applicable to all areas of science and engineering, to ensure that the metrics are properly defined. We also draw on definitions and concepts which have evolved in the last few years within software engineering. In particular this includes those definitions which have been developed within the SCOPE project. Finally we describe the limitations to what we are able to conclude from analysing software product metrics.

4.1 CONSISTENT METRICS COLLECTION

The term *software metrics* means simply measurement applied to software. Measurement is fundamental to almost every area of science and engineering. Without it, it is impossible to apply quantitative mathematical techniques to scientific observations. Since software engineering is the attempt to impose the rigour and discipline of traditional engineering on to software production, it would seem obvious that software metrics should play a key role. Regrettably, software metrics have not yet been fully integrated into software engineering. Many software projects still use no metrics at all and there are few organizations that use metrics comprehensively throughout the software life cycle. This is in part due to the difficulties associated with collecting and using them.

There is a marked difference between using metrics informally on a single project, and setting up a metrics collection scheme over a whole series of projects. On a single project there will be a number of people working together who will develop a common culture. Many ideas and concepts will be implicitly understood. There is likely to be a small range of hardware, programming languages, specification and design notations and tools to support them. Although applying software metrics is never a trivial matter, standardizing metrics on a single project or within a small organization is far easier than for a metrics scheme over a large organization or group of organizations.

Our approach to metrics collection differs from other approaches where the information gathered is only used locally. There are two principles we observe.

1. Any metrics used for assessment or QA must have some scientific basis for the inferences that are made. They must fit into some theoretical framework.
2. The data collected from different projects must be consistent so that a common attribute can be captured in a way independent of the peculiarities of that product or process.

Of course, if measures are collected in this consistent way within a metrics scheme, they can still be used locally within that specific project. But there are added advantages for consistent metrics collection. We can make comparisons with other projects and make use of historic data.

It is not sufficient for data to be collected consistently. The data has also to be useful, and has to fit into some framework which allows inferences to be made from it. It is important for such a framework to be in place before any data collection is started. If we try to define and collect metrics in an *ad hoc* way, we have little chance of collecting the right data.

We use the term *metrics framework* to mean a set of well-understood concepts and definitions and a strategy for making meaningful inferences from the data we have. This chapter sets out such a framework.

4.2   MOTIVATION FOR A FRAMEWORK

The framework which we now establish for metrics collection has three key features:

1. A terminology for describing what we are doing
2. A motivation for collecting the metrics
3. A set of principles for ensuring that the inferences made are valid

Before we can start to define measures or state theories which relate them, we need a terminology to describe the various key concepts. Many words and expressions in software engineering have very different meanings within different organizations. For example, the word *module* to some can mean a single procedure in a program and to others it means a group of procedures or even a piece of hardware. Such ambiguity will lead to distortions to metrics collected at different sites since the definitions of these metrics will be interpreted differently. It is particularly important to be able to identify various types of software product and process and various types of software metric applied to them. Software metrics is a relatively new area, and it has evolved in a haphazard way; so the terminology tends to be inconsistent. Pieces of work in diverse areas such as cost estimation, complexity metrics and reliability modelling all developed independently, and have little in common except that they all attempted to quantify some aspect of software. Work at City University has attempted to unify these diverse areas. Norman Fenton in his book *Software Metrics: A Rigorous Approach*[64] has for the first time provided a consistent set of definitions and terms for describing these and other types of software metrics. Where possible we will use his terminology.* Other terminology has evolved from SCOPE and earlier projects for ideas and concepts not covered by Fenton's work. We define these terms in this chapter.

Collection of software metrics, or indeed any other type of measure, is never an end in itself. It is a means of gaining information about the software product or process. Our motivation for collecting the metrics is that the metrics can fit into our quality model and be used to assess the quality characteristics of a given product. We should be clear how any given metric relates to them. The same principle should apply to any use that we might have for metrics. If we were collecting the metrics for cost estimation, not only would we need to believe that the metrics collected will influence cost but we would also require some underlying cost model. If we were attempting to evaluate different methods then we would need an experimental model.

When we claim that a particular metric is related to a given characteristic by means of a decomposition into sub-characteristics we in are fact stating a *theory*. These characteristics are by their nature difficult to measure directly and the existence of such theories is fundamental to the assessment of

---

* Fenton uses the term 'measure' rather than 'metric' throughout his book. To be consistent with SCOPE and other projects we shall use both words; metrics are applied only to software, measures can pertain to any field.

software. Even so, such theories are often not explicitly stated. Whenever metrics are used to make some assessment or prediction, there is always some underlying theory relating different attributes of the software even though it may be implicit. If we wish to assess maintainability by measuring the amount of program documentation, then we are making use of the (obvious but rarely stated) theory that program documentation makes the program easier to maintain. Some theories may be expressed by means of equations which can precisely describe the relationship between the metrics we have collected and the characteristics we wish to assess. But, given that we are working in such a new and immature discipline, in most cases we will only have informally stated theories where the precise relationship is not well understood. Nevertheless the fact that a relationship exists means that assessment can be performed on this basis.

4.3 PRODUCT AND PROCESS MODELS

Software metrics can be applied to three classes of objects: products (code and documents), processes (the actions which created them) and resources (people, machines, buildings which were used to make them). We are specifically interested in the first two of these, products and processes. Our approach to assessment is based on the software product, but often we will want to use process data to test and calibrate the product-based assessment methods. Before we can start to define metrics on these various products and processes, we need to be able to identify exactly what they are. We therefore propose basic models of the products and processes of the software.

4.3.1 Types of data models

There are numerous life-cycle models such as the waterfall model, the spiral model, incremental design and the transformational model (for formal development). Any of these could be used as a basis for defining the products and processes for any given life-cycle type. However, these models are prescriptive, saying how software ought to be developed. Since our metrics scheme is general, it should be applicable to any number of different software development styles, from the sequential waterfall model to incremental design. These models are only really meaningful when the software has been developed in that particular way. To restrict the assessment techniques to software produced in a prescribed way would be unduly restrictive.

The SWDL and REQUEST projects attempted to produce general and comprehensive software data models that could cope with nearly any software process. These models were typically object-oriented and aimed to capture every product part and process event that could occur. The purpose of the SWDL project was to collect a large amount of metrics data to build up a library of data and so this approach was perhaps justified. REQUEST planned to use the data to validate models of the COQUAMO (COnstructive QUAlity MOdel) type.[98,99] But since the quality models were being formulated at the same time as the data was being collected, there were no clear data requirements when the data model was being designed. So the project tried to collect as much data as it could. The complexity of the resulting data model proved to be a problem and created difficulties in implementing a repository to store the metrics. Any metrics repository will have a structure which mirrors the models of the data collected and so a complex data model leads to a complex repository structure.

In SCOPE we found that a model based on vastly simplifying the REQUEST and SWDL ones was sufficient for our purposes. This is described here. But first we shall consider some of the problems of identifying product parts, which we refer to as *components*.

In Chapter 1 we defined software as computer programs and their associated documentation. There is no doubt that source and object code will count as parts of the software, but the difficulty comes when categorizing the other components. Most would accept that the specifications, user manual and test data were part of the software, but what about the contract or licence, publicity material, programmers' notebooks and so on? What about the metrics themselves? Are they part of the software product? Some researchers[75] have created baroque software models which can capture all these components. However, for our purposes, there is no need to be concerned about such things because the assessment methods which we currently have only apply to the executable (source and object) code, specification, design, test data and usage instructions. It is possible that in the future other components may be used for software assessment, but until such techniques can be developed and validated, there is no point in collecting the data. It is unwise, and counter-productive, to collect data on the grounds that it might be useful one day. Any data collection incurs a cost, in both the collection and storage of the data. The amount of data we could conceivably collect from a software project and which might be useful one day is almost limitless. So unless the data collected has a clear purpose, there is no point in collecting it. It is for this reason that our product model is based on those software components which are analysable.

Figure 4.1 shows the product model which we used to define metrics within SCOPE. We now look in detail at the definitions of the product and process parts.

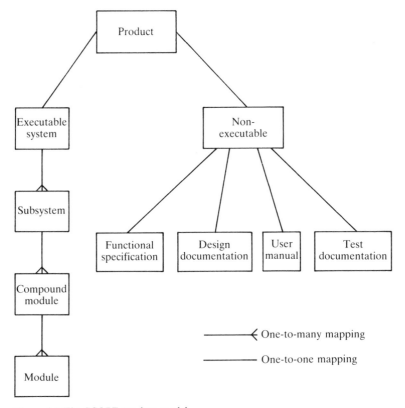

Figure 4.1 The SCOPE product model.

4.3.2 Executable components

This category consists of source code and executable (binary) code. If the language of implementation is interpreted and not compiled (as is PROLOG) then source and executable code are precisely the same thing. Often the software will be coded in a programming language such as Pascal or FORTRAN (source code) and then compiled into object code. Difficulty arises in our classification when code is generated from a higher-level representation. Increasingly, software developers are making use of code generators which produce output in languages like COBOL or C from a higher-level representation. This output is then fed into a standard compiler to produce executable code. There are two ways in which this technique may be used and the identification of the executable components depends on which of these is chosen:

- All development and modification is done at the higher level; the intermediate code is never altered.
- The intermediate code is generated once only and then subsequently altered by hand.

In the first case, where the intermediate code is *never touched by human hands*, we consider the higher-level representation to be the source code. Although the developers of these generators often claim that the 'code is generated automatically from specifications or designs', in our classification this is still just a different type of source code. It is the quality of these representations that will clearly affect the maintainability and portability of the software.

In the second case where the intermediate code is altered we consider the intermediate code as being the source code since its quality will affect the maintainability.

Many of the techniques we wish to apply are not applied to the whole source code but to a part of it. So we need some way of breaking the code down into smaller components. We use the terms *system, subsystem, compound module* and *module* to refer to successive decompositions of executable components. *System* refers to a number of computer programs performing a common service, that is, all the executable components in a given product. So all the executable components in an operating system or a word processor may be considered to be a system in this sense. Any system will consist of one or more separate programs; we refer to these as the *subsystems*. A *subsystem* can be separately compiled (if this is necessary) and executed. Each subsystem will consist in turn of one or more software procedures, functions, subroutines, etc. We collectively refer to these as the *modules*. In languages such as FORTRAN and Pascal, the structure of the language provides that there are in any program the main body and a number of subroutines, procedures, etc. In this case the main body, minus its procedures is itself considered a module.

Within larger subsystems, the modules may be grouped together because they perform a common function or set of functions. Sometimes this grouping is supported by the language of implementation which groups these modules together using a syntactic device. For example, in CORAL 66, modules may be grouped together in one or more *segments*. We use the term *compound module* to refer to this grouping. The compound modules in a subsystem should be mutually exclusive and collectively exhaustive. Each module should be in one and only one compound module. Unlike the definitions of system, subsystem and module, the boundaries of the compound modules are not immediately obvious and are open to interpretation. It depends on the way that the software developer has organized the program. For example, where the source code is contained in a number of different files, and the modules in each file relate to a particular purpose (file operations, output routines, syntax checking) then these files will define the compound modules. If no such structure manifests itself within the software, then the default is to define a single compound module as being conterminous with a subsystem.

In the most degenerate case of this model, the 'hello world' program which prints the phrase 'hello world' on the screen may be considered a system, consisting of one subsystem which has in it one compound module containing one module.

4.3.3   Non-executable components

Non-executable components comprise all the documentation associated with the program such as functional specifications, design documents, test plan, user manuals, etc. These documents may be written in a natural language such as English, a formal notation such as Z,[122] a semi-formal notation like SSADM,[61] or have diagrams and tables of data. It is precisely because these components can be heterogeneous that they are often difficult to assess.

Identifying and naming these documents is more difficult than for the executable components. Often a specification or user manual will consist of many documents. In SCOPE, one case study provided a document which contained the functional specification and design merged together. Our task of identifying the components would be somewhat easier if documents were identified in a clear manner, for example, if all specifications had the words 'Functional Specification' on the front page. But again because terminology is not standard, different organizations will call their documents different things. One case study provider working in the area of data processing called their functional specification a *business area analysis*. Thus when we talk about a functional specification, design document, etc., we are referring to a *conceptual* document which may in reality consist of part of an actual document or else several actual documents. We use the following IEEE definitions[86] for identifying these conceptual documents.

Functional specification A document that specifies the functions that a system or component must perform.
Design document A document that describes the design of the system or component.
Test documents These are called the *test case specification* in IEEE terminology. It is a series of documents that specify the test inputs, execution conditions and predicted results for an item to be tested.
User manual A document that presents information necessary to use a system or component to obtain desired results.

4.3.4 Process

The software process consists of a number of *tasks* punctuated by a number of *events*. A *task* is a deliberate human activity by one or more of the project staff contributing towards the construction or modification of the software. Examples of tasks are writing a specification, testing a module and fixing a fault. Events are the identification of suspected problems usually caused by using the software product itself either during construction or after release. Tasks are classified as *planned* or *unplanned*. Planned tasks are precisely the construction and testing of all the software products and the management overhead to control them. Unplanned tasks are the responses to an event such as investigating a problem or making a change to overcome such a problem. Although any software manager may plan and budget for some unplanned tasks, they are still unplanned in that no one can anticipate exactly what they will be until an actual event occurs.

An event arises from a perception by someone (a developer or a user) that the software is in some sense wrong. This can range from a full system crash to finding a typographical error in the user manual. An event consists of the following sequence of steps.

Incident This is the perception by someone that the software is not performing as expected. This perception may be right or wrong. Often incidents are in fact misconceptions on behalf of the user. Some software developers provide 'fault forms' or 'problem forms' for users to fill in or a telephone hotline to deal with problems perceived by users. These are, in our terminology, *incidents*. During testing or inspection, the development staff may themselves discover incidents.

Failure After an incident has been investigated, it may be decided that the software was indeed incorrect. The incident is then classified as a failure of a software component. Note that we do not care whether the software was at this stage consistent with its specified behaviour or not. An error or omission in the functional specification can still lead to a failure.

Fault After a failure has occurred, the developer may investigate the failure and attempt to find the fault that caused it. A fault is the result of an error that has been made by someone constructing the software. A failure will be due to one or more faults in the software. These faults will reside in specific software components.

Change If it is decided that the fault should be fixed then this will lead to a change which is a modification of one or more software components. A change is a type of unplanned task. Changes may also be due to an alteration in requirements or a realization by the developer that a fault existed, even if it had not yet created a failure.

The events of greatest interest in software metrics are usually those that occur during the execution of the software since measuring these can enable us to estimate the reliability of the software. However, any component may fail, whether or not it is executable. A design document which is rejected by a review meeting has in this sense failed.

4.4   MEASUREMENT THEORY

We consider that in software engineering 'metric' is a synonym for the word 'measure'. If we accept that measurement in software engineering is essentially the same as measurement elsewhere then we are bound by certain rules which are common to all types of measurement. The word 'metric' cannot mean just any numerical quantity that has some relationship to software.

Measurement is fundamental to almost anything we do both in the scientific domain and in everyday life. It would be very strange indeed if software measurement were unique in being different from all other types of measurement. Of course it may be argued that techniques devised for measuring the real world are not applicable to software since it is intangible and not governed by physical laws. However, economists and psychologists have been performing measurement on intangibles for years and, it should be noted, have usually done so within the obligations of measurement theory.

Measurement theory is the body of knowledge which shows how to construct a measure from the observation that there is some attribute that can be represented as numbers. There are several expositions of measurement theory and the interested reader is referred to the review by Finkelstein.[66] We do not intend to describe measurement theory in full here but we shall explain the main principles that impinge on data collection. In particular we use it to guide us in the definition of meaningful and useful measures.

4.4.1   Defining measures clearly

Any measure should objectively describe some attribute of an object or event in question. In software, these objects or events are the products or processes. This means that subjective ratings of an object or event cannot be considered as proper measurement.* There should instead be a well-defined procedure for arriving at a particular numerical value capturing a named attribute. Often this procedure will have human judgement as an integral part. For example, if we are counting the number of failures in some software then we need a human to identify what exactly is a failure. Other

---

* We can, of course, measure opinions but that is not the same as measuring the objects or events themselves.

metrics will be calculated automatically by tools. In this case the procedure is embodied in those tools.

The attribute that we are measuring should exist before a measure is defined. So if a new metric x were proposed it would only be valid if it described an identifiable attribute. It is not acceptable to first define a measure and then say that it measures x-ness.

The measurement procedure should preserve the relationships imposed by the attribute in question. So, for example, any measure of temperature should yield a higher value for boiling water than for ice. In terms of measurement theory these are known as the *representation condition* and the *uniqueness condition*.

Only when we clearly understand what a particular metric is measuring can we draw valid conclusions from the software. Failure to do this can lead to confusion or erroneous conclusions, as the following example shows. One of the most well-known metrics is McCabe's cyclomatic number.[118] It can be defined from the flowgraph of a module (i.e. procedure, subroutine, etc.) and is equal to the number of decisions plus 1. It is thus a metric of the number of decisions, which is an attribute of the control flow structure. However, in the past it has been claimed that it is a measure of complexity and maintainability. It is reasonable to suppose that the number of decisions will influence these attributes but is quite wrong to claim it measures them. Consider two software products with the same cyclomatic number; would this mean that their maintainability or complexity is bound to be the same? This is unlikely to be the case since there are so many other factors which will influence maintainability. Of course we can be sure that the number of decisions is the same.

The measurement procedure should also be repeatable. This is why subjective judgement cannot be considered as proper measurement. Metrics which can be calculated automatically are very likely to be repeatable. For example, the cyclomatic number can be calculated by a program analyser.* However, there is a large class of metrics which cannot be calculated in a purely automatic way and these still require some human input. These can still be valid measures where efforts are made to keep the human judgement as objective as possible. Any measurement is subject to error and human error is simply one source of this. Even with the automatic calculation of metrics, an error may be introduced by a failure of the tool in that it calculates the wrong value.

Any measure should be defined on an appropriate measurement scale. The type of measurement scale will affect the types of inferences that may be made from the measures and we deal with this in detail in Chapter 6. There

---

* This assumes that we specify which tool, since there are discrepancies between tools based on the underlying assumptions about control flow.

are five common scales of measurement. As far as we know, any software measure can be defined on one of these scales.

Nominal This refers to data that categorizes the objects of interest where there is no ordering of the classes; the only property is equality. If classification is carried out in an objective way, this can be considered measurement. Examples of nominal measurement are language of implementation (C, COBOL, Pascal, etc.), or type of application (commercial, real-time, software tools, etc.).

Ordinal An ordinal measure is one where the values of that measure have an ordering. We have the notions of greater than and less than but no notion of difference. Examples are the classification of failure severity into classes such as minor inconvenience, loss of some functions, and total loss of service. The version number of components is also an ordinal measure.

Interval Interval measures have a notion of difference, but no zero point. The only interval measures in software are those related to the date, such as date (and time) of a product being created. The choice of time zero is purely arbitrary. In everyday life it is the supposed birth of Jesus.* In the Unix operating system, zero time (known as the epoch) is defined as 1 January 1970.

Ratio Ratio measures have a notion of difference and also a zero point. For instance, all measures of component size such as number of characters, pages, or lines are defined as ratio measures. Elapsed time (as opposed to date) is also a ratio measure. So, for example, *time between failures* is defined on a ratio scale.

Absolute This is simply counting. For example, number of modules in a subsystem is an absolute measure.

It is usual to represent the value yielded by a measure as a numerical value.† However, it is often more useful in the case of nominal and some ordinal measures to use names rather than numbers. This is simply a convenience. Any nominal or ordinal measure can be expressed as a number; we just need to assign numbers to each of the classes. In the case of nominal measures the allocation of number can be arbitrary; for ordinal measure it must preserve the ordering. For our example above: minor inconvenience = 1, loss of some functions = 2, total loss of service = 3.

The scale of measurement will determine which statistical techniques may be meaningfully used with which measures. We will come to this point in Chapter 6 but, in general, any technique that can be applied to one scale can also be applied to other scales further down our list. We can show the importance of applying the right techniques to the right scale in the following example. As an example there are three definitions of the notion

---

* Some scholars now believe that Jesus of Nazareth was born in 4 BC or before.
† More generally measurement theorists talk about a set of symbols rather than numbers.

of central tendency: mean, median and mode. The mean can be applied to interval, ratio and absolute measures. Median can be applied to ordinal measures and below, whereas mode is applicable to all measures. It is totally meaningless in, say, a nominal scale to try and apply the mean. Let us suppose that we have six products implemented in different languages: three in C, one in FORTRAN, one in PL/1 and one in COBOL. We can arbitrarily assign the numbers 1–4 to the respective languages (C = 1, FORTRAN = 2, PL/1 = 3, COBOL = 4). The metrics values for the projects are $\{1,1,1,2,3,4\}$. The mode (the most common value) is 1 (C); this is a meaningful statement. The mean is

$$\frac{1+1+1+2+3+4}{6} = 2.$$

Does this imply that the mean language over the six projects is PL/1 ? Clearly not. If we do not pay attention to the measurement scale, we are in danger of coming to nonsensical conclusions.

4.4.2 Data granularity

The term *data granularity* refers to the level at which product and process metrics are collected. For example, data collected for an entire system will have a coarser granularity than data collected for each module. When we are defining our metric collection procedures, it is not only necessary to specify the definition of a metric but also the granularity at which it is to be collected. For some metrics the granularity is implied by the definition of that metric. Metrics based on the control flowgraph are by their nature collected at module level, whereas metrics of the call graph must be collected at either compound-module or subsystem level. Other metrics, such as number of faults discovered or lines of code, can, in principle, be collected at any level. If metrics are collected with a fine granularity, then they can always be aggregated. If we know the number of faults in each module of a system, we can add these up to give a total for the system. The reverse is not possible. However, if the granularity is finer, the quantity of data will be larger and so a greater cost will be incurred in its collection and storage.

The metrics we collect for product assessment will generally be at a fine level of granularity—down the module level where possible. This is a major difference between metrics for product assessments and metrics-for-managers which are usually collected at a coarse level of granularity such as at the system level.

4.4.3   Internal and external attributes

To quote Fenton:[64]

Internal attributes of a product, process or resource are those which can be measured purely in terms of the product, process or resource itself. *External attributes* of a product, process or resource are those which can only be measured with respect to how the product, process or resource relates to its environment.

Metrics which capture these respective attributes are called *internal* and *external* metrics accordingly. The quality characteristics which we wish to assess are external attributes. These attributes are difficult to assess directly. Usually we will want to assess software before it is released and certainly before the end of its life cycle. But the only way we could directly measure these characteristics would be to observe the software during its entire life cycle. How maintainable was it? How often did it actually fail? First, collection of this kind of process data over the whole life cycle is costly but, secondly, and more to the point, any such information is irrelevant since the software will then, by definition, be out of service. It is possible to observe the software over part of its life cycle and infer that future behaviour can be predicted from past behaviour. This approach is used in reliability prediction. But software certification will usually be applied before the first release. QA should certainly be applied prior to the first and subsequent releases. Historic information about porting or maintaining the software may not be available at this time.

Internal attributes are usually much easier to measure, but are of no *direct* relevance to either the user or the consumer. The only motivation for collecting the internal attributes is that we can infer something about the external attributes. This assumes that there is a theory which relates them by means of a quality model.

To relate an internal attribute to one or more external attributes we need to construct a theory based on our observations of the real world. We can debate and attempt to validate or refute specific theories based on experience, statistical evidence, or counterexamples. For example, we might argue that if all operating system calls in a system were commented then the software would be easier to port between operating systems. We then might find an example of such comments that were incorrect or irrelevant and this would lead to a refined statement that only meaningful and correct comments would improve portability and so on. But underlying our whole framework for data collection is the assumption that there are some theories which are valid. We are assuming that the internal attributes of the software do relate in some way to the external attributes. This assumption is in fact fundamental not only to metrics collection but to most of the work in software engineering that has been done over the last 25 years, even though the point is rarely made explicit.

Many of the numerous techniques which aim to improve software quality, such as specification techniques, design methods, testing strategies and so on work precisely because they alter the internal attributes of the software. If the internal attributes did not matter, managers would simply say to their programmers, 'Go away and write the software in any way you like.'

4.4.4 When are metrics valid?

A metric is valid if it properly measures the attribute in question. We can determine if a given metric is valid by carefully arguing that it preserves the relationship on the set of objects implied by that attribute. It is a purely theoretical exercise and does not require actually using the measure or collecting data. The fact that we may have used a given measure and made inferences from the data thus collected would in no way assure us that it measured the attribute claimed. Authors have often talked about validating metrics by experimentation, usually by finding a correlation with one or more other metrics. This confusion has been caused by a lack of agreed terms. What they were actually doing was validating an (often unspecified) theory.

When we have two or more metrics of different attributes, we can relate them by means of a theory. For a very simple example we may state that larger programs take longer to code. The size of programs and the elapsed time to code can be measured, and we can easily define valid measures of both attributes. If we collected data from a number of different projects then it would be possible to validate this theory by correlation of the two quantities. We could thus validate the above theory.

To illustrate how we can draw false conclusions from badly defined measures, we use again the example of the cyclomatic number, which is one of the best known and most widely applied metrics. Figure 4.2 shows a graph correlating the cyclomatic number with the lines of code for all modules in one of the SCOPE case studies. We can clearly see a correlation. If the cyclomatic number were a measure of complexity we might conclude that size affects complexity. Larger modules are more complex than smaller ones. However, if we understand the true meaning of the metric (that it measures the number of decisions), then our conclusion is that large modules have more decisions in them—a more correct but less startling conclusion.

4.5 ASSESSMENT AND PREDICTION

Ideally we would like to make *predictions* of the external attributes and use these as a basis for QA or certification. Alas, this is generally not possible.

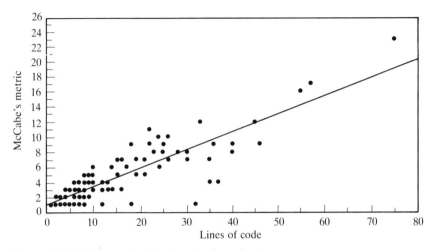

Figure 4.2 McCabe's metric plotted against lines of code.

We can make a quantitative prediction only for reliability. There are a number of *reliability models* which allow us to infer from its previous failure history how often a system will fail. In this instance we are making a prediction of an external attribute from external metrics. We might be able to say that the expected mean time to failure is 10 hours of CPU execution time. We cannot yet do this for the other characteristics: maintainability, functionality, portability, efficiency and usability. It is not possible to infer that, say, the mean effort to fix a fault will be three person-days from the information available from the product. It will also depend heavily on the maintenance environment and the nature of the maintenance. We can only assess attributes that are known to affect these characteristics. In effect we are saying that if the right attributes are present, the software is more maintainable than it would otherwise have been.

The idea of making an assessment which cannot produce a quantitative prediction is common to other areas of science and engineering. Consider the following two examples.

In most countries motor vehicles must undergo regular road worthiness tests. In the UK it is the MOT test, which consists of a number of measurements of the internal attributes of the car such as the amount of rust, the effectiveness of the brakes, how many of the lights work, etc. There is an assumption that these factors affect the safety of the car, and that a car that passes is safer than one that fails. There is no attempt to quantify how much safer, or predict the 'mean time to road accident'. Furthermore, it would be difficult to validate any predictive theory. We might release a number of vehicles which have failed their MOT, and attempt a statistical study on the number of accidents. But the probability of an accident would depend on a whole number of factors which cannot be predicted by an MOT test such as the amount of mileage or the drunkenness of the driver. Yet the MOT test, and its equivalent in other countries, are widely respected and essentially use product measurement for assessment.

Even where statistically significant results are available to relate metrics, it is not always possible to transfer this result to a specific prediction. Numerous studies have shown that smoking, diet, amount of exercise and other factors influence health, and that this will affect life expectancy. But this does not mean that we can accurately predict the lifespan of anyone based on that information. The most clean-living person could fall under a bus.

How then should we formulate theories on which to base assessment? We can identify three possible approaches.

Predictive theories Where we can actually make predictions from a validated model such as the stochastic reliability models, we can predict the behaviour of the software from the data we have collected. This is applicable only for reliability (as yet).

Quantitative correlations We may be able to establish a relationship between internal and external attributes under controlled conditions. For example, metrics of software structure may be shown to affect the time to fix a fault. However, we cannot generalize the predictive result to all software. We can state that these internal attributes will affect the external attributes and base our assessment on this fact.

Common sense and experience We have good reason to believe that certain internal attributes will affect the external attributes even if no statistical correlations have been found from historic data. For example, a user manual with an index makes the software more usable than one without. It would be difficult and perhaps pointless to try and validate theories of this kind.

Without doubt, predictive theories are the most useful and powerful kind of theories. Theories which have been statistically validated are likely to carry more weight than those that have not. But we have to accept that in software engineering we do not yet have the kind of well-understood relationships between quantities that exist in other fields such as, say, physics.

One of the first advantages gained from any type of measurement is that we are able to record our observations accurately and then communicate them in a way that is free of ambiguity and value judgements. Only when we can do this can we start to establish norms for quality on which we can base assessments.

SUMMARY

If we wish to use metrics for QA or certification, the metrics must be standardized. This means that we must be sure of what we are measuring and how this quantity will be used in analysis. We also need to be sure on what scale the metric is defined and at what granularity it will be collected. There should be an agreed terminology to define the metrics and we need to be able to identify the different parts of the product and process on which the metrics are defined.

The data should be collected with a clear purpose and be related to the characteristics we wish to assess by means of theory. For most of the quality characteristics we use internal metrics of the software products to make assessments, but precise quantitative prediction of future behaviour is not yet attainable. Only for reliability can we make quantitative predictions of future behaviour, but as we shall see this is not possible for high-reliability systems.

5

ASSESSMENT TECHNIQUES

Supposing that a piece of software arrives at a testing lab, what can we do to evaluate it? Our product-based approach relies on collecting metrics and using these to assess the quality characteristics. We know from the previous chapter that whatever metrics we wish to apply should be valid and fit into some theory, but how do we choose the appropriate metrics? Furthermore, when we have selected these metrics, what techniques do we use to collect them? In this chapter we discuss precisely these questions, and outline a simple mapping from the quality characteristics to a set of metrics that we know we can collect. We specifically focus on the techniques used within SCOPE. For this reason, we have a feasible set of metrics and techniques that can be used to assess all six characteristics, but we do not claim the set to be exhaustive.

5.1 CLASSIFYING THE ASSESSMENT TECHNIQUES

The usual approach for selecting metrics proposed by McCall[119] and others is essentially top-down. They divide a given quality characteristic into a number of attributes which then are captured by one or more metrics. A major drawback with a top-down approach is that it often leads to the definition of metrics which are difficult to collect. Literally thousands of software metrics have been proposed in the past 20 years, yet only a small number of these are actually used in practice. This is because only a limited number of techniques for collecting metrics have been shown to be both practical and cost-effective. It follows that any form of metrics-based software assessment will have to be built around these tried and tested metrics. Thus we take a bottom-up view, first examining what is currently feasible, and then attempting to relate this to our quality characteristics.

There are basically three things we can do to assess software products:

- Use tools to measure the components without running them
- Run the executable components
- Analyse the components by hand

These three activities are known respectively as *static analysis, execution analysis* and *inspection*. In addition we may also wish to collect certain process information, not for assessment itself but to calibrate the product-based techniques. These process metrics are usually collected by hand. We now look at the three basic techniques in further detail.

5.1.1 Static analysis

Static analysis is the analysis of software products by other pieces of software (static analysers) where the software under examination is not actually executed. A key feature that makes static analysis readily applicable to software assessment is that, unlike execution analysis, there is no need to simulate the environment in which the software will be used. This technique is often associated with the analysis of source code, but it has much wider applications than this and may be applied to specifications and designs in a formal or semi-formal notation. It may even be used in a limited capacity on documents written in natural languages. There are four types of static analysis which we have used on SCOPE:

Anomaly checking This applies only to formal languages and specifically to source code. Anomaly checking identifies in the components those features which might be faults. It can also check for non-portable features of the source code. It may be used to assess reliability and portability.

Textual measurement Measurement is based on the count of tokens or words in the document. In the case of natural language documents it can be used to determine the readability of documents and for source code it can be used to derive metrics which relate to maintainability (for program documentation) or usability (for users' documentation).

Structural analysis This applies principally to formal notations such as source code or formal specifications. Structural models such as flowgraphs or call graphs are derived from the code and from these various structural metrics can be derived. These can be used to assess maintainability.

Test cross-referencing The test cases and functions of the software as described in the documentation can be cross-referenced to give measures of the functional coverage of the tests for gauging functionality. It is only possible to apply this technique to specifications and test plans where they have been specially instrumented.

5.1.2   Execution analysis

Execution analysis (also called *dynamic analysis*) requires running of the software either on its target machine or on a host machine which simulates its eventual operation environment. We need to differentiate two approaches to dynamic analysis. *Black-box* (also known as *closed-box*) analysis is where we examine the relationship between the inputs and outputs and pay no attention to the internal workings. *Glass-box* (also known as *white-box* or *open-box*) analysis is where we do examine the internal workings, that is, which statements, modules variables, etc., are used while the program is being run.

We use the term *testing* to refer to where a subset of all the possible inputs is selected, and actual outputs produced by the software are compared with the expected results.* It is widely accepted that testing is an important part of the software development cycle. Even in the most *ad hoc* software developments, the two key activities always present are coding and testing. Testing not only checks the correctness of the software with respect to the specifications or implied requirements, it also serves to identify faults which can then be fixed before release.

The amount of testing (measured, say, as effort or number of test runs) is not itself so important as its effectiveness. There are numerous testing strategies which may be followed to ensure that the effort used in testing is spent in an efficient way, and descriptions of these have been published.[27,55,56,76,125] But, for product assessment, we are not specifically concerned with which actual strategy was used, since this is a process issue. Our interest lies instead with the effect that any such strategies might have on the products themselves. We do, however, need to make one important distinction between *operational testing* where the type and distribution of test data mirrors the intended use of the software and *non-operational testing* where it does not. This will determine whether we can use this testing to estimate reliability. Some testing strategies try and systematically select inputs to cover various parts of the input space or else force various parts of the program to be executed. They are in this sense non-operational. *Ad hoc* testing where test cases are arbitrarily chosen by the programmer is also deemed non-operational.

---

* Some authors use the term 'testing' to refer to any form of assessment of the software products. For example, the IEEE definition[86] would include static analysis and inspection. We use the term here in a more restricted way. The EN 45000 series of standards consider *static path analysis* as a test method. It is a form of non-destructive testing.

Clearly, the effectiveness of testing will have a bearing on the final quality, and more specifically the reliability and functionality, of the software. It is therefore natural to try and measure the test effectiveness to gauge these particular characteristics. According to Grady,[72] testing uses around 34–39 per cent of the development effort on the set of 132 software projects that he looked at. It is clearly not feasible to re-create the whole testing phase except for very small or very highly critical products. It would simply not be cost-effective. There are three ways dynamic analysis can be used to assess the testing without re-doing all of it:

1. Collecting data during the testing phase
2. Rerunning the test cases which were prepared during the testing phase
3. Performing selected testing during the assessment procedure

Note that the effectiveness of testing may also be assessed using static analysis or inspection of the test documentation.

There are two types of product data we can collect during the testing phase. We can automatically trace the execution of the program and determine how the software was executed for glass-box analysis. We can also collect the time between failures during the testing phase. Failure data of this type is only useful for reliability predictions if the testing done is operational testing and the inputs are randomly selected.

It may be that no data was collected during testing, or for some reason the data is not considered suitable. In this case we can re-create the test runs. A large part of the effort during testing is consumed in thinking up test cases, calculating the expected results and then comparing these with the actual results. If this has already been done and we have a set of inputs and corresponding outputs, then re-executing the test data will only take a small proportion of the total testing effort. As the test data is re-executed, it is possible to apply glass-box analysis techniques to measure how the software was actually executed. We cannot, however, use this opportunity to collect failure data for reliability estimation since the inputs have not been randomly selected.

We may wish to perform a small amount of testing ourselves. This can only be justified in terms of cost if the testing is highly focused. For example, we can compare the descriptions given in the user documentation to the actual behaviour of the software. We can thus measure the functionality and usability of the software. In both these cases, the selection of the test cases needs to be structured in such a way as to yield a metrics value. This can be done by means of checklists in much the same way as for inspection as described in the next section.

As we can see, dynamic analysis is not a synonym for testing; it includes testing but also includes collecting the data associated with it. There are three techniques identified here:

Black-box testing This is where the executable components are tested against the functional specifications or user manuals using a checklist.
Failure data collection We collect data concerning the type and frequency of failures during execution.
Test coverage The amount of source code executed during testing is measured automatically.

5.1.3 Inspection

The term *inspection* covers a whole range of activities based on evaluation of the software by humans. Walkthroughs and reviews[67,158] are two ways in which the software may be inspected during its development. However, neither of these techniques will necessarily produce the kind of software metrics that can be used in the assessment. One approach that has been used in many companies and was adopted by the SCOPE project is to add structure to the inspection by using checklists. Checklists comprise a number of questions, for which there are a finite number of specified replies. Each reply has a score associated with it and some questions can be weighted to give them a greater contribution to the final score. Adding up the scores for the applicable questions will yield a total for that checklist. Provided that the questions are objective and relate to a specific attribute, we can consider the checklist score as a valid metric.

As we shall see later, checklists can be used to drive inspection and certain types of black-box testing. In principle checklists can be used as a means to collect metrics for assessing any technique. For example, McCall's[119] or Bowen *et al.*'s[33] quality models used checklists for all metrics. We should be careful about taking a *checklists-for-everything* approach since it is rather like a golfer who uses only one club. Consider the following example. Suppose a checklist asked the question 'How many modules have more than 50 lines of code?' (We shall assume for the time being that *lines of code* is a well-defined measure.) We could derive this measure by hand, which is time-consuming, or we could use a tool. However, if we use a tool we can transfer the actual metrics for each module electronically to a central repository without using a checklist. Therefore when we use checklists to provide a unifying framework for whatever kind of measurement we should remember that not only does the global rating need to be recorded but also the raw data has to be kept and stored separately.

5.1.4 Modelling

We use the term *modelling* to mean creating an abstraction of the software on which assessment may be performed. The essence of modelling is that the model is a simplified representation of the actual component. A good model loses irrelevant detail but captures the attributes of interest. Modelling in this sense refers to representations of the software such as Petri nets or finite-state automata. We can apply our three basic techniques: execution analysis, static analysis and inspection to the model rather than to the software directly. Note that applying execution analysis to a model is usually called *simulation*.

5.1.5   A mapping from characteristics

Figure 5.1 shows how the different measurement techniques can be classified. Table 5.1 shows which techniques may be used to assess which

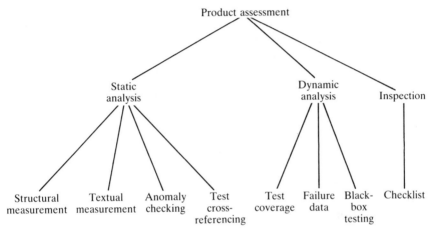

Figure 5.1 Categorization of assessment techniques.

Table 5.1 Mapping of techniques to characteristics

Characteristic	Static analysis	Execution analysis	Inspection
Functionality	Test cross-referencing	Black-box testing	Checklists
Reliability	Anomaly checking	Reliability modelling	Checklists
Usability	Textual measurement	Black-box testing	Checklists
Efficiency		Black-box testing	Checklists
Maintainability	Textual and structural measurement		Checklists
Portability	Anomaly checking		Checklists

characteristics. We note that all characteristics are covered, that most characteristics have at least two methods of assessing them and that no one method can assess everything. This is a key feature of the SCOPE approach and it differs from some other schemes by using many different techniques. For example, the Gütergemeinschaft Software (GGS)[100] scheme uses only black-box testing and checklists and the original McCall scheme relied solely on checklists. We now examine each of these techniques in more detail.

5.2 ANOMALY CHECKING

An *anomaly* is any undesirable feature of the code that may lead to a fault. Anomaly checking is a technique where software tools (static analysers) search for certain classes of anomaly that reside in the source code. For example, if there is a path through the program where a variable is read (referenced) before it is written (defined) this may be a fault which under certain circumstances will lead to a failure. What actually happens will depend on the programming language, the compiler and the state of the machine. It may be that the particular path through the program is in fact unfeasible, in which case the anomaly is benign. But any anomalies found, should at the very least be checked out to see if they can cause a failure.

One particular type of anomaly is the use of non-portable language features. This may cause difficulties when the software is ported to a different platform.

5.2.1 Relation to characteristics

Reliability

The software will fail due to the presence of faults. Any technique that can identify faults and cause them to be removed will increase the reliability of the software. Anomalies that can be detected by tools will only account for a small number of all the possible faults but if we can be sure that this type of fault is absent then the software will be more reliable than it would otherwise have been. We certainly cannot produce any quantitative estimates of reliability from anomaly checking.

Portability

We can consider non-portable features of the code as anomalies. It may be that these features will behave differently when run on different platforms, or else the code may fail to compile on a different machine. The greater the number of non-portable features, the greater will be the effort required to port the software to its new platform.

5.2.2   Data collection

Many compilers perform some types of anomaly checking, and there are in addition some free-standing tools which will do more extensive searches through the code. These free-standing tools will, of course, only support certain languages. Within SCOPE we used the tools lint and flint* (for C and FORTRAN respectively) which are provided with some versions of Unix.[93,157] These tools can provide a report indicating each of the anomalies and where such anomalies can be found in the code. It then requires manual inspection to identify which of them are benign and which indicate actual faults. For example, the tool lint produces the following information:

1. Functions that are never called
2. Statements that can never be reached
3. Variables declared but never used
4. Variables that may be read before they are written
5. Inconsistent type declarations in parameters and returned values
6. Functions that return values that are never used
7. Null-effect operations like assignments in conditional expressions; in C, the valid statement:

   `if ( a = b ) ...`

   does not compare a to b but assigns b to a
8. Precision lost in assignments
9. Non-portable or questionable comparisons,
10. Precedence confusions (where the order of evaluation is undefined)
11. Illegal indirections, assignments and combinations
12. Problems with size
13. Shadowing and redefinitions

Figure 5.2 gives an example of the output of lint for a simple program. The tools SPADE[135] (which is a development tool) and MALPAS[138] perform more extensive checking but only on language subsets. They also provide facilities for formal proof.

If a particular software house defines its own language standard in which certain language constructs are forbidden, then this will in turn require constructing an anomaly checker. A simple example of this is banning the use of the GOTO. However, we will see in structural analysis that there are more effective ways of capturing this attribute.

---

* The Unix operating system is case-sensitive, and Unix tools such as lint, flint and tcov are always written in lowercase even though they are proper names.

```
ckwart.c(296): warning: possible pointer alignment problem
ckwart.c(485): warning: main() returns random value to invocation environment
ckwart.c(653): warning: possible pointer alignment problem
malloc, arg. 1 used inconsistently llib-lc(441) :: ckwart.c(635)
strcpy value declared inconsistently llib-lc(672) :: ckwart.c(636)
exit value declared inconsistently llib-lc(236) :: ckwart.c(650)
fprintf returns value which is always ignored
putc returns value which is always ignored
ungetc returns value which is always ignored
fputs returns value which is always ignored
printf returns value which is always ignored
strcpy returns value which is always ignored
```

Figure 5.2 Example of output from lint.

If we wish to collect metrics such as the number of certain types of anomaly, then this in turn requires some modifications of the tools since many tools just produce a list of the anomalies as they are encountered.

5.2.3 Proposed metrics

There are two types of metrics that might be collected with information on anomalies: first, simple counts of the anomalies (defined on the absolute scale) and secondly conformance or otherwise to a language subset (on the nominal scale). Such a subset may be supported by a standard. For assessing reliability, the kind of anomalies listed above will be generally applicable. In some applications where time and space are of the essence, restrictions on recursion and dynamic arrays may be appropriate. For portability, any non-portable feature will be of interest. Examples are:

- Language extensions
- Non-standard library functions
- Calls to the operating system
- Embedded assembler code

5.2.4 Advantages

This form of analysis is very cheap to perform once the tools have been set up. Checking whether or not the anomalies are benign may take more time and effort. In order to cut out most spurious warnings, it is a good idea to filter automatically the output produced by standard tools.

5.2.5 Drawbacks

Very often a large number of the anomalies will be benign. In general as anomaly checking becomes more intensive and larger number of anomalies are identified, there is a law of diminishing returns as fewer and fewer of these turn out to be faults. We partially overcame this problem by building a tool which filters the output of lint. This is described in Chapter 7.

5.3 TEXTUAL MEASUREMENT

There are several metrics based on counts of the lexical items (words and symbols) that make up the software components. The three main types are:

- Measures of size such as lines of code
- Software science measures
- Readability indices

Size measures give us information about how large the components are and how large certain sections within them are. In particular, in the case of source code we can measure the size of modules or the density of comments.

Software science measures are based on the work of Halstead.[74] These measures are based on the source code and aim to predict the effort and difficulty associated with understanding the program. Many of the assumptions which underlie the theories are questionable, specifically the view that the software was only the code. Also many empirical validations[48] of Halstead's theories have cast doubt on some of the theories he proposed. But at the simplest level of counting the operands and operators of the program, these metrics can indicate size and amount of vocabulary.

Readability indices are defined on natural languages and have been applied specifically to the English language. They indicate from the length of words and the length of sentences, if the text is difficult to read. Spelling checkers can find faults in code comments.

5.3.1 Relation to quality characteristics

Maintainability

An important part of the maintenance task is understanding how the existing software works. Only then can the correct changes be made. Many factors will contribute to the ease with which the software and in particular the code can be understood, and these factors are often referred to as the *complexity*. We will be very careful with this word since in the past it has caused a lot of confusion. In particular there are a number of proposed complexity metrics which measure only one aspect of complexity. Among these factors are the size and structure of the modules. If the modules are too large then it becomes difficult to understand them. If on the other hand they are too small the maintainer will have to constantly switch attention between different parts of the code. Textual measures can be used to measure the size of the modules.

One of the metrics proposed by Halstead is the *vocabulary*, that is, the total number of distinct symbols used in the program. This may also be used to gauge maintainability, since more symbols mean more complexity. Comment density will determine whether there are comments present in the code. It will not of course determine whether they are accurate or meaningful.

The program documentation (functional specifications, design documents, etc.) will of course affect the maintainability of the software. Textual measures can be used to measure the size of the documentation, and the readability indices can be used to indicate whether it is comprehensible.

Usability

The quantity and quality of the user manual(s) will clearly have a bearing on the product's usability. Textual metrics may be used to assess both the size of user documentation and its readability.

5.3.2 Data collection techniques

Calculating textual metrics requires some kind of static analyser. It is not practical to do the calculations by hand. A number of commercial tools such as Logiscope[154] currently calculate many textual metrics such as Halstead's measure and comment density from the source code. This facility is provided along with structural analysis which is covered in the next section. For analysis of natural languages there are a number of text analysers available. Style[79] is a utility on certain versions of the Unix operating system. Right Writer is a free-standing tool which runs on a PC and accepts text input from various word processors. Simple measures like lines of code can be derived either from the operating system or from small tools that can be readily constructed.

5.3.3 Proposed metrics

Simple measures of size can be defined such as:

- Lines of code or text
- Number of characters
- Number of pages

In the case of lines of code, some conventions need to be agreed such as whether to include comments and/or blank lines. Comment density can be measured as the ratio of comment to the amount of code.* Any of these

---

* Often the comment ratio is calculated by dividing the length of comments by some measure of structure.

measures may be defined at different levels of granularity, and for determining the modularity based on the size of the modules these metrics will need to be defined at the module level.

The Halstead metrics are based on counts of the number of operands and operators in the code. *Operands* are the variables, labels and constants used in the program, and *operators* are the key words, arithmetic symbols (+ , - , * , /), brackets, comparison operators (= , > , <= , etc.), and other symbols (like , and ;). Names of functions and procedures count as operands where the function is being defined, but as operators where it is being called. Comments and declarations are ignored. We thus define the four base metrics:

- N_1 The total number of operators
- N_2 The total number of operands
- η_1 The number of distinct operators
- η_2 The number of distinct operands

We than can derive the size of the vocabulary η;

$$\eta = \eta_1 + \eta_2,$$

and the length of the program

$$N = N_1 + N_2.$$

These measures may again be taken at different levels of granularity, although Halstead always intended that the metrics be defined over the entire program. Halstead asserted a number of predictive theories based on these measures. In particular he maintained that the amount of effort to write the program, the language level and the difficulty of the program could be determined from these simple counts of operators and operands. Several years ago some software development units used Halstead measures (the effort metric) to decide whether a program could easily be maintained or whether it was time to rewrite it. Given the weight of published studies[6,14,50] against these theories, we no longer can accept their validity, nevertheless the simple counts of operators and operands are still useful metrics.

The style tool calculates the following readability indices, detailed descriptions of which are given by Cherry:[40]

- Kincaid Reading Grade
- Coleman–Liau Reading Grade
- Flesch Reading Score

In addition several measures of sentence-type and word-type occurrence are calculated.

5.3.4 Advantages

These metrics may be derived easily and cheaply once the tools have been acquired. Collecting the metrics is a mechanistic process and does not require any specialist skills and the metrics are derived objectively. Some metrics such as lines of code can also be used for cost modelling using such models as COCOMO.[30]

5.3.5 Drawbacks

Many of the metrics have no standard definition. This is particularly true for lines of code. Merely altering the layout of the code can alter this metric substantially. This can bring about a funny situation where a bespoke software product is paid for by lines of code. Yet this attitude still persists. The Halstead metrics also have no standard definitions of what constitutes an operator or an operand.

There is a problem inherent in any static analyser in that it cannot necessarily cope with all languages and all the different versions of a given language. Many languages are not defined by any standard; even where a standard exists many compiler builders choose to ignore it. For this reason different versions of the tools are needed for each language dialect. Logiscope, for example, provides a number of different versions for each different dialect of a given language. Even where standards are followed, they only define the features a language must have. Many compiler builders choose to add extra features, and a static analyser ought to be able to cope with these. Static analysers sometimes fail because a non-standard feature is encountered in a particular piece of code.

It is not possible to parse natural language fully, and indeed there are reasons to believe that it will always be impossible. So text analysers will often make mistakes when parsing natural language and this may distort some of the readability indices. The style tool is claimed to work with 95 per cent accuracy.

5.4 STRUCTURAL ANALYSIS

Structural analysis is based on deriving directed graph models of the software and then calculating metrics from these models. The metrics are known as *structural metrics*. The most common models used are the following:

Control flowgraph captures the algorithmic structure of a given module; Fig. 5.3 shows an example.
Call graph captures the interrelations between the modules in a compound module or subsystem; Fig. 5.4 shows an example.

Flowgraph of module 'shell_sort'
in file 'drawer.i'

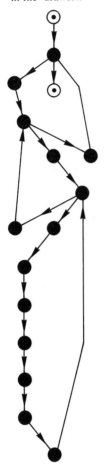

Figure 5.3 Example of a flowgraph.

There are also some metrics defined on the data flow, but tools for this kind of analysis were not readily available to the project.

Structural models can be defined on many formal or semi-formal notations. However, it is not possible to perform this kind of analysis on natural language text. Most commonly these models are applied to source code, but this need not be the case. The metrics thus defined capture various structural attributes such as depth of nesting and use of structured programming. The term *complexity metrics* (and for call graphs *system complexity metrics*) is often used, in our view misleadingly, to describe these metrics. We will avoid these terms, but instead refer to specific structural attributes.

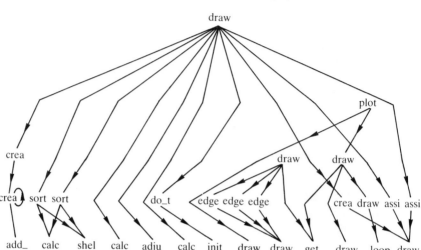

Figure 5.4 Example of a call graph.

5.4.1 Relation to quality characteristics

Maintainability

The structure of the various software components will affect how easy they are to understand and test and this in turn will influence the maintainability of the software. One of the main reasons that there is any design process at all in the development life cycle is that it divides the problem into a number of smaller and more easily understood parts. The fact that developers should wish to perform unit testing before integration testing again supports the general divide-and-conquer approach which is prevalent throughout most software production. Development methods such as object-oriented programming and structured programming work precisely by imposing discipline on the software structure. Structural metrics can capture many, although not all, of the key structural attributes which these methods aim to achieve.

5.4.2 Data collection techniques

Structural analysis requires a static analyser, since it is not practical to perform the calculations manually. The static analysers for this purpose typically have two parts: a *front end* and a *back end*. The *front end* reads in the source code, specification, etc., and outputs intermediate files. Front ends are always specific to a particular language. The *back end* reads in the intermediate files, calculates the metrics and displays them. It may also display flowgraphs and call graphs. Many tools allow the user to view the control flowgraphs and call graphs (or parts of these). Thus, for a given tool, a number of different front ends supporting different languages can be used with a common back end. The graphs displayed by the back end can be used to create documentation or for the purposes of inspection. It is possible to judge certain structural attributes by simply inspecting the graphs. However, the layout of the graphs will depend heavily on the particular graph layout algorithm implemented within that specific tool. Sometimes an apparently simple graph can be drawn in a contorted way. So we rely on the metrics to assess the structural attributes rather than the graphs themselves. These metrics may be displayed as tables of numbers and many analysers also provide some simple statistics for interpreting the metrics, such as bar graphs, histograms and Kiviat diagrams used to represent multi-dimensional data.

The two tools used in SCOPE were Logiscope and QUALMS. Logiscope also calculates textual metrics. Both support a large number of different languages. There are in addition a number of other tools available such as Qualigraph[47] and Metropol[49] which perform a similar form of analysis.

There is a popular misconception that these techniques apply only to traditional third-generation programming languages. Within SCOPE, structural measurement has been applied to fourth-generation languages such as RULER and SQL. In the COSMOS project front ends have been developed for specification languages such as Z, SDL and LOTOS.

5.4.3   Proposed metrics

There are a very large number of structural metrics that have been proposed in the literature. A survey by Züse[159] defines over 100 metrics based on the flowgraph alone. We will define here some of the metrics defined on SCOPE. From Logiscope, the following metrics are defined directly from the flowgraph:

Number of nodes The number of nodes in the flowgraph
Number of edges The number of edges in the flowgraph
Cyclomatic number This is defined as *edges − nodes + 2*
Number of levels The maximum number of nesting levels of control-flow constructs within the flowgraph

QUALMS takes a different approach to defining metrics based on the Fenton–Whitty theory of flowgraph decomposition. This was an attempt to unify the various diverse views of control-flow structure and produce a general theory (see Fenton[64] and Chapter 10 of Bache's thesis[11]). A control flowgraph is *decomposed* into a hierarchy of *prime flowgraphs* known as a *decomposition tree* where the primes represent the basic control-flow constructs. The size and frequency of these primes characterize the use of structured programming. This provides a language-independent means of determining whether a program is well structured. In many languages such as FORTRAN, it is still necessary to use GOTO statements to provide the full range of structures needed to implement an algorithm. Yet GOTO may be used in a structured or unstructured way. This can be characterized by the primes. Furthermore a number of metrics can be defined on the decomposition tree. Such metrics would be difficult to calculate directly from the flowgraph itself. Examples are:

Depth of nesting Similar to the Logiscope levels metric.
Is D-structured Yields the value 1 if the module is written in accordance with the rules of structured programming, 0 otherwise.
Biggest prime Indicates the worst instance of unstructured programming.
Cyclomatic number Same as Logiscope.
Testability metrics These estimate the minimum number of paths needed to attain certain glass-box-test coverage strategies such as statement and branch testing.
Occurrences of a named prime This is the number of times a given prime flowgraph (corresponding to a control-flow construct) appears in a given module.

Both QUALMS and Logiscope calculate a number of call graph metrics. From Logiscope examples are:

Testability Characterizes properties of the call paths which relate to the difficulty of selecting test data.
Hierarchical complexity* Average number of modules on each level of the call graph.
Structural complexity Average number of calls per module.

From QUALMS the following metrics may be calculated:

Maximum depth of call How far down the calling graph the least reachable node is.
Number of recursions Number of modules that call themselves.
Yin and Winchester metrics A family of metrics which calculate how much the call graph deviates from a tree.
Re-use metrics Determine to what extent modules are called by many different other modules.

---

* The word 'complexity' appears in the metric name which was not chosen by the authors.

5.4.4 Advantages

Structural metrics are easy and cheap to collect once the tools have been obtained. Using the tools requires no great expertise and the metrics derived are objective.

5.4.5 Drawbacks

Structural metrics share many of the same difficulties as textual metrics. Different versions of languages are likely to cause difficulties. Furthermore there is another problem concerning the modelling of flowgraphs: there is no agreed convention for mapping the statements of the language to the nodes and edges of a graph. For this reason, different analysers may generate different graphs from the same program module. Even when tools calculate the same metric like the cyclomatic number (which is implemented by a number of analysers) the differences in the underlying graph may yield different numerical values. Figure 5.5 shows the same module as Fig. 5.3 but modelled in a different way.

Structural metrics cannot of themselves assess everything about maintainability. A program which is ill-structured will be difficult to maintain, but a well-structured program may be difficult to maintain for other reasons such as poor or inaccurate documentation.

5.5   TEST CROSS-REFERENCING

Test cross-referencing is a technique that connects functions of the product with specific test cases so that it is possible to obtain the measure of the functional coverage attained by the execution of those tests. It is a static technique since it is based on analysing non-executable documents. In fact it calculates the level of coverage that would be obtained if the actual testing followed the documented plans.

This technique is based on the following steps:[39,110]

- Extraction of the functionality from the documents describing the functional behaviour of the product (i.e. functional specification or, when this is not present, user manuals). This is the most important step and implies both the *underlining* of all functions described explicitly in the functional specification and the insertion of *hidden* functions (threshold values, negative behaviour, etc.)
- Specification of test cases, with indication of the functions that are covered by each of them
- Computation of functional coverage on the basis of tests and of their relationship with functionalities

72

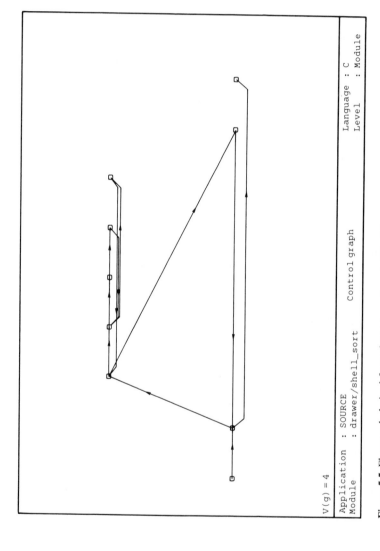

V(g) = 4

Application : SOURCE   Control graph   Language : C
Module   : drawer/shell_sort   Level   : Module

Figure 5.5 Flowgraph derived from the same code as in Fig. 5.3.

The technique is oriented to the definition and monitoring of testing activities, captured by instrumentation of functional specification. The next logical stage is to perform the actual (black-box) testing to determine whether the test cases pass or fail.

We can see that the idea is simple and does not require a large overhead on the testing activities. Its key feature is that it creates a strong link between specifications and test documents (by means of the list of functions) and it gives a coverage measure that is closer to the user's perception than glass-box coverage measures.

5.5.1 Relation to quality characteristics

Functionality

The technique is a particular application of black-box testing with a functional coverage approach. Therefore it is mainly directed to the verification that all the functions that are expressed in the specifications of the product work correctly.

5.5.2 Data collection techniques

Even if it is possible in principle to apply this technique without tools, their usage is highly recommended, especially when the product to test is large.

The collection of data from test cross-referencing was done in the SCOPE Project using TEFAX,[62,111] a tool supporting the testing and quality-control activities performed on a software product. It also manages the actual testing of the software as well as test cross-referencing. TEFAX is useful during assessments because:

- It produces a standard environment to develop quality-control activities.
- It helps in pointing out all functionalities to check, organizing tests and managing the results provided by the tests executed.
- It automatically manages quality-control activity documents.
- It provides useful statistical information about the progress of test activities and of related costs.
- It provides information about test results.

TEFAX also makes the test-maintenance activity easier. In fact, after software product specifications and/or tests change, it allows us to automatically create updated test documents and reports.

5.5.3 Proposed metrics

Among the various metrics gathered by TEFAX, the ones related to assessment concern test structure and functional coverage.

Test-structure metrics (which give us an indication of whether the test design was good) are:

Test redundancy Average number of tests covering a functionality
Test power Average number of functionalities covered by a test

The (static) coverage measure calculated is the *percentage of tried functions* which is the percentage of functions that would be tested if the test plan were actually executed. Two related execution metrics which we include here for completeness are:

Test progress Percentage of tests actually executed
Functional coverage Percentage of passed functions, that is, functions that were tested without causing a failure

5.5.4 Advantages

The advantages of this technique can be summarized as follows:

1. Well-defined relationship between development and testing
2. Definition of user-perceivable metrics
3. Independence from the hardware/software platform of the product to be assessed
4. Careful analysis of functional specifications, which usually brings us to the early detection of ambiguities and faults (this is very useful when it is applied as a quality assurance and control activity)
5. Applicability to large systems[116]

5.5.5 Drawbacks

The main drawbacks of the technique are:

- It is labour-intensive and thus costly unless it is embedded in the testing phase of the product. Therefore it is normally not cost-effective when applied to already released products; rather it is well suited for *concurrent* assessment (that is to say, assessment carried out in parallel with development).
- The extraction of functionalities can suffer from subjectivity.

Research is moving towards the automatic identification of functions when specifications are expressed in a formal[28] or semi-formal way.[5,16]

5.6 BLACK-BOX TESTING

Black-box testing is testing against the specification or some other document like the user manual. Any testing has to be performed on either the target machine or some simulation of it. Black-box testing checks for consistency between the documents provided and the actual execution of the code. The usual way to systematically assess this consistency is by applying a checklist. Within SCOPE we used a particular checklist which has become a German standard DIN 66285[59] and is the basis of the Gütergemeinschaft Software scheme (GGS). We subsequently refer to this particular technique. Many of the features of this standard are based simply on inspection of the documentation such as checking that the user manual has a table of contents. This is inspection by checklists as described in Sec. 5.9. We concentrate here on those aspects which are based on execution analysis.

The standard specifies a technique and a uniform way of preparing and recording the test data to ensure that all the functions of the software are tested at least once.

5.6.1 Relation to quality characteristics

Functionality

The checklist ensures that every function described in the specification is tested and that everything performed by the software is described in the specification. This includes the installation instructions.

Usability

The standard checks that the functions of the software are described in the user manual. It also checks aspects of the user interface such as whether information is presented to the user in a uniform manner and that the error messages produced are useful.

Efficiency

Even though not covered at present by the GGS scheme, efficiency can also be assessed by means of black-box testing. For example, we can look at the response times and compare them with the performance requirements.

5.6.2 Data collection techniques

The method of data collection is similar to that used by inspection based on checklists. There are in addition several forms that have to be filled in with the description and results of the testing performed.

5.6.3 Proposed metrics

The metrics collection is the number of failures discovered during the testing of the product. There are two types of errors:

Class I are the most significant errors like a system crash or a function not implemented or data corrupted during the test run. If one of these is found the product is deemed to have failed the test.
Class II are minor failures such as bad representation of data or error messages.

These errors are further classified according to which component they were found in (e.g. user manual, specification, etc.).

5.6.4 Advantages

The technique is very thorough in that it aims to cover every function of the software. It also covers the installation of the software which is something not captured by coverage measurement.

5.6.5 Drawbacks

The technique is very labour-intensive, and in the case of a complex product with a large number of functions, it would take a long time to perform. There are the obvious problems of interpreting what exactly constitutes a function of the software, although the instructions provided with the checklist give some guidance on this. Unlike test coverage, it is not possible to re-use test data provided by the developer.

5.7 FAILURE DATA COLLECTION

The software developer will often record failures which occur both during testing and after release. This can be used to ensure that the corresponding faults have been fixed. However, a record of failures cannot be used by itself to assess the software unless we know also the amount of usage the software has had. Failure data collection for software assessment means recording the first manifestation of each failure and the time between the occurrences of each failure. Time in this sense means a measure of the amount of usage rather than of calendar time.

5.7.1 Relation to quality characteristics

Reliability

The only way we can currently estimate the reliability of software (by which we mean the probability it will run for a given period of time without failing) is by analysing the past failure history. Although there is good reason to believe that many of the internal attributes, and specifically the presence of anomalies, will affect the reliability, there are as yet no quantitative theories which allow us to make predictions from these results. There are, however, a large number of *reliability models* which can make quantitative estimates from past failure data. These are discussed in the next chapter.

5.7.2 Data collection techniques

Failure data can only be collected while the software is being run. Furthermore such data can only be used to estimate reliability if the software is run using the same kinds and frequency of inputs that will occur during its actual usage. So we can collect failure data either during operational testing with randomly selected inputs or else while the software is actually being used for its intended purpose. Normally we will wish to assess and certify software before it is released and so this second source of data will not usually be available. But we can use failure data from actual operation for other uses such as assessing already-released software or planning maintenance effort. In the latter case effort used in corrective maintenance will depend on the number of faults discovered during operation and this can be estimated from the history of past failures.

During testing, we run the software until it fails. We then debug the program and create a new version in which the offending fault *may* have been fixed. We then run the software again until it fails. The data of interest is the time until the first manifestation of each failure. Sometimes the faults will not be fixed individually but in batches. In this instance we collect failure data but must ignore repeated occurrences of the same failure. If the software is not being repaired at all then we take a quite different approach. We still collect the total number of failures (repeated or not) that occur during a given period of execution, but the methods of analysing this last kind of data are appropriately different.

Failure data can be collected with pen, paper and stop-watch, but this approach tends to be time-consuming and error-prone. Within the SCOPE project we developed a semi-automatic method of collecting failure data from the operating system. Methods of automatic failure collection are addressed in Chapter 7.

In addition to collecting the time between failures, it may be useful to collect the class and severity of each failure. We can then analyse subsets of the failure data to determine reliability in terms of certain types of failure. If, for example, we were assessing a safety-critical system we might exclude certain classes of failure such as spelling errors on the screen and estimate the mean time to a serious failure.

5.7.3 Proposed metrics

The metrics needed to make reliability estimates are the times between failures. If this data is not available then an approximation can be made with the number of failures that occur in given time periods. This is possible if, for example, we know how many failures occurred each day and how much time the software was run on each day. Reliability estimates can still be made, but the results are less accurate. We should be careful about using calendar time unless the software is being run continuously.[41] If we do we might find that the software appears to be more reliable at weekends and on public holidays. Fewer failures are likely to occur when the software is used less. There are various measures of time we can use, and the one chosen will depend on the type of software:

CPU time This has to be measured by the hardware itself.
Elapsed time This is the time between the start and stop of the program.
Number of transactions This is applicable for certain data-processing applications.
Number of test runs (sessions) This may be used if each test run is of similar length in CPU time.

In addition to this we may wish to collect the class and severity of the data. The class of failure will be different for each application and is defined on a nominal scale. Severity is defined on an ordinal scale. An example of such a classification is as follows:

- Trivial inconsistency
- Minor inconvenience
- Significant loss of functionality
- Total loss of service

5.7.4 Advantages

Failure data can be used in reliability models to make predictions about the software after release. It is in this sense the most powerful technique we have. If the data is collected automatically then the overhead during testing is small.

5.7.5   Drawbacks

The failure data can only be useful if the testing was conducted in a particular way. Specifically we need to simulate the way in which the software will actually be used. This is often difficult.

Collecting failure data can be difficult. If it is to be collected by hand then it requires the full cooperation of the development staff who will have to record every time the software is run during testing. If the data is collected automatically, then this imposes limitations on the kind of operating system and hardware that can be used. It is worth noting that very few sets of failure data have been published.

As we shall see in Chapter 6, we cannot use failure data to assure high-criticality systems.

5.8   TEST COVERAGE

Test coverage is a way of measuring the amount that the code has been exercised during testing. It is a form of glass-box execution analysis. Data is gathered on the paths of the program that have been executed. From this we can determine which parts of the code have been tested and which have not. Test coverage may be used during testing to guide the selection of test cases. If the developer finds that certain parts of the program have not been executed then test cases can be created that force execution of these specific paths. However, for assessment purposes we are interested in the measures of coverage which enable us to determine whether the testing was done effectively.

Test-coverage measures are usually based either on the control flowgraph or on the call graph. There are a number of coverage measures also defined on data flow but in general these are not supported by tools.

5.8.1   Relation to quality characteristics

Functionality

Test coverage in fact measures the quality of the test data rather than of the code itself. If the test data has been executed without any failures then this gives us a degree of assurance about the code. The relationship between the functions provided by the software and the structure of the code is a complex one. Nevertheless, if part of the code has not been tested, then the functionality that this part provides cannot have been tested. The converse is not true. Just because all the code has been executed does not mean that all the functions have been tested. Also test coverage gives no indication of functions that have failed to be implemented.

5.8.2 Data collection techniques

Test coverage requires a dynamic analyser. Often these analysers are free-standing tools such as Logiscope and Testbed. In other cases they are add-ons provided with a compiler. In SCOPE we used the tools Logiscope and tcov. The second of these, tcov, is a facility provided with certain versions of Unix which together with the C compiler supports coverage measures.

To collect coverage measures, the code has to be altered so that in addition to performing all its usual functions it also records which statements have been executed. This is done by *instrumenting* the code: extra statements are added to track the path followed and the information thus derived is written to a file which is later used to calculate the coverage measures. In the case of Logiscope, collecting coverage data proceeds by the following stages:

1. To the source code is fed into a facility which creates the instrumented source code with the extra statements added. This instrumentation tool is different for every language version.
2. The source code is then compiled in the usual way and is linked with certain extra library modules provided with the analyser.
3. The object code is run with the appropriate set of test data. A file of results is automatically created.
4. The results file is then fed into a dynamic analyser back-end which calculates the coverage measures.

In addition to providing the coverage measures, some tools draw control flowgraph and call graphs which indicate the unexecuted paths. Other tools such as tcov give a listing of the source code with the unexecuted statements clearly identified. This information can be used for inspection or creating additional test cases.

5.8.3 Proposed metrics

All coverage metrics are of the form:

$$\frac{number\ of\ items\ executed}{total\ number\ of\ items} \times 100$$

and differ only in which items are counted. A coverage of 100 per cent means that every item has been executed at least once. The most commonly calculated coverage measures are:

Statement coverage Every executable statement. People are, of course, likely to argue over what is an executable statement.

Branch coverage Every branch in the control flowgraph. If 100 per cent coverage has been attained then every decision has been evaluated as both true and false.

DDP coverage A decision-to-decision path is any set of consecutive edges between any two decisions, start nodes, or end nodes. Note that 100 per cent DDP coverage is the same as 100 per cent branch coverage.

LCSAJ coverage A linear code sequence and jump is a consecutive set of statements and jumps with no branching.

Basic block This refers to Algol-style languages such as Pascal and C. A basic block is either a single statement or a set of simple (i.e. non-control) statements enclosed in BEGIN and END (or { and } for C). The term *basic block* can also mean any one-entry-one-exit structure; however, we adopt the terminology used by tcov.

Procedure coverage Procedure in our terminology is a module.

PPP coverage Procedure-to-procedure paths are the edges in the call graph between any two modules.

Within SCOPE we collected three coverage measures: PPP coverage and DDP coverage from Logiscope and basic-block coverage from tcov.

5.8.4 Advantages

Coverage measures can be calculated automatically and so the effort to collect them is not great. Furthermore, if the dynamic analyser is used during the testing phase, this data can be provided by the developer.

5.8.5 Drawbacks

As with textual and structural measurement, the instrumentation tools are language-specific. A non-standard feature in the code may cause the tool to fail. This might create an incorrect program, i.e. the functionality of the actual program will be altered.

The instrumented code is generally larger (up to 50 per cent or so) and slower. In one instance it was found to run at one-tenth of the normal speed. The instrumentation statements need also to write to files and these files can become quite large. For this reason dynamic analysis is not suitable for some real-time applications, nor for embedded systems where space is at a premium and there may be no file-handling facilities.

Certain types of fourth-generation languages use diagrams and tables to generate the object code automatically. In this case it is difficult to instrument the code unless a feature has been provided by the compiler maker.

5.9   INSPECTION VIA CHECKLISTS

Checklists provide a structured way of performing inspection. We can apply inspection to many software components such as function specifications, design documents, user documentation and source code. Checklists look for the presence or absence of features which will contribute to the quality characteristics. Each checklist consists of a number of questions. Each question has a number of specified replies which in the simplest case can be 'yes' or 'no'. There may be several checklists assessing different aspects of a given document.

Two kinds of checklist are normally used. The first is document-oriented so that it looks for several characteristics in a particular software component. These are useful for QA or assessment conducted in parallel with development. The second is characteristic-oriented so that it looks at specific characteristics or sub-characteristics across several software components. These are used for validation, traceability and consistency inspection and are particularly useful on a released software product.

5.9.1   Relation to quality characteristics

Functionality

By applying checklists to the specification and test documentation we can find out if the functions provided by the system are clearly described and if the test data addresses these functions. We can also find out if there are omissions in the specification such as error messages, details of the user interface, or real-time constraints. If important items are unspecified, the final product may deviate substantially from the intended product.

An example of checklists developed in SCOPE and related to safety aspects of functionality has been published by the SCOPE consortium.[101] Checklists for security can easily be derived from the ITSEC document.[44]

Reliability

Checklists can be used to assess technical aspects of fault tolerance and recoverability in areas such as restart, rollback, data integrity, validity checking of users' inputs, robustness to hardware failure, degraded service, redundancy and so forth.

Usability

There are certain features that user documentation should have, such as a general description of the product, a table of contents, an index and a list of error messages. The checklists can check for these. The checklists can also look for inconsistencies in the documentation and assess whether documents are written at a suitable level for the target audience. An example of a usability checklist is provided by the US Air Force.[54] Checklists for human–computer interface can be easily derived from graphical user interface guidelines. The MUSIC project has also developed checklists.[95,134]

Maintainability

Checklists can be applied to the source code and design documentation to ensure that the software is easy to understand. Such features as meaningful identifier names, a description of each module, and modules performing a simple well-defined function will all make the software easier to maintain. These things are impossible to measure using static analysis. Comprehensive examples of checklists inspecting maintainability are provided by the SCOPE project,[102] among others.[33,53,68]

Portability

Certain features will make the software easier to move to a new environment. It is rarely possible to make the software totally portable, so those parts which are non-portable need to be clearly identified and documented. Checklists can check that this has been done. A good example of a portability checklist was created within the SCOPE project.[141] It is specifically oriented towards C and is based on earlier checklists developed by partners.[93,157]

Efficiency

Checklists can be used to identify those features of the software that will affect its efficiency. These include choice of algorithm (some algorithms are faster than others) and optimization of certain parts of the code such as using assembler for the most critical parts, avoiding using constant assignments in loops, avoiding constants in conditional expressions, not using redundant variables, using iteration rather than recursion, using special registers and so on.

5.9.2 Data collection techniques

Any checklist can be applied using pencil and paper. The checklist scores can then be derived by hand. However, it is possible and indeed desirable to automate this process by means of a set of data entry forms. Such a tool can check for consistency and store the checklist data in an electronic format. Of course, deciding the responses to the questions still requires considerable human input. In Chapter 7 we describe how checklists were automated by means of the *checklist manager*.

In a large software project, the components to be inspected may be very large, and thus the effort to inspect them will also be large. The effort used in inspection can be substantially reduced by sampling, that is, only applying the checklists to randomly selected parts of the components.

5.9.3   Proposed metrics

The metrics generated by checklists are the scores derived by adding up the values associated with each answer. This can then be divided by the maximum possible score and multiplied by 10 to give a range of values from 0 to 10. (The choice of the range 0–10 is purely arbitrary.) A score of 10 indicates that all the desirable features are present. Often some of the questions in the checklist may be irrelevant, and in this case they are excluded from the total score.

5.9.4   Advantages

The use of manual input in applying the checklists means that many important features can be measured in a way that is impossible for the purely tools-based methods. There is no need for any outlay on tools although the use of automated forms can be justified in that it reduces the likelihood of errors. Checklists are not sensitive to different languages, operating systems, or target environments in the way that tools-based methods are.

The derivation of checklists is very easy and cost-effective where a standard already exists. A special case is when a documentation standard is adopted by a project and the checklist can be used to check aspects such as traceability, consistency, completeness, or adherence to the standard. Such a checklist can be used both for assessment and to support management and QA activities.

Another advantage is that checklists, unlike tools, can be easily modified and reissued in the light of experience. Where ambiguities are felt to exist, the questions can be rephrased or definitions may be added.

5.9.5   Drawbacks

The use of a human making judgements inevitably introduces the problem of human error and some degree of subjectivity. Indeed the definition and application of checklists is heavily influenced by human factors.[150] These problems can be mitigated by the way in which the checklists are drafted. For example, if there is an odd number of replies, the assessor may always plump for the middle value. Providing an even number forces a non-neutral judgement to be made.

Checklists are not completely repeatable in the same way as the tools-based methods. In Chapter 9 we give an example of how two different assessors applied the same checklists to the same components.

Checklists also require an expert to perform the inspection and this may be expensive. For this reason the cost of applying checklists can be high. The necessary level of expertise can be reduced if each question is supported by explanatory text (typically about half a page). This approach has been adopted by SCOPE and increases the effort needed to prepare the checklists.

One way to reduce the effort needed to apply checklists is to use sampling techniques where only part of the component is actually inspected. This is particularly relevant to very large projects with perhaps hundreds of pages of documentation and hundreds of thousands of lines of code.

5.10 MODELLING

Modelling is not a technique on its own but rather an intermediate step that may be used before the above techniques are actually applied. Models are essential when software products are extremely large or complicated.

Once we have a model of a software product, we can apply almost all the techniques that we would apply on the product itself. Execution analysis, for instance, can be applied when we have a model of the behaviour of the software system; in this case, we normally use the term *simulation* which means the representation of selected characteristics of the behaviour of one physical or abstract system by another system. Simulation is very useful in assessing efficiency[65] when direct measurements (by means of benchmarking, sampling, or profiling) are not possible; this happens for instance when the software product is not yet fully available or cannot be accessed or instrumented. Simulation is also used for assessing the functionality of software systems, typically for event-driven or concurrent ones. In the SCOPE project we used Petri nets[133] and communicating finite-state automata as modelling techniques.

Obviously static analysis can be applied on a model. We can apply anomaly checking to see whether all the underlying rules of the adopted modelling technique are respected, to check the consistency of the representation, or to assess its balancing. For instance, if we adopt a modelling technique that allows some form of levelling, we can check whether all the events produced or consumed at one level are also represented with the same meaning at the lower level. Structural analysis is also applicable, since most models are based on such graph notations as processes and flows. An example of classical static-analysis metrics is one applied to Petri nets.[19] To this end those tools (including CASE ones) that extract metrics from the supported technique are very useful.

Finally, it is obvious that inspection techniques can be applied to any model and furthermore that a model of a software product is a good starting-point for testing. Thus, techniques like test cross-referencing keep their validity.

5.11 MIXING TECHNIQUES

There is no reason why each of these assessment techniques should be used in isolation. It is often possible to combine two complementary techniques in order to assess a particular characteristic. The tools-based methods such as static analysis and test coverage are quite cheap but many important attributes of the software cannot be measured automatically. Checklists, on the other hand, get around this problem but are labour-intensive. A mixture of the tools-based and inspection-based techniques can lead to a more efficient use of effort during assessment.

For example, let us suppose that we are assessing the maintainability of the source code for a large software product, where it may not be practical to inspect all of it. By applying textual and structural measurement to the whole project we would be able to use Pareto analysis where, for example, 20 per cent of the modules were causing 80 per cent of the difficulties, to identify those modules which were particularly large or badly structured. These modules are likely to be the most difficult to maintain. We could then apply inspection via checklists to these specific modules to determine if in reality they were difficult to understand and as a consequence difficult to maintain.

Another example of mixing techniques is one where a scheme for usability evaluation is given that merges execution analysis with inspection (based on expert judgement or guided by checklists), and with modelling.[109]

5.12 PROCESS DATA COLLECTION

We will from time to time wish to collect process data to validate the theories that underlie product-based assessment. Having collected the product-based metrics from the software we will sometimes want to determine if the assessments based on these metrics were justified. By collecting the process data during development and after release we can calibrate the assessment criteria based on the product metrics. More specifically we can use the process data to determine what pass/fail thresholds should be placed on the various metrics.

We do not propose that the process data should be used to assess the software itself. For one reason, the process data will not be available when we want to certify the software. Nor do we propose that every piece of software subjected to product assessment needs to be followed up with process data collection.

The two types of data we wish to record are:

Data on tasks such as maintaining and porting the software
Data on events such as the type and location (in the software) of faults

This type of data needs the cooperation of the developer. The data also has to be collected with a large degree of manual input. The data-collection process can be automated by electronic forms, but it requires programmers to record the location of faults and the amount of effort to perform various tasks such as finding and fixing them.

The proposed metrics defined on tasks are:

- Amount of effort
- Type of task (enhancement, fault fix, etc.)
- Elapsed time to perform task

As far as data on events is concerned, for faults we collect the location of the fault and the type and severity of the failure it caused. To be most useful this data should be collected at the finest granularity, that is, at the module level.

SUMMARY

We have proposed eight methods of product assessment. Our criterion for choosing these eight was that they have all been applied successfully on one or more SCOPE case studies. Each of these techniques applies to the software components that are available prior to release and each will yield a set of measures. Some techniques necessitate the use of tools and all of them can be supported by tools in some way. We would maintain that there is no one method that can be used by itself to assess all aspects of quality. Furthermore, for any one characteristic there may be more than one technique used to assess that characteristic. At no point do we wish to suggest that these should be seen as substitutes. For example, portability can be assessed by anomaly checking and inspection but inspection will reveal many features that the static checker cannot find. To try and use a checklist to look through the entire code for non-standard language features would normally be impractical.

However, there is more to assessing software than just generating numbers. These numbers have to be interpreted so that conclusions can be drawn about the quality of the software. In many cases quite a large amount of data will be produced from assessing a software project. In the next chapter we consider how we can make sense of this data and arrive at definite conclusions.

6

METRICS ANALYSIS

WITH MARTIN NEIL

As we have seen in Chapter 5, there is a wide range of techniques that we can use to assess internal attributes of the software product. All of these techniques produce data and, as we have argued in Chapter 4, all this data can be expressed in numerical form. But collecting data should be seen as only the first stage of software assessment. We also have to analyse the data to make deductions about the quality of the software product and determine if it is sufficiently good to be passed by the QA staff or issued a certificate.

The quantity of data we collect will often be quite large. Many textual, structural and test coverage metrics are defined at the module level. If we collect, say, 20 metrics for each module and we have 100 modules in a system, then we will have 2000 data points, excluding metrics defined at the subsystem and system levels. It would be difficult to imagine a software assessor simply gazing at pages of figures and rationally arriving at a pass/fail decision for that particular product. We need to use statistics to understand the numbers, to make deductions and then produce evidence to support those deductions. In many cases simply expressing the data in pie charts and histograms can reveal a great deal about the software. Nevertheless, if we wish to uncover the relationships between metrics to validate theories, methods like regression and correlation will be more appropriate. However, when applying any kind of statistics we need to be very careful. Software metrics data is often considered to be unusual in that it does not conform to the normality assumptions on which many statistical tests and methods are based. However, this does not preclude the meaningful application of statistical techniques. We have many tests at our disposal which can accommodate other distributional assumptions. It is therefore important for the researcher to determine the specific statistical tests and methods needed for each analysis in turn. Furthermore, analysing failure data needs a very particular type of statistics and there is a range of models which are specifically used to predict future reliability. Nevertheless, there are limitations to the kind of predictions we can make about reliability.

6.1 USING STATISTICS FOR PRODUCT ASSESSMENT

The primary purpose of applying statistics to metrics data is to gain understanding. Therefore the choice of statistics we use will ultimately be determined by the audience for whom the statistics are intended. If we are providing an evaluation of a software product for project managers then generally we will want to use simple *descriptive statistics*. We can use simple graphs and tables to point out areas of high and low software quality and make comparisons with other projects or predefined target values.

We will also want to use the metrics data collected from different projects to define and refine the criteria on which the assessments are made. This means deciding the ranges of values that the metrics ought to have. Such an activity is essentially one internal to the QA department or test laboratory. In this case there is no need to restrict ourselves to simple descriptive statistics, although these will still have a role. There are other more powerful techniques such as regression, correlation and multivariate techniques.

The advent of commercial statistical packages over the last few years has meant that statistics can be readily used by people who have little or no knowledge of the underlying mathematics. Many of the complex calculations which in the past had to be done manually or hard-programmed into specific tools are no longer a concern. One particular facility provided by many such packages is the ability to generate graphs and diagrams automatically. Some packages are compatible with word processors so that these diagrams can be 'cut and pasted' into assessment reports.

The fact that statistical packages are so easy to use gives rise to the danger of applying inappropriate techniques. We still need to understand the assumptions on which a particular technique is based. If these are ignored then the conclusions are likely to be erroneous. It is all too easy to produce plausible-looking diagrams or correlations that are, in reality, totally meaningless.

We shall assume that within our test lab or quality assurance group we have all the data both from past products and the particular software product under examination. The precise details of how to do this are given in later chapters, but for the time being we assume that the data exists and can be readily accessed. This will enable us to do the following:

Outlier analysis for a given product to look for 'unusual parts' that may require further examination

Norms and thresholds to use past data to establish assessment criteria

Comparison across projects to try to find out why the quality differs between projects

Regression and correlation to uncover relationships between the internal and external metrics to support a particular theory or hypothesis

Reliability estimation to make quantitative estimates of reliability

Statistics is a large body of knowledge and it would certainly not be possible to describe all the methods that would conceivably be used with software metrics. We do describe here a range of techniques that have been specifically used in SCOPE on data from the case studies. These are:

Summary statistics such as mean, median, maximum and minimum

Graphical representations such as histograms, pie charts and box plots

Principal components analysis to reduce the number of variables being analysed

Regression and correlation techniques for uncovering relationships in the data

Reliability models for predicting future reliability—these are very different from the other techniques and are described separately in later sections of this chapter

We want to see how each of these techniques can be used to interpret particular metrics data. But before we show how we can actually apply the statistics we explore why software metrics are different from other types of data on which statistics have traditionally been applied.

6.2 PROBLEMS WITH METRICS DATA

Most statistical methods and tests make a number of assumptions about the data being analysed. For example, the use of F-tests in testing the significance of *simple least-squares regression* (fitting a straight line to two variables) assumes that the data for both variables is at least interval and that the errors are approximately normally distributed. Both of these assumptions will often be false for many of the metrics we consider and so we should check carefully before applying any such technique.

6.2.1 Normal distribution

Many statistical tests are based on the assumption that the data under analysis is drawn from a normally distributed population. The frequency distribution for normal data has a bell-shaped curve as shown in Fig. 6.1.

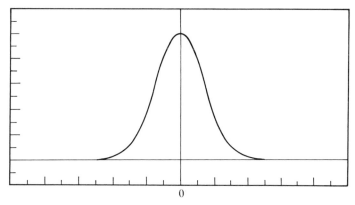

Figure 6.1 The normal distribution.

Many types of physical measurement data have been shown to follow this kind of distribution and for this reason it underlies many techniques. However, this is often not the case for software metrics. Figure 6.2 shows the frequency histogram for two different metrics, drawn from two SCOPE case studies. These are manifestly not normal. In fact *none* of the data collected during SCOPE for *any* of the metrics could be shown to be normally distributed.

This has implications when considering testing for equivalence of mean averages from different samples. When using the *t*-test for this purpose it is necessary that the sample variable be normally distributed. We can also circumvent this problem by using *robust* techniques. These robust techniques (often called non-parametric) require few distributional assumptions or perform just as well even when their assumptions are violated. When wishing to test the equivalence of means, if normality cannot be assumed, then other, non-parametric, tests can be applied such as the Wilcoxon signed rank test.

Alternatives to parametric statistics are also available in linear regression analysis when ordinal data is being used (again we cannot assume ordinal data is normal). Spearman's rank correlation coefficient and Kendall's robust correlation coefficient are appropriate replacements for Pearson's linear correlation coefficient, especially in cases where the data is ordinal in nature and there is no suggestion of an underlying continuous distribution.

6.2.2   Outliers

An outlier is a data point which is outside the normal range of values of a given population. In non-software data, outliers are often due to errors in measurement or are caused by systematic bias. For this reason they are frequently removed from the data set and subsequently ignored. In software

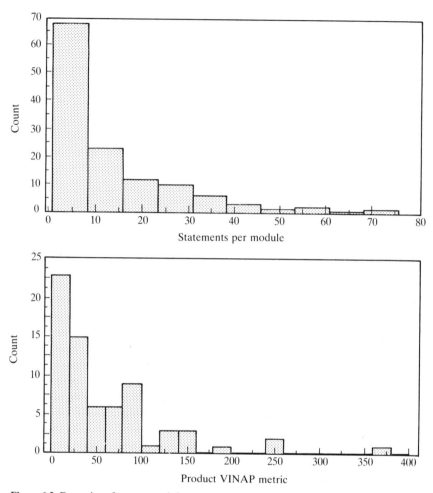

Figure 6.2 Examples of non-normal data.

metrics data, however, the outliers are often the most interesting data points. For example, if we are measuring module size, it is not uncommon to have a single software module which is 10 or 20 times larger than any other module. It is precisely these large modules which may give rise to problems in maintainability and so they should certainly not be removed from the data set.

6.2.3 Measurement scales

The scale on which metrics are defined will generally determine which statistics can be meaningfully applied. Most physical measures are ratio, e.g.

length, mass, voltage, pressure. Therefore people would be forgiven for assuming the same about software metrics. This is often not the case.

To decide which scale a particular metric is defined on, we need to go back to the actual definition of the metric and reason about the relationship imposed by the attribute being measured. However, we provide here some simple and informal guidelines. First we make three observations:

1. Nominal metrics are usually obvious since the values correspond to unordered categories.
2. With the exception of calendar time, interval metrics never occur in software.
3. Virtually any statistic that can be applied to absolute metrics can be also applied to ratio metrics and vice versa.

So we only need to worry about distinguishing ratio/absolute measures from ordinal measures. If we have ratio/absolute measures we can apply *means, standard deviation, Pearson's linear correlation coefficient*, etc. On the other hand, for ordinal metrics these techniques are not applicable, except under certain conditions.

To decide whether a measure is ratio/absolute or ordinal we ask the question, *is it meaningful to double the metric*? If the answer is *yes* then the metric is ratio or absolute. For lines of code or any size measure the answer is clearly 'yes'. But for test coverage the answer is 'no'. For example, if a module has DDP coverage of 80 per cent is that twice as well tested as if it had only 40 per cent coverage? Certainly, twice as many DDPs have been executed, but that is not the same thing. Our view is therefore that the following metrics should be classed as ordinal:

- Test coverage
- Checklist scores
- Readability indices
- Certain flowgraph metrics such as biggest prime
- Certain call graph metrics like testability, re-use and Yin and Winchester metrics

Most others will be ratio or absolute.

Generally a metric which is ratio or absolute is more useful in terms of mathematical manipulation than one which is ordinal or nominal. The application of parametric statistical techniques assumes that the measurements used are at least interval in nature. However, practitioners of statistics do not generally take a fundamentalist approach to measurement theory and apply techniques on the basis of practical usefulness and understanding. When choosing a statistical test or model it is important to consider its power. If the model used is incorrect or the measurement requirements are not satisfied the power is reduced. However, as the sample size increases the power of the non-parametric test approaches that of the corresponding parametric test. Thus, with large samples, the measurement theory assumptions can be avoided, especially in the case where the ordinal variable is approximately continuously distributed (little chance of value ties and large number of categories). In statistics it is therefore not uncommon to apply parametric statistical techniques to ordinal data provided the above provisions apply. An example of this would be where Pearson's correlation test could be substituted for Spearman's rank correlation test where the sample size is large and the data is spread over a wide range.

6.2.4 Multicollinearity

Many multivariate techniques such as *multivariate regression* require that the variables (i.e. metrics) are independent of each other. *Independent* in this sense means that they do not correlate with one another. Unfortunately most static flowgraph and textual metrics are correlated with size. It does not mean that these metrics all measure size—they measure many different attributes like number of decisions or nesting—but these attributes tend to be highly correlated with size and by implication with each other. This is because a module with a high number of decisions or a high level of nesting is also likely to be large. The same phenomenon of multicollinearity exists for coverage metrics, so branch coverage will be highly correlated with statement coverage, DDP coverage, etc.

The solution to this is to use either *factor analysis* (FA) or *principal components analysis* (PCA) to reduce the set of metrics to a smaller set of independent components. FA usually requires the data to be normally distributed, which, as we know, is rarely going to be true. PCA on the other hand is a robust technique because it relies on no distributional assumptions.

PCA is applied to data in order to reduce the number of measures used and to simplify correlation patterns. It attempts to solve these problems by reducing the dimensionality represented by these many related variables to a smaller set of principal components while retaining most of the variation from the original variables. These new principal components are uncorrelated and can act as substitutes for the original variables with little loss of information.

6.3 AGGREGATING METRICS

There are two reasons we may want to aggregate metrics. First we may want to combine several different metrics for the same component to create a composite metric which captures a higher-level attribute. Secondly we may want to combine the same metric for a number of different components to yield a metric value for a larger component which comprises the smaller ones. In this sense we are reducing the granularity of the metric. It is this second type of aggregation we consider here.

If we have data collected at a fine level of granularity, then it is always possible to derive data values at a coarser level. So, for example, if we know the size of each module, we can calculate the size of each compound module or subsystem and of the system as a whole. The way in which we aggregate the metrics will depend on the measurement scale. For ratio and absolute scales we simply add up the values to produce a sum. The difficulty arises with nominal and ordinal data. The fundamental problem is that nominal and ordinal metrics *cannot* be added. McCabe's cyclomatic number presents a different problem still: since it is defined as the number of decisions plus 1, an adjustment needs to be made when this metric is added. We therefore propose four ways in which these kind of metrics may be aggregated.

Creating a new category

We can add an extra value to a nominal metric to cope with the situation when a component contains several heterogeneous sub-components. For example, the language in which a module is written is a nominal metric where the values are all the possible languages. When aggregating this metric for a system or subsystem, we should create a new language category called *mixed*. So if all the modules were written in C then the language of the system is C, but if some are written in C and some in Pascal then the metrics value for the system will be *mixed*.

Recalculating the metric

For coverage measures and readability indices, we need to go back to the raw data and recalculate the metric over the larger component even if we know the metric values for sub-components. For example, if we wish to know the branch coverage for a subsystem, we cannot derive it directly from the coverage measures for each module, instead we have to use the formula

$$\frac{Branches\ executed\ in\ the\ subsystem}{Total\ branches\ in\ the\ subsystem}$$

Adjusted sum

The cyclomatic number is defined as

$$v(G) = e - n + 2$$

where e is the number of edges and n is the number of nodes in the flowgraph G. This number is equivalent to the number of decisions plus 1.*

* If you have case statements then this is not quite true unless you consider that a case with n choices represents $n - 1$ decisions.

It would be much easier if the metric were defined as $e - n + 1$ because then by summing up the metric we would get the total number of decisions. However, to remain consistent with the historic definition we aggregate the number in the following way:

$$\sum_i (v(G_i) - 1) + 1.$$

Using other statistics

In some cases a statistic such as the maximum, median, or minimum should be used as the aggregate value of an ordinal metric. The choice here should be based on considering the nature of the attribute being measured. For certain flowgraph metrics that capture overall structure, the aggregated metric should be the median of all the values. For the *biggest prime* metric which itself is a maximum value, the aggregate should be the maximum.

6.4 THE COMMON POOL OF DATA

We will often want to compare metrics from one software product with typical values observed in many other products. This requires creating a common pool of data from previous projects. If metrics are defined at the system level then we will have one value per software project. However, metrics defined at finer levels of granularity will contribute to the common pool in varying degrees. The pool of metric values defined at the module level will be influenced more by those software projects which have a greater number of modules. When establishing the common pool we need to be aware of three points:

1. The selection of projects should be representative and not all come from a single application domain or development style. The exception is when the common pool is used by a QA department with a fixed range of developments or a defined process.
2. No one very large project should be allowed to dominate the pool; this is less likely as the number of projects increases.
3. For some projects, certain metrics may not have been collected; we should ensure this is not a source of bias.

Only when these three points are satisfied can we be sure about making comparisons with the common pool.

6.5 OUTLIER ANALYSIS

When we collect metrics at the module level, outliers will be those modules that have exceptionally large or small metric values. These modules can be considered as abnormal in some sense and may be rejected on quality grounds or subjected to further investigation. This is suggested by the Pareto principle where 20 per cent of the components yield 80 per cent of the faults. The metrics to which this approach is most appropriate are the textual and structural (flowgraph) measures. Normally we are interested in those modules which have particularly high metric values since this indicates modules that are either very large or very ill-structured. On the other hand for checklist scores or coverage measures (where high values are a good thing) we will be interested in those modules with abnormally low values.

We can identify outliers from the data of a single project. But we really should also compare the outlier value against the distribution of metrics from the common pool.

6.5.1 Using descriptive statistics

To identify an outlier for a single metric we can use simple graphical techniques such as frequency histograms or box plots. Although box plots are the most appropriate technique here, many non-statisticians find histograms easier to read.

Figure 6.3 shows a frequency histogram for the *number of nodes* metric from QUALMS from one of the case studies. It captures the size of modules in terms of the size of the flowgraph. We can see that there are a few very large modules which we would consider to be outliers. However, because

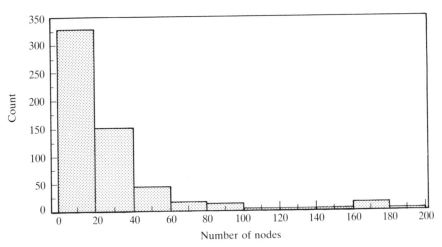

Figure 6.3 Frequency histogram of 'number of nodes' metric.

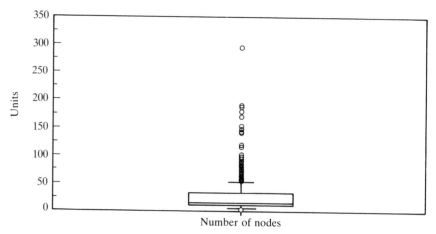

Figure 6.4 Box plot of 'number of nodes' metric.

these modules are so large they do contribute to a large proportion of the total size. Another representation useful for this purpose is the box plot shown in Fig. 6.4. The box in the middle shows the data points between the upper and lower quartiles. The line in the middle of the box is the median and the lines extend to the upper and lower deciles. The circles represent outlier values. In metrics which capture the size or structure of models we are specifically interested in outliers that have high values since these modules will be difficult to understand and may cause maintenance difficulties.

6.5.2 Multi-dimensional outliers

It may be necessary to examine patterns of outlier behaviour for more than one variable. Scatter-plots have often been used to visually detect those points which deviate from the typical pattern in two dimensions as in Fig. 6.5. The points at the bottom left are outliers. However, this is a fairly simplistic approach which relies on detection of the outliers *by eye*. By using sophisticated statistical techniques this scatter-plot approach can be generalized to *n* dimensions. The stages involved in this approach are:

Principal components analysis (PCA) This is a necessary first stage to ensure that multicollinearity is negated.
Cluster analysis (CA) This involves automatically grouping observations on the basis of their principal component values. The groups involved may be the typical observations and the outlier observations.
Discriminant analysis (DA) By using this technique we can derive an 'assessment criterion' function which will discriminate between the two

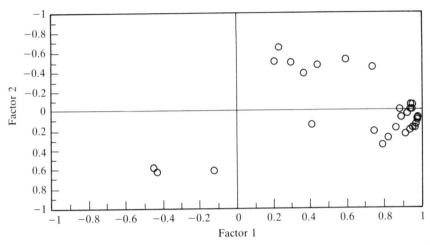

Figure 6.5 A scatter plot showing two principal components derived from QUALMS metrics of one of the case studies.

groups identified in CA and allow automatic allocation to future observations to the outlier or typical groups based on their measurements.

6.6 ESTABLISHING THRESHOLDS AND NORMS

We use *thresholds* as a basis for passing or failing software components with respect to a particular metric or combination of metrics. They define an acceptable range of values that a given metric should have. We should know from our understanding of a particular metric whether to define an upper bound, a lower bound, or both. For example, it would clearly be counter-productive to set an upper bound on checklist scores or the coverage metric. Outlier analysis techniques can help detect these thresholds for assessment purposes.

A *norm* on the other hand is a value or range of values which metrics from the software are expected to have. Within an organization, quality assurance staff may publish a set of norms which the development staff are expected to adhere to. Thresholds are used for quality assessment, whereas norms are intended for quality improvement, and if followed will help ensure that the software products are subsequently approved during QA. Note that thresholds can only be applied to metrics that are at the very least ordinal; for nominal metrics they are meaningless. For nominal metrics we simply define a set of acceptable values. For those nominal metrics which have only two values (e.g. conforms to Standard Pascal or not), which is obvious.

There is little enough agreement within the software engineering community about which metrics should be collected. It is not surprising therefore that there is no consensus at all as to what target ranges we should set for specific metrics. Some software houses have tried to restrict the cyclomatic number to 10 or below. But if this were applied to the SCOPE case studies, all products would have failed miserably.

In the future we might expect some consensus on acceptable ranges to emerge, perhaps through standards, but at the present time test laboratories and quality groups still have to establish their own norms and thresholds. We can think up values based on intuition and experience. But such values are likely to be subjective and arbitrary. Furthermore the thresholds may be too weak or too stringent. If they are too weak, nearly all products will pass and the bad products will not be weeded out. If the thresholds are too stringent then too many products including the good ones will fail. We can establish thresholds for a single metric by looking at the frequency distribution of the common pool and setting thresholds at the upper and lower deciles (the values which separate the top and bottom 10 per cent from the rest of the population).

We can set thresholds for a number of related metrics by using a multi-dimensional outlier approach as explained in Sec. 6.5.2. Within SCOPE we used the QUALMS data from the case studies in the first phase to derive an assessment criterion function. This was then used on some of the case studies in phase 2; details are given in Chapter 9.

Once thresholds have been established, we will then want to determine how particular products fare when the assessment is applied. One technique used for representing this data is a Kiviat diagram. The example in Fig. 6.6 shows static analysis data from Logiscope. The 'spokes' of the diagram represent the different metrics and the inner and outer circles are the lower and upper threshold values.

6.7 COMPARISON ACROSS PROJECTS

Comparing projects reveals similarities and differences between the internal metrics. By examining these differences together with external attributes, we can build up an experience base of how internal attributes relate to other observable factors. For example, suppose we compared two projects, A and B, and found that the internal metrics differed markedly. Suppose also that we knew from anecdotal evidence that project A had caused problems because of say, cost overrun, or unsatisfied customers due to poor functionality. Project B, on the other hand, had caused fewer problems. We may be able to explain these differences as causal relationships. This in turn means that in future we will know how to spot troublesome projects before they are released.

AXIS	LOWER	UPPER	MEAN
NB_STMT	2	31	15.51
NB_COM	1	32	2.04
ETA2	5	79	44.26
N2	1	35	16.24
ETA1	6	104	55.70
N1	1	23	12.90
P_LENGTH	0	40	99.97
V_SIZE	0	10	29.14
P_SIZE	0.00	5354.00	119.76
P_VOLUME	0.00	200.00	522.35
INT_CONT	11.59	48.16	26.42
NB_ERROR	0.00	0.30	0.15
P_LEVEL	0.03	0.31	0.13
DIFFICUL	3.17	26.24	17.03
EFFORT	143.16	96400.00	13970.00
P_TIME	0.00	250.00	776.11
L_LEVEL	0.00	8.50	2.46
NB_ARCS	1	37	19.51
NB_NODES	2	27	16.24
P_NODES	0	2	0.24
VG	1	8	5.51
C_D	0.16	0.30	0.21
NB_LEV	1	4	3.07
NB_DEG	1	5	3.34

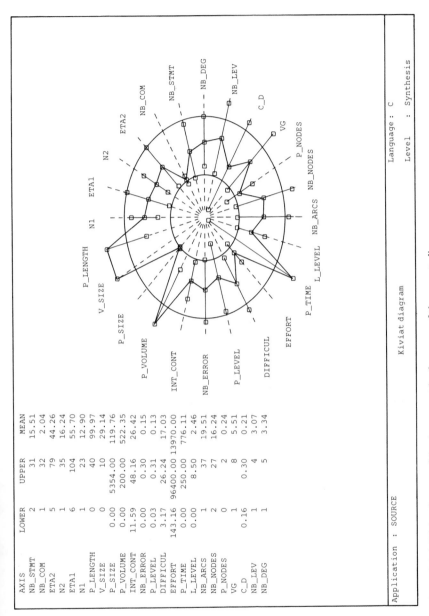

Application : SOURCE	Kiviat diagram	Language : C
		Level : Synthesis

Figure 6.6 A Kiviat diagram of Logiscope metrics from one of the case studies.

We can also explore how different development methods will alter the internal attributes and provide useful information to managers. We might discover, for example, that object-oriented design leads to greater modularity, as measured by static metrics. This would then justify some of the claims made by the supporters of that method.

It would be foolish to treat this kind of evidence from only two projects as conclusive proof, but rather it contributes to our collected experience, which in time gives us greater confidence in these theories.

We cannot use this type of comparison directly for quality assurance or certification, but it does have a role in uncovering the underlying theories relating internal and external attributes, on which the assessment is to be based.

Data across projects may be compared by descriptive statistics such as histograms, pie charts, box plots, etc., to spot differences visually. The experience, from the SCOPE data sets, is that means and standard deviations of data will contrast greatly.

6.8 RELATIONS BETWEEN METRICS

Correlation means determining whether two or more variables are related to each other. *Regression* is where we attempt to fit a curve or a straight line to the data so that we can make future predictions. Generally we will use internal metrics as the independent variable (or variables) and an external metric as the dependent variable. The external metrics we are interested in are measures of faults, changes and effort data. The number of faults can indicate how much a part of the software deviates from its functionality; the number of changes will indicate how much maintenance has been performed on particular parts of the software. Effort figures can reveal how portable or maintainable the software was.

6.8.1 Approaches to validation

The history of software engineering shows that metrics and their related theories are seldom validated. In few cases was it demonstrated that the metrics really were useful, that is to say that they measured the quality attributes they were purported to. It is important for metrics to be validated before they are used to assess and certify the quality of software products. To be considered valid, a metric should both satisfy sound mathematical criteria (algebraic validation of the metric) and demonstrate a high degree of association with the quality factor it is intended to represent (empirical validation of the theory relating metrics). These two forms of validation are complementary and are both useful.

The algebraic approach[147,160] is pragmatically applicable when it is possible to perform a *mathematical* proof based on a formal model and its behaviour. Although this approach is theoretical, it provides some interesting practical side-effects, like the unambiguous definition of the counting rules and a sound foundation for the development of data-collection tools.

The second approach (the empirical one) is more widely known and conforms to most people's perceptions of validation. We need to understand clearly that when talking about validation in the software assessment context, at least three distinct areas are relevant and must be distinguished from one another:

- Identification of factors that will influence quality attributes
- Relationships between sets of metrics
- Theories, mapping characteristics to metrics

Irrespective of which class of validation we are going to attempt, we are in all cases trying to test hypotheses that we derive from our intuition. Hypothesis testing usually follows this experimental procedure:[48]

1. State the null hypothesis (that we hope to reject).
2. Choose an appropriate test.
3. Specify a significance level as criterion for rejection.
4. Compute the chosen statistical test and determine its probability value.
5. Reject the null hypothesis if, and only if, the probability value is less than or equal to the significance level. In this case our theory is validated against the specified criterion.

A comprehensive validation methodology has been proposed,[145] in which the following properties are deemed important for metrics to be used in software assessment:

- Association between the metric and the intended factor, so that it is possible to use one as a substitute for the other, as can be done by means of linear correlation coefficients.
- Capability of tracking changes in the product quality (i.e. if the perceived quality changes, the related measures must also change and vice versa). This can be done by means of the coefficient of rank correlation.
- Consistency, for a set of software components, between the ranks of the factor values and the ranks of calculated values for metrics.
- Predictability of the factor values with a good accuracy.
- Discriminative power between high-quality components and low-level ones; this is done by means of the Mann–Whitney test or the chi-square test.

- Repeatability of the above properties (association, tracking, consistency, predictability, discriminative power) for a high percentage of the applications of the metric.

A similar general scheme is under discussion at international standardization level.[83] If a metric does not pass all the validity tests, it should be used only in accordance with the criteria of the tests successfully passed. It is important to notice that validity is not a static, one-time property. A validated theory is not necessarily valid in other environments or future applications; conversely, a hypothesis that has been refuted by statistical evidence may be valid in other environments or different applications. Validation is a continuous, optimizing process.

6.8.2 Testing a hypothesis

Before we start correlating metrics, there should be a clear hypothesis to test. Given a collection of data with a sufficiently large number of metrics, trying to relate everything with everything else will sooner or later turn up a spurious correlation. For example, we might construct a hypothesis such as:

Modules with a high test coverage have fewer faults.

Execution analysis can be used to determine the test coverage attained during the testing phase. We then have to collect fault data during usage of the software. However, we should note that we are collecting the number of faults that have been discovered to date, not the total number of faults, which is always unknown. We would then attempt to correlate these two metrics.

One correlation often cited in metrics papers is between structural metrics and number of faults. There is reason to believe that modules with high structural metrics (implying they are large and/or ill-structured) do have more faults. However, the number of faults present will depend on the degree of testing. As the software is tested, so faults will (hopefully) be removed. Some parts of the system may show few faults simply because they have never been tested thoroughly and this will distort any such relationship.

Linear least-squares regression analysis can be used in two ways:

- To provide a predictive equation
- To assess the usefulness of a variable for prediction

It is the second of these that is more useful for assessment. We should, however, be wary of using regression equations derived from one data set to make predictions for another product since there may be many other factors that have not been captured in the regression equation.

There are a large number of regression analysis methods, but traditionally linear regression analysis in combination with Pearson's correlation coefficient has been the most popular. Linear regression analysis involves fitting a line (when we have two variables) which minimizes the sum of squared errors (difference between predicted value and actual value). When this best-fit line is achieved we determine whether the errors are distributed normally. If they are, we can then go ahead and test the significance of the equation as a whole and for each of the coefficients, using F-tests and t-tests. Furthermore, it is common practice to employ Pearson's correlation coefficient to also determine the *goodness of fit* of the equation to the data. A satisfactory fit usually results when the correlation coefficient is near $+1$ (positive correlation) or -1 (negative correlation).

It should, however, be noted that the application of Pearson's correlation coefficient is not dependent on normality and that the assessment of the *goodness of fit* depends on an absence of multicollinearity and on the equation making sense.

The non-parametric alternative to Pearson's correlation coefficient is Spearman's rank correlation coefficient. This technique, as the name suggests, is based on the assessment of similar rankings for observations from two variables. It is useful for ordinal measures and is less sophisticated than Pearson's statistic in that it does not imply linearity nor can it be used for prediction.

6.9 RELIABILITY ESTIMATION

The techniques we use to analyse failure data are quite different from those mentioned above. Unlike other techniques, we have data that refers to a number of versions of the software products over a period of time (time-series data), whereas with static analysis or checklist data we have metrics which refer to different parts of the same version taken at the same point in time.

Many techniques have been devised specifically to analyse failure data and these are known as *reliability models*. These models allow us to predict the time to next failure from the history of previous failures. Of course we have to assume that the software is being used in a consistent way. The term *operational profile* refers to the frequency with which the various inputs to the software will occur. A prediction of reliability is only valid for a given operational profile. This is precisely why reliability estimates can only be derived from operational testing and/or actual use in the field.

6.9.1 Reliability growth and stability

We assume that we have collected failure data from a software product during operational testing, actual use, or both. We will have a set of data points $t_1, t_2, \ldots, t_n$, where $t_i\,(i = 1, 2, \ldots, n)$ is the machine time between the first occurrence of two failures. These may be either the first occurrence of a given failure, or all the failures in a particular version. The former is used to estimate reliability growth. After each failure has been encountered, we ignore all subsequent failures until a new version has been created. We assume that some attempt has been made to fix the fault that caused the failure and a new version is then released. The latter case is for estimating *current* reliability of just that version.

Our aim is to estimate the expected time to failure t_{n+1}. The statistic we usually derive is the median time to next failure. Reliability models are simply statistical methods for estimating the mean or median time to failure and other related statistics such as the accuracy of the estimate and the parameters used in each model. Some models estimate both the mean and the median; others estimate just the median since the mean is deemed infinite.*

Some models have, as a parameter, the number of faults left in the software. But we should not take this quantity too literally. If, for example, a model estimated that there were three faults left in the software, we would be mistaken in thinking that, after three more fault fixes, the software would be fault-free.

We usually assume that the software has a finite number of faults. Each of these faults may lead to a software failure with a given set of inputs. As the software is executed, these faults will, with a certain probability, manifest themselves as a failure. When new versions of the software are created, some of these faults will usually have been removed, so the number of remaining faults will decrease and the reliability will grow. We can see from the data whether the reliability is actually growing because the time between failures will generally get bigger. If the time between failures is not increasing then we have the situation of stable reliability. In this case we do not need to use elaborate models at all. We can estimate median time to failure as:

$$MTTF = \frac{number\ of\ failures}{total\ execution\ time}$$

If we have only a small number of failures (say, four) then it is not practical to use the growth models, and we adopt the above formula. If we only collected the total occurrences of failures from a single version of the software, then again we can assess only stable reliability. The formula will not work for software that has never failed, so Littlewood and Strigini constructed a Bayesian argument to cope with this case.[106] If the software has run for a period t without failing then, under reasonable assumptions, the expected median time to failure is t.

---

* These models assume that there is a finite chance that the last bug has been removed and reliability is infinite. Even if this chance were very small (0.0001) it would still imply that the mean time to failure was infinite.

6.9.2 Choosing the right reliability model

If the reliability of the software is growing, there are a large number of reliability models which predict the next time to failure. They vary in the assumptions made about the frequency distribution of failures and the effectiveness of bug fixing. The key problems in applying reliability models are:

1. Choosing the 'best' models to give reliability predictions since they will generally give different results
2. Determining the value of the parameters needed to initialize the approximation routines
3. Actually performing the calculations since these models are not supported by ordinary commercial packages

The following models were used on data collected within the SCOPE project.

Jelinski–Moranda This model assumes that failures are purely random and that each fault has the same probability of occurring. Fault fixes are assumed to be perfect. Reliability estimates are usually very optimistic.

Goel–Okumoto Similar to Jelinski–Moranda except that the failure rate improves continuously with time.

Musa–Okumoto Similar to Goel–Okumoto except that later fixes have a smaller effect on reliability.

Duane This assumes that failure rate changes continuously with time.

Littlewood Similar to Jelinski–Moranda except that faults have differing probabilities of occurring. The *large* faults which occur most frequently tend to be removed earlier than the *smaller* ones.

Littlewood non-homogeneous Poisson process (NHPP) Similar to Littlewood but assumes that failure rate improves continuously with time.

Littlewood–Verrall The improvement of reliability after each fix varies randomly, and so accommodates the notion of imperfect fix.

Keiller–Littlewood This is similar to Littlewood–Verrall but uses a different form of reliability growth.

It has not been shown that there is any 'best' model since different models perform with varying degrees of accuracy for different data sets. The view taken by Brocklehurst and Littlewood[34] is that, rather than trying to match the assumptions of the models to the particular circumstances of the software product, the data should be used to choose the best model. That is, each model is applied to the failure data and the one that fits the data best is chosen.

The reliability models described above cannot be calculated by hand— the volume of calculations is too great. The approximation methods used to derive the results are highly mathematical and require a considerable level of specialist knowledge. It is also not really practical to build tools for this purpose ourselves. There are a number of specialist packages currently available which do perform this kind of analysis. These are intended primarily for research and so do not have sophisticated user interfaces. Extensive work at City University has developed the algorithms for making the reliability estimates. Within SCOPE we used the SRM package produced by Reliability and Statistical Consultants Ltd. based in London.

The SRM package produces raw numerical results and simple tables constructed out of ASCII characters. For use in SCOPE we built a simple graphical interface to control the SRM package and display its results using proper graphics. The interface was implemented on the Sunview windowing system. Figure 6.7 shows a screen dump from the package where the predictions made by the various models can be compared to the actual observed failures.

6.9.3   Analysing failure data with simple statistics

An alternative pragmatic approach to prediction is to plot time to next failure against the number of failures and fit a straight line using ordinary least-squares regression or use a moving averages model. This can be done with most standard statistics packages. The estimates produced in this way are usually close to the ones produced by the reliability models although, of course, the models have a theoretical underpinning. Figure 6.8 fits a straight line to a failure data set collected within SCOPE. This approach has very little theoretical justification but does produce estimates very close to the more elaborate growth models.

6.10   LIMITS TO RELIABILITY PREDICTION

Although we are able to make predictions of reliability from past failure data, we should be aware of the limitations of these predictions. In particular we have no way of assuring the reliability of software for very high-reliability systems from failure data.

6.10.1   Software that has never failed

If we use reliability growth models, as basic rule of thumb, to assure that the software has a failure rate of 10^{-x} per hour we need to test for at least 10^{x+1} hours. So to attain a failure rate of 10^{-4} (one failure every 1000 hours) we need to test for 10 000 hours. This assumes that the software has failed during testing and that attempts have been made to fix the faults. The best result that we could achieve during testing was that the software had never failed. Even then we would still need to test for 1000 hours. Many safety-

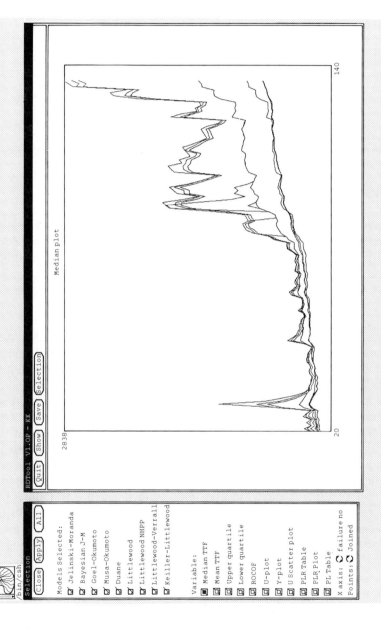

Figure 6.7 A simple user interface for the SRM package based on Sunview.

109

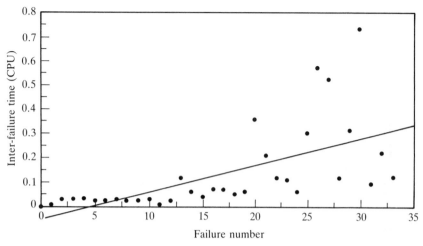

Figure 6.8 Fitting a straight line to failure data.

itical systems require a reliability exceeding 10^{-9}. For this we would need to test the software for hundreds of thousands of years. If the testing were done concurrently over a reasonable period (e.g. 1 year) we would need hundreds of thousands of machines.

6.10.2 Increasing estimates with prior belief

The reliability models described above are *black-box models* in that they make assumptions about neither the internal attributes of the software nor the process that created it. We should expect that software produced and quality assured with the best methods should be better than software made in the back of a garage by an amateur. Yet these models assume that we know nothing about the software. We can improve our estimate by stating a *prior belief* about the software, that means we have some belief about the reliability of the software based on the internal attributes or the process or both, prior to testing. Let us assume that we wanted to increase the reliability estimate by an order of magnitude. From 10^x hours of failure-free execution we wanted to arrive at a reliability estimate of $10^{-(x+1)}$ failures per hour (assuming that the software had never failed). According to results by de Neumann[130] and Littlewood and Strigini[106] this would require a prior belief so strong before testing that we would hardly need to do the testing in the first place.

6.10.3 Use of formal methods

A software product fails because it contains faults which manifest themselves. If we could be sure that it was fault-free then we could use this to estimate the reliability (which would be infinite). Proponents of formal methods have advocated that using them will guarantee fault-free software by mathematically proving the code against its formal specification. This approach makes two doubtful assumptions.

- The formal specification is itself correct. Since software may fail due to a fault present in the specification, we have to assume that the specification is itself flawless. This is a bold assumption.
- The proofs are correct. If the proofs are constructed by hand there is a possibility that these may themselves contain errors. Even proofs produced by respected mathematicians and published in refereed mathematics journals have been known to contain mistakes. Automatic theorem-provers are not yet mature enough to construct full proofs for complex systems without some human intervention. Even if they were, they are, after all, pieces of software that may fail and generate erroneous proofs.

If we could accept these assumptions, there is still a further problem. Any formal specification will state a number of *axioms* which describe the behaviour of the system. If two or more of these axioms contradict each other, the resulting proofs will be meaningless. In mathematical logic, from a set of inconsistent axioms, it is possible to construct a valid proof of any statement. We can prove that a statement A is true, and then construct an equally valid proof that A is false. For a system specified with x axioms, we need to prove that every combination of axioms does not lead to a contradiction. For a system with x axioms the number of such proofs will be 2^{x-1}. De Neumann[131] has shown that for a reasonably sized system with perhaps 100 axioms, it would take millions of years to prove that the axioms were not inconsistent.

SUMMARY

Statistics are necessary to present and interpret software metrics data. In many cases, simple descriptive statistics are adequate for this purpose. There are occasions when more sophisticated techniques such as correlation and regression are called for, but in these cases we need to be aware of the peculiarities of software metrics data and where possible use robust statistics. Failure data should be analysed by reliability models and from these models we can make predictions of future reliability. Nevertheless these models cannot be used to assure very high levels of reliability and, given the current level of technology in software metrics, nor can any other technique.

7

TOOLS FOR DATA COLLECTION

For data collection to be efficient, cost-effective and reliable, it must be supported by tools. Past experiences have shown that paper-based data collection is both time-consuming and error-prone. In an ideal world we would start from scratch and design and build a full set of integrated data-collection tools which satisfied our precise requirements. In the real world where time and money are scarce we have to construct our data-collection scheme from as many existing components as possible. Some tools construction is necessary but this can be minimized by adapting existing tools. In this chapter and the next we explain how data collection and storage were automated within the SCOPE project. The scheme we set up was usable and allowed us to analyse a large number of products. In Chapter 10 we look at how tools could be more closely integrated in the future and how automation can be extended to the assessment procedure itself.

7.1 REQUIREMENTS FOR DATA COLLECTION TOOLS

For product-based assessment to be generally applicable and cost-effective we can state the following two principles of data collection.

1. Data collection should be automated, and never be performed with pen and paper.
2. Assessment should cope readily with new languages and notations.

It would be untrue to claim that SCOPE *never* collected metrics on paper. Often data collection had to start before the tools were completed and so paper-based collection was used as a stop-gap. Nevertheless even limited use of paper forms led to not a few difficulties. Our aim was to move away from paper-based collection, and this end was achieved by the end of the project in that all techniques were fully supported by tools.

We should make a distinction between *automatic* data collection where the whole measurement activity is conducted by the tools and *automated* data collection where some manual input is required. Many of the techniques described in Chapter 5 such as static analysis and test coverage are simply not practical without some tools, these are typically the cases where data collection can be done automatically. Checklists, black-box testing and failure collection do not strictly speaking *need* tools, but their use is highly desirable. These are cases where the data collection can be automated but is not automatic.

Although a number of metrics tools were available to us, the problem was that the tools often did not precisely fit our requirements and alterations were needed. In Table 7.1 we summarize the tools used on SCOPE that were produced outwith the project.

The five basic areas where tools did not exist or were not adequate were:

1. Collection of failure data
2. Application of checklists
3. Anomaly checking
4. Textual and structural measurement on some languages
5. Static analysis of large quantities of source code

Checklist data and failure data can be collected by hand. But using a pencil and paper for this type of data collection leads to a number of problems,

Table 7.1 Existing tools used in SCOPE

Technique	Tool	Languages supported
Anomaly checking	lint	C
	flint	FORTRAN
	Compilers	Various
Textual metrics	style	English
	Right Writer	English
	Static Logiscope	Various
Structural metrics	QUALMS	Various
	Static Logiscope	Various
Test cross-referencing	TEFAX	Any
Test coverage	Dynamic Logiscope	Various
	tcov	C

such as consistency checking and transcription errors, which occur when data is converted to an electronic form. In the case of failure data a large number of errors are introduced because programmers simply forget (or are too busy) to record failures.

Some commercial anomaly-checkers such as lint produce a very large volume of information about anomalies, and we found that this information was difficult to comprehend; we therefore built a tool to filter this output.

Static analysers that performed structural and textual measurements were used extensively in SCOPE, but they often required a great deal of human interaction to derive the metrics from the source code. This was a particularly acute problem with larger case studies with tens of thousands of lines of code. Furthermore, many of the analysers did not support all the languages which we had to deal with, in particular the newer fourth-generation languages.

SCOPE therefore had to build a number of tools itself. We did not duplicate existing work and construct tools where alternatives were readily available. All the tools described are novel in that they provide functionality that had not previously been implemented.

The tools described in this chapter are:

1. A *session data collection system* to capture failure data from operating systems
2. A *checklist manager* to automate checklists used for inspection
3. A *filter* for the lint tool
4. New *front ends* for existing static analysers
5. *Batch mode* facilities for static analysers

In addition various data-transfer tools and mechanisms for inputting other data were developed but these are described in Chapter 8, along with the database.

7.2 SESSION DATA COLLECTION SYSTEMS

It is worth noting that the number of reliability models published in the literature actually exceeds the number of published data sets on which these models may be used. This is because failure data has historically been very difficult to collect. It is time-consuming and generally inconvenient to collect software failures manually. Perhaps this is why most of the failure sets have been collected by those programmers or project managers who were themselves interested in metrics research.

Since reliability models are the only predictive technique that we can use in software assessment, and they assess one of the most important characteristics, it would be a shame if we could not use this technique simply because the data could not be collected. The session data collection system (SDCS) was an attempt to solve this problem. All the SDCSs used on SCOPE were built by Kenneth Kirkwood who also conceived the basic architecture and has published a description of the SDCS.[97]

7.2.1   Principles of the SDCS

A *session* is an occasion on which an executable system or subsystem is run. *Session data* is the information collected from that particular run such as the execution time, how the execution ended, and the version of the executable component. From session data it is possible to derive the inter-failure times that can then be analysed with a view to predicting reliability. A *session data collection system* (SDCS) is a tool which captures the session data and then derives the inter-failure times. SDCSs be may used either during operational testing of the software or during actual use in the field since these are the two occasions when failure data can be usefully collected.

SDCSs rely on the fact that much session data is already recorded by the operating system. There will be records of certain classes of failure such as program crashes and also information about versions, dates and machine time. The SDCSs that we developed work on multi-user operating systems such as Unix and VMS.

The collection of data using an SDCS is not completely automatic; some human input is required. Although it is possible for the operating system to detect when the program crashes* and certain classes of abnormal exit, there will still be a large class of failures which can only be spotted by a human. For example, a menu may fail to appear or a numerical value may be incorrect; there is no way that these kinds of failure can be detected automatically. This is when we use the *fail tool*. When a failure is identified the user must exit the program and type the command 'fail'. This tool then prompts the user for the class and severity of the failure.

7.2.2   High-level architecture

An SDCS has essentially two parts: a front end and a formatter.† The first stage of applying an SDCS is to record all executions of the software in question. This information is written in a file, known as the SESSDATA file. There are number of *front ends* which produce the SESSDATA file and these will vary between operating systems. Indeed there will generally be different front ends for different variants of the same operating system. The

---

* A program written to test the operating system or hardware may deliberately cause a crash and this would not be regarded as a failure, but this is a rare situation.
† At one stage we referred to the statistics package as the back end and the formatter as the 'middle end'.

format of the SESSDATA file will always be the same no matter which front end or operating system is used.

From time to time we will want to make a reliability estimate from all the sessions that have occurred to date. At this point we use a *formatter* which reads in the SESSDATA file and produces the file of inter-failure times. In our implementation, the output of the formatter can be fed directly into the SRM package which supports reliability growth models but the format of this output could easily be altered for any statistics packages. Figure 7.1 shows the global architecture of the failure collection and analysis system.

Because terminology varies between operating systems, we will henceforth use Unix terms to describe the details of the various implementations of SDCS. Many of the concepts are equally applicable to other multi-user operating systems.

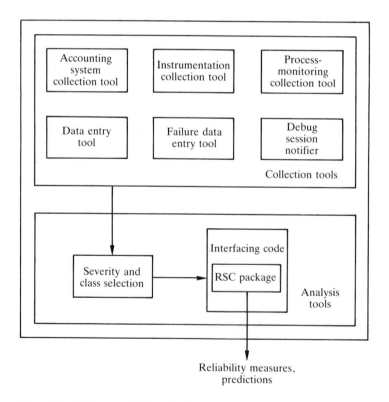

Figure 7.1 Architecture of failure data and analysis system.

7.2.3 Measures of time

The SDCSs calculate several different measures of execution time. *Elapsed time* is the amount of time the program actually runs. However, this includes time taken waiting for input from the user. It could be heavily distorted if the person testing the program had a tea break while the software under test waited for a user response. *User mode time* is the amount of CPU (central processor unit) time taken to run the software under test. *System mode time* is the CPU time taken by the operating system to service the software, such as when system calls are invoked. *Total CPU time* is the sum of user and system mode time. It is the last of these that is usually used for reliability estimates.

In principle SDCSs could be built for single-user operating systems such as DOS. But it would be difficult to record CPU time. Of course elapsed time would be straightforward.

7.2.4 Design of SDCS front ends

There are three ways in which session data may be collected:

1. Internal instrumentation
2. External instrumentation
3. Using the accounting system

Each of these three methods has advantages and drawbacks and the choice will depend on the system under test and the way in which the operating system has been configured. All three methods make use of the *fail tool* which must be invoked by the user after any failure to record the severity and class of failure. Even when the program crashes, and the failure is recorded automatically, the fail tool ought to be invoked. The formatter will make sure that the same failure is not counted twice.

Internal instrumentation

This involves altering the source code. The programmer must add an extra procedure call as the first statement in the program. In addition, there may be certain paths of the program which deal with exception handling and these are only executed in the event of a failure. An extra statement should be added on each of these paths too. An extra set of SDCS library functions has to be linked on to the executable image.

Figure 7.2 shows the architecture of the instrumentation-based system. When the program is executed it records its start and termination and records any abnormal exits and, in particular, program crashes. If at any time during testing or usage we wish to generate the SESSDATA file we invoke the session data processor.

Instrumented application   Instrumentation software

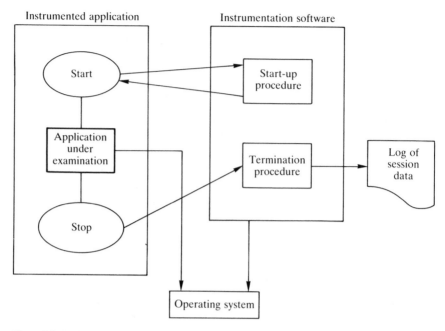

Figure 7.2 Architecture of the instrumentation front ends.

There are three problems with the internal instrumentation. First, the recording of the session information itself contributes to the execution time. Secondly, removing the instrumentation at a later stage will mean altering the source and this may inadvertently result in a fault being introduced. Thirdly, it cannot be used with certain languages such as Standard Pascal* (it may work with extended Pascal) or languages where procedure calls are not possible (e.g. PROLOG).

External instrumentation

The software which records the session data is in this case a separate executable image. Therefore the user does not invoke the program under test directly but instead invokes another program which starts a separate *process* to record the session data and then invokes the program under test. The architecture for the external instrumentation is much the same as for internal instrumentation. The only difference is that the SESSDATA file is altered by a separate program and not by the software under test.

---

* Standard Pascal does not allow separate compilation, and the internal instumentation is usually shipped as object code. Even if the source code were provided (in Pascal) it would not compile since Standard Pascal cannot deal with system calls. But then no language standard supports system calls.

External instrumentation is preferable in that it does not require changing the source code to remove the SDCS and it does not itself contribute to the execution time like the internal instrumentation. However, it cannot trap exception-handling failures.

Using the accounting system

The accounting system records details of program executions by users. It is an optional feature of the operating system which may be turned on or off by the systems administrator. The accounting system is usually used to charge users for the amount of machine time they have used. However, the data recorded in the accounting file contains all the necessary session data except for user-recorded failures.

Figure 7.3 shows the architecture of the accounting-system front end. The front end extracts the information from the accounting file and failure log file to produce the SESSDATA file which can then be read by the formatter.

For the accounting system to be used, the systems administrator will need to configure the system kernel to ensure that the accounting system is maintained by the operating system. In an organization where users are neither charged nor rationed in their use of machines there will be little incentive to instigate the accounting system other than to run the SDCS.

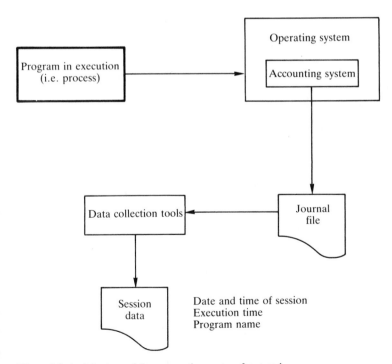

Figure 7.3 Architecture of the accounting-system front end.

The accounting system does impose an overhead in terms of slowing down the operating system and using considerable file space. Other users of the system may not be prepared to accept this. Also the accounting system method cannot detect failures that are due to exception-handling features.

7.2.5 Formatting the session data

The formatter converts the session data, which contains the details of each execution, into inter-failure times. Since the SDCSs collect several different measures of time, the user has to select which measure of time to use. For each version of the software, the formatter sums up the (chosen) execution time for each execution of one version until a failure occurs. It then ignores all sessions after that failure until a new version is created. In Unix, each executable component is simply a file. For each file the SDCS knows the time at which that file was created; the information is recorded as the number of seconds since the beginning of 1970. This (very large) number is used to identify which version of the software is being executed at any particular time.

The SESSDATA file is a text file and therefore may be transferred easily between different machines and operating systems. For this reason, the formatting can be done on a different machine, and perhaps at a different site from where the software is being run. Furthermore, the formatter is simply a file processing program and so, unlike the front ends, can be readily ported. It is usually best to run the formatter on the same machine that hosts the statistical analysis package (e.g. the SRM package runs on a Sun workstation).

The formatter can select subsets of the failure data for statistical analysis and output the set of inter-failure times in a way that can be read in by a statistical package. We can also derive inter-failure times for certain classes or severities of failure: for example, we might wish to estimate the mean time to a system crash or mean time to a failure that gives an incorrect calculation.

7.2.6 Debugging versions

If the software under examination is being tested and fixed on the same machine then, after a failure has occurred, the programmer will try to identify and fix the fault that caused it. If the cause is not obvious, the programmer will try to re-create the failure to find out how it was caused. This debugging activity is not testing, and certainly will not conform to the normal operational profile. Since all executions after a failure are filtered out by the formatter we do not need to worry about this kind of distortion. However, one problem that can arise is from *debugging versions*.

When a fault has been identified, the programmer will attempt to fix it by altering the source, and then recompile. But if the programmer cannot find the fault, he may create debugging versions. These are not attempts to fix the fault but rather to make its cause more obvious. Debugging versions may, for example, print out the values of certain variables, or print messages to show that a particular path is being executed. These debugging versions are not part of testing and must not be allowed to distort the session data. This problem can be easily solved by asking the programmer to give the executable image of any debugging version a different file name. However, the SDCS can also deal with this by calling the *debug notifier* which causes all debugging versions to be ignored by the formatter.

7.2.7 Examples of SDCSs

Several versions of SDCS have been implemented for a number of different operating systems. To date these are:

1. SUNOS running on Sun workstations
2. DYNIX running on a Sequent
3. HP-UX running on Hewlett-Packard workstations
4. VMS running on a VAX station

7.3 CHECKLIST MANAGER

The checklist manager is an automatic tool used to guide the evaluator through the various questions of those assessment elements composed of questionnaires and to produce suitable outputs. Since, at the time, inspection driven by checklists was the most widespread and flexible assessment technique available, this was (together with static analysers) the most used tool.

7.3.1 Definition of a checklist

First of all, we need to define what constitutes a valid *checklist*. It is obviously a list of questions, but we must pay attention to define it in a way such that questions are easy to understand and focused enough to minimize subjectivity. Our experience has shown that each question must be detailed in terms of specific attributes and that the format of checklists must be consistent. First, questions must be numbered; this would seem obvious, but has proven to be a serious limitation for some checklists we tried to use. Secondly, questions might have an optional weight so that the reply to each question will have a different contribution to the total checklist score. We felt that three weights (low, medium and high) were enough. A special case of weighting is when we decide to promote a question to *mandatory* or *key*. In order to pass the assessment this answer has to receive a positive evaluation. This approach is used both by the SEI process assessment scheme and by the experimental product-quality certification scheme set up in Italy and described in a later chapter. Finally, the type of the value of the possible replies must be clear. All the checklists we know can be answered using one of the following predefined types:

Type	Example metric
text	What language was used?
integer	What is the value of the cyclomatic number?
real	What is the average length of procedures?
percentage	How many documents adhere to the predefined standards?
boolean	Is the module D-structured?
enumerative	What severity class does the failure pertain to?

Of course a question must be expressed by text; we found out that five lines (400 characters) were enough in the great majority of cases. If this is not the case then it is likely that either the question is confused or more than one topic addressed. The checklists were drawn up by a number of SCOPE partners and one of them needed explanatory text accompanying the questions and guiding the assessor.

Any reasonable checklist manager must be able to store several checklists composed of questions which conform to the above types. In addition to this it must also support the assessor in filling in the checklist during a product assessment. This means storing the value of each answer, its weighting and notes explaining the reasons for the evaluation decision.

Once a checklist has been completed, the checklist manager ought to process it by applying a predefined algorithm in order to derive a pass/fail decision. This is normally achieved by means of weighted averages combined with the check of *key* questions. Special care has to be paid to the evaluation of questions that were considered not applicable by the assessor for the specific product.

7.3.2 Using a commercial spreadsheet package

All the above functions can easily be supported by a spreadsheet package. Indeed our first experience in handling questionnaires made use of off-the-shelf spreadsheets. However, problems arise when you have a quality model structured on several levels and embodied by hundreds of checklists each composed of many questions. These problems are compounded when the checklists to apply vary greatly from one assessment to another. Further features that were needed on SCOPE were:

1. Configuration and version control
2. Ability to maintain integrity of the overall structure
3. Shared data
4. Production of customizable reports

For these a spreadsheet is not sophisticated enough.

7.3.3 Implementation of a checklist manager

In order to cope with these problems, a custom-built checklist manager was defined and used; this had the following main functions:

Set-up (data definition): this allows the definition of the underlying assessment environment in terms of the characteristics model, individual checklists and a customized view for the assessment of a specific software product. This means defining quality characteristics, the quality model structure, checklists, weights, ratings, evaluation criteria, types of usage, report layout and templates.

Assessment support (data manipulation): starting from the definition of an assessment session, it completely supports the assessor in the inspection activities conducted by means of checklists. This involves opening, handling, closing and deleting assessments. Within any assessment we need to define the nature of the assessment, complete the checklists, derive assessment results and produce reports.

Historic viewing (data management): it allows us to perform various kinds of data analysis on a local database accumulated during the previous assessments.

Utilities such as back-up and restoration data, definition of users' access-control rules, import and export of definition data, packing data, customization reports, etc.

The checklist manager used within the SCOPE project was a customization and enhancement of an existing tool called Mac System and produced by IAMA in Italy. It should be noted that the tool is completely independent of the content of the assessment. It could equally well handle checklists related to product assessment, process assessment, or a market survey for washing machines.

7.4 A FILTER FOR LINT

Lint[51] is one of the most useful free-standing tools for performing anomaly checking in a cost-effective way. Despite its maturity (lint dates from the first versions of Unix) and its widespread use by both novice and experienced C programmers, lint has some drawbacks that may prevent successful use in a software assessment activity. Specifically, lint has the following deficiencies:

1. Lint is not standard: this means that the application of lint to the same source code transferred to different Unix (or Unix-like) systems can produce different results. Differences can be present at the following levels:

   - number of messages produced
   - wording of messages
   - semantics of messages

2. Lint is very sensitive to the environment; that is to say if appropriate libraries are not well defined, we might be overwhelmed by hundreds of meaningless messages.

3. Results are dependent on the parameters specified when calling it. Parameters can be specified for enabling or disabling specific checks but, unfortunately, these are not standard. As a matter of fact, consistency is carefully avoided both in semantics (the same parameter can have utterly different meanings on different platforms) and in strategy (on some platforms lint is weak and parameters are used to strengthen checking, whereas on other platforms lint is by default extremely strong and options are available to bypass useless checks).

4. Lint is very seldom well documented; it is very uncommon to find details about the messages produced and their meaning.

5. Lint produces too many spurious messages; especially at inter-file checking level, most of the messages are warnings that are usually useless. This reduces the effectiveness of the use of the tool, since you lose a lot of time in analysing and understanding spurious warnings. Worse still, if lint 'cries wolf' too often the important anomalies may be ignored.

These problems can seriously affect the usage of lint when we have to apply it on large products (typically for internal QA) or when we have to achieve reproducibility and repeatability (essential for third-party evaluation and certification). In order to overcome these drawbacks, it is necessary to set up the environment carefully, to identify the messages and to pick out the relevant ones and, last but not least, to define strategies and design tools able to filter messages out.

7.4.1 Setting up the environment

Figure 7.4 shows a general scheme for using lint in a controlled and systematic way. First of all, we must provide an environment that is flexible and takes the configuration data as parameters; moreover, lint libraries and function prototypes must be present and accessible. When the appropriate

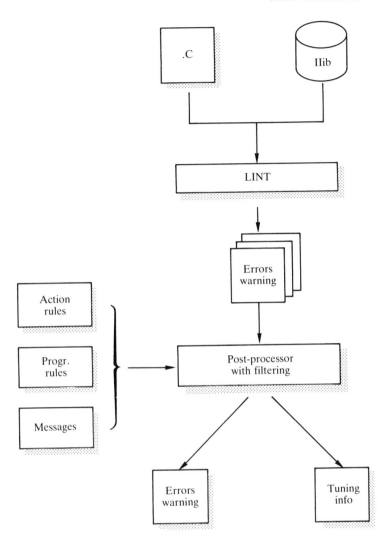

Figure 7.4 An environment for using lint.

command is issued, output is collected and filtered in accordance with predefined rules. Finally, pass/fail criteria are applied to assess the quality of the software analysed.

7.4.2 Selecting useful messages

We have seen that the messages produced by the specific lint are usually not explicitly stated. At the same time we need to have a list of messages in order to decide the filtering strategy. How can we deal with this problem? In

Fig. 7.5 we propose a possible approach that combines a theoretical top-down approach with practical bottom-up trial usages; it is not particularly sophisticated but it has been shown to work.

The top-down activity combines the messages of the specific lint version with the set of *generic lint messages* and with the evaluation rules. By *generic lint messages* we mean the set of statements with a given format that correspond to a given situation, e.g. `<function name> used (<file name>)` `but not defined`. These are used to categorize the specific messages extracted. We did not rely on technical documents but, rather, on stripping out and analysing the lint executable and looking for any string contained in it. Of course, you need a simple program to do this.

Evaluation rules represent the specification of the situations that have to be checked; in the case when we are applying lint for the QA, the rules are in fact the programming rules adopted for the project. The combination of these three inputs produces a list of messages that are relevant in principle. Before freezing the environment, this set has obviously to be cross-checked with outcomes of practical applications of lint to instances of source code. This is covered by the bottom-up approach that requires selecting a sample of source code (as far as possible representative of the overall product), running lint on it, collecting messages and evaluating their relevance by means of analysis of the source code. The steps can be repeated several times until we feel that all typical situations have been covered.

7.4.3   Defining filter strategies

All messages have to be assigned a class to determine their relevance. This defines which messages are to be shown (the useless ones which are by far the most frequent are suppressed), and how we have to deal with them. The following situations can occur:

1. We identify a message that embodies a programming rule. In this case the message can be ranked in accordance with the priority of the rule (for instance, mandatory or suggested).
2. A lint message is raised but no corresponding rule exists. This can be due to one of three situations: the message corresponds to a compiler error, the message is not relevant, or the message is relevant and thus shows us the inadequacy of the rules.
3. A rule is defined and lint ought to pick it out but does not (i.e. an anomaly of this kind is present in the sample examined). This normally tells us that the specific lint version is somewhat lacking. Therefore, if we want to automatically check the anomaly we have to forget about lint and build a specific parser. Unfortunately, this situation happens more frequently than one might suspect.

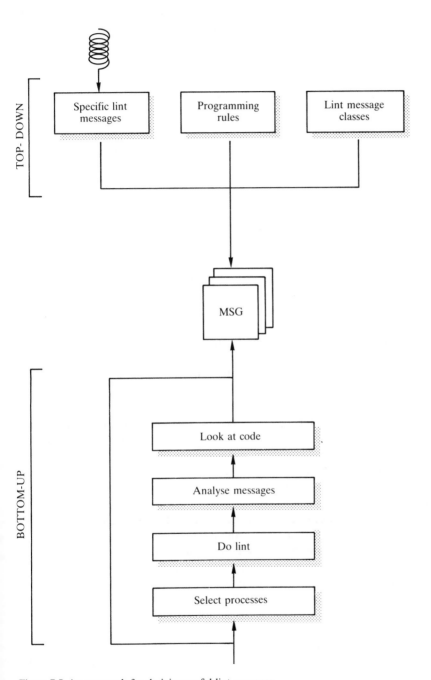

Figure 7.5 An approach for deriving useful lint messages.

Table 7.2 summarizes the most interesting situations among the possible ones, attaching a class (numbered from 1 to 4) to the various cases.

Table 7.2 Ranking messages from lint

Message has been identified?	Is a rule defined for the case?	Is the message relevant?	What is the priority?	Class
Yes	Yes	Yes	Mandatory	1
Yes	Yes	Yes	Suggested	2
Yes	Yes	No	—	3
Yes	No	To be decided	To be decided	4

All messages belonging to class 1 have to be notified in order for programmers to solve anomalies and for assessors to derive a judgement on the quality of the code. Messages belonging to class 2 might be related to anomalies and therefore have to be reported in order for programmers to evaluate them on a case-by-case strategy. QA has to perform statistical analysis on the number of warnings of this kind that have led to a change in the code or a software failure. If the rate is very high this means that the rule may shift from suggested to mandatory, whereas if the rate is extremely low the message could well be moved to class 3. Class 3 covers in fact all the situations that are mostly spurious and that represent *noise* in the output. This means that these kinds of messages have to be filtered and not reported. Messages of class 4 represent unknown situations; for this reason it is good not to report them to programmers but to notify QA staff to evaluate them and decide to which class (1–3) they have to be assigned and whether a new rule has to be issued. As a matter of fact, messages of class 4 represent the tuning information introduced in Fig. 7.4.

The filtering strategy can be further refined. For instance, messages can also be filtered in accordance with the related software characteristic. Lint messages in fact cover more than one characteristic: mainly portability (usage of old-fashioned operators or non-portable comparisons) and reliability (null-effect instructions or illegal pointer combination), but also to a much lesser extent efficiency (assignment to constant inside loops) and maintainability (names defined but not used or statements not reachable).

We have mentioned in this section a tool which only processes C code. There is a lot of software written in C, but nevertheless it does restrict the applicability of the assessment technique. The same system could be applied to flint which reads in FORTRAN or to other anomaly checkers.

Many of the ideas proposed here could be incorporated into specifically built anomaly checkers rather than constructed around an existing tool.

7.5 EXTENSIONS TO PROGRAM ANALYSERS

The SCOPE project ran about 25 case studies in which commercially produced software was subjected to the numerous assessment techniques detailed in Chapter 4. We wished to choose as wide a range of case studies as possible in order to show that our assessment methods were generally applicable. It would have imposed an intolerable restriction on our choice if we had only been able to analyse those languages which were supported by the tools we had at the time. In particular it would have ruled out analysing software written in the newer fourth-generation languages which are not yet supported by the existing commercial program analysers. We also wished to establish the principle that tools-based methods can cheaply and rapidly be adapted to accommodate new languages and notations.

The two tools to which extensions were added are QUALMS and Logiscope. We now briefly describe how they work.

7.5.1 QUALMS

QUALMS (QUality AnaLysis and Metrication System) is a static analyser which performs structural analysis. There are many variants of QUALMS in existence but the main features common to all versions are that it:

1. Displays the flowgraph
2. Derives and displays the decomposition tree which is another representation of the control flow
3. Derives metrics from the decomposition tree
4. Displays the prime flowgraphs which give an insight into the program structure

QUALMS arose out of research at CSSE (Centre for Systems and Software Engineering), South Bank University and has been used on numerous research projects. It is not sold as a commercial product and supported in the same way as other analysers. Licence holders are given full source code and documentation and it is part of the QUALMS culture that users should add their own enhancements and perform their own maintenance.

The architecture of the system is that there are two parts to the QUALMS system, a number of graph modellers (front ends) which extract the flowgraph and call graph information from source code in a specific

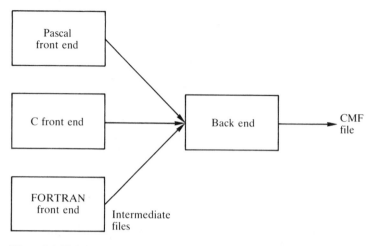

Figure 7.6 High-level architecture of QUALMS.

language and two analysers* (back ends) which display the graphs and calculate structural metrics as shown in Fig. 7.6. QUALMS runs on Sun workstations and PCs.

An attempt was made to extend QUALMS to cover data-flow metrics, but this work was highly experimental and is a long way from any commercial exploitation.[94]

At the time of writing, a commercial version of QUALMS, called *Prometrix* had been built by Infometrix Software. Prometrix overcomes many of the problems we encountered using QUALMS by adding an advanced user interface. Also Prometrix includes many of the descriptive statistics described in Chapter 6 such as histograms, pie charts, box plots and one of the multivariate tests developed by Neil. There are in addition many new call graph metrics. This version is supported by full user manuals and maintenance and is available for C, Pascal, Ada, COBOL and FORTRAN.

7.5.2 Logiscope

Logiscope[154] is a software engineering product designed, developed, marketed and maintained by Verilog. It is an automated source-code analyser which provides textual and structural analysis and coverage

---

* There is no agreed terminology for the component parts of program analysers, which is why we use the terms front end and back end. The word *analyser* means different things in QUALMS and Logiscope. The QUALMS analyser is the back end whereas the Logiscope analyser refers to the front end.

analysis. Logiscope supports several languages (standard and other versions) such as Pascal, C, Ada, FORTRAN and COBOL. As with other analysers, the front ends are language-specific and the two back ends (static and dynamic) are language-independent. Static Logiscope:

1. Displays flowgraphs and call graphs
2. Calculates metrics from these graphs and from the text
3. Compares the metric values against predefined criteria and thresholds
4. Identifies anomalous modules
5. Displays some simple statistics of metrics

Dynamic Logiscope:

1. Calculates coverage measures
2. Displays flowgraphs and call graphs showing which paths have been executed
3. Provides information to help the user derive extra test cases

Logiscope runs on several stations such as Apollo (under both Aegis and Unix), Sun (Unix), HP 9000/3XX (Unix), WS 2000 (VMS), VAX (VMS) with 32793 terminals and GDDM libraries. The actual languages supported are: Ada, Assembler 68000, Assembler 8086, Atlas, C, COBOL, FORTRAN, Ltr 2, Ltr 3, Modula 2, Pascal, Pdl, Pl1, Plm86, Rap86, Rtl 2, Rtl 3, Xal, Xar.

7.5.3 Interfacing with existing analysers

It is possible to adapt for new languages simply by building new front ends. One case study used the database query language SQL. Since neither QUALMS, Logiscope nor any other tool we knew about supported SQL we decided to build a Logiscope front end for this language to derive the textual metrics only (SQL has no control flow).[4] It should be noted that the Logiscope licence prohibits building new front ends without the prior permission of the supplier (Verilog). Luckily, Verilog was the prime contractor of the SCOPE consortium.

Like Logiscope, the interface between the two parts of QUALMS is an ASCII text file, although the format of this file is quite different. Within SCOPE, front ends were built for many languages including CORAL 66, BCPL and RULER. The last of these is particularly interesting since in many ways it is not like traditional programming languages.

A programmer who is developing a program in C, Pascal, FORTRAN, etc., uses an editor to create source-code files and then feeds these files to a compiler to generate the executable code. To perform static or test-coverage analysis these sources files are fed into a program analyser, rather than the compiler, to generate either metrics or instrumented source code which is then itself compiled. Even when the compiler has its own editor, the programmer can still 'intercept' the source-code files for this purpose. However, many newer fourth-generation languages are not like this; some of the information used to generate executable code is not in the form of standard source code but is represented as diagrams or tables of information. Even when information is stored in a textual form, it is not always possible to intercept it before it reaches the compiler. In building the RULER front end we encountered many of the problems associated with supporting new languages and so it is given here as a paradigm.

7.5.4 A front end for RULER

RULER is a fourth-generation language which is used for developing commercial data-processing applications and is produced by Phimac. It is a development environment which allows the programmer to rapidly construct an application by using series of menus. There are also within any RULER program a series of *rules* which are algorithmic descriptions of the program operation. These rules are in our terminology *modules* and since they have an algorithmic structure, they can be represented as control flowgraphs and have metrics calculated on these graphs. Although the RULER package contains its own editor and compiler bundled together, it is possible to dump the set of rules together with other information into a text file. Once this other information is stripped out, this file provides the necessary input for the front end. It is not possible to pass the source code back to the compiler. So it would have been totally impossible to perform coverage analysis or use the internal-instrumentation-based SDCS.

To build any front end for a static analyser, we need to have an unambiguous description of the language syntax. This is usually expressed as syntax rules in a formal notation called BNF (Backus–Naur form). The documentation provided with RULER did not provide such a description although each of the language commands was itself described. From this information we *reverse-engineered* a full BNF description of the language.

The front end itself was built using the code generators yacc and lex which are tools provided with the Unix system. These produce a language parser which together with some additional code will extract the flowgraph information from the RULER text file and create the input for the QUALMS back end. The new front ends for program analysers took typically 1–3 person-months of effort to build and test; for RULER it was only 1 person-month. This figure was comparatively low because first, RULER is a small and simple language (in terms of syntax rules), and secondly because by this time we had built up considerable experience of building front ends. For more details the reader is referred to the technical report.[12]

7.5.5 Remote analysis of source code

It is always necessary to have access to the software components in electronic form to perform static and test-coverage analysis. However, sometimes the owner of this data may not be prepared to hand over documents such as source code for fear of having them copied. In two case studies, the providers were unwilling to release the source code to the case-study partners for exactly this reason. This of itself is no obstacle to performing an assessment.

Since the front and back ends for the program analysers are separate, we can supply the provider with their own copy of a front end. Running a front end does not require any great expertise, so this can be done by the providers themselves. The intermediate files are then handed over to the case-study partner who runs the back end, calculates the metrics and makes an evaluation. The analysers have been designed in such a way that the original source code cannot be recaptured from this intermediate file.

7.5.6 General principles of front ends

By describing the specific implementation of front ends for two named tools, we have established a number of principles which extend beyond QUALMS or Logiscope. For example, the separation into front and back ends is common to many other analysers. The main principles are:

1. New languages and notations can be easily accommodated
2. There is no need for a testing lab to have access to source code
3. The cost of extending tools is relatively low

7.6 RUNNING ANALYSERS IN BATCH MODE

When we are performing a software assessment we will generally wish to collect all the metrics first and then use statistical techniques to interpret them. Since the metrics will come from a number of different tools, we will often store all the metrics in a central repository and then extract data from this repository, rather than use the metrics directly from the tools. So we have a requirement to calculate all the metrics for a given product *in one go*.

Commercial analysers such as Logiscope are intended to be used by the programmer as the software is being developed. They provide the programmer with interactive menus to view the system file by file, module by module. For our purpose we want to run these tools in a *batch mode* where the set of files is fed in and the set of metrics (in a text file) output with minimal user interaction. The versions of tools used on SCOPE did not support this.

One particularly large case study had several hundred modules which were stored in a hundred or so files. To have run Logiscope on the whole case study and calculate all the metrics would have required literally thousands of keyboard operations. Apart from being tedious and time-wasting, this kind of procedure is likely to introduce errors. It would be all too easy to forget to enter one or two files, or enter the same file twice.

Our solution to this was to implement batch options for these tools. In the case of QUALMS this was quite straightforward since we could alter the source code and add a new batch function to the analyser. However, Logiscope source code was not available so we adopted a different approach. A Logiscope usage manager was built. This tool invokes and issues appropriate commands to the various parts of the Logiscope system in the same way that a user would. The Logiscope usage manager was implemented as a Unix shell script and relied on the fact that in version 2 of Logiscope all commands are entered via the standard input. Any analyser which is operated by a mouse-driven interface could not be controlled in this way.

The new version of Logiscope (version 3) does support a batch facility and in this sense the Logiscope usage manager is now redundant. Nevertheless there are many analyser and other metrics tools which do not provide a batch option and the approach taken here would be applicable in these cases.

SUMMARY

The lesson of this chapter is that it is often possible to adapt existing software (including operating systems) for data collection, even if we end up using the software for a purpose very different from the one originally intended. This is more effective than either building tools from scratch or using no tools at all. The tools described in this chapter fill gaps that existed in the data-collection scheme. Apart from explaining how specific problems were overcome, we have also shown principles of how to collect data in an automatic way. The fact that many of these tools can be built cheaply means that any test laboratory or QA department attempting product assessment can build these tools or else contract someone else to build them.

8

A METRICS DATABASE

At the heart of any metrics scheme there needs to be somewhere to store the data. Until now we have used the term *repository* to describe this so as not to prejudice any implementation. We will now show that, for the kind of metrics scheme we propose, this repository needs to be a database.

Once we know the underlying model of the data we are collecting, constructing a database is relatively straightforward. However, problems arise when we try to transfer large quantities of data from different sites into the database. Although it might seem a simple matter, data transfer is not at all trivial. Perhaps the main difficulty that has beset many previous metrics projects is that those involved did not realize the importance of transfer mechanisms until too late into the project and then had difficulty in analysing the data. Although this fact is rarely broadcast by the participants in these projects, our research has shown that it is a quite common phenomenon.

One of the major achievements of the SCOPE project was that we were able to solve this problem. This enabled us to collect and analyse data from the case studies as we describe in Chapter 9. Many of the difficulties that we have overcome will occur again and again with different metrics schemes. For this reason we now describe how the SCOPE database was constructed and why it was built in that way.

8.1 WHY A DATABASE?

The purpose of the SCOPE data repository was to store the data from the case studies. Each case study derived its data from applying some or all of the assessment techniques, each of which was supported by one or more different tools. We therefore had data coming from a number of different *sources*. In order to perform the various types of analysis described in Chapter 6 we needed to collect together the data from different sites and different sources and store them at a central site. There are three ways that metrics data can be stored which are in increasing order of sophistication:

1. On paper forms in a filing cabinet
2. In electronic flat files
3. In a database

For very small amounts of data, paper forms are the cheapest and easiest means of storage. However, the quantity of data from the case studies would make this approach totally infeasible. Also paper forms are very difficult to back up. Making a complete copy of the repository for archiving would mean photocopying each sheet of paper. Backing up electronic data is very much easier.

If we are only storing data from a single source (i.e. from one tool) then we could store the data in the form of flat files. A *flat file* is a text file in which data is represented in the form of a two-dimensional table. Each data point is stored as a record and these records are typically delimited by new-line characters. Each record is a list of data values usually delimited by commas, spaces, or some other character. Figure 8.1 gives an example. Flat files offer the following advantages over paper forms:

1. Most statistical and spreadsheet packages can import and export flat files.
2. Flat files can be stored electronically and readily copied and backed up.
3. Flat files can be concatenated so that data can be combined, but only where the set and ordering of metrics stored in each respective flat file is exactly the same.

Flat files do not limit the amount of data that can be stored but they do limit its complexity and our ability to manipulate it. In particular, if we wish to

```
"main",1,23,5.7,44,8
"proc1",2,34,6.3,33,9
"proc2",3,46,10.0.23,12
etc.
```

Figure 8.1 Example of a flat file.

combine data from two or more sources, merging the flat files becomes very difficult. Before the SCOPE database had been completed we did use flat files as a stop-gap measure. We found we could easily examine the data from any one metric source but not from two or more sources. For example, we could not combine the data from, say, QUALMS and Logiscope except by manually editing the flat files. For thousands of data points this is simply not practical. We did once consider building a tool specifically to merge flat files from different sources, but this would, in fact, have been a sort of crude database anyway.

Since flat files and paper forms were not adequate for our purposes, a database was needed. We used a relational database, although other types of database may well do the job equally well. A relational database consists of a number of tables of data which can be cross-referenced. If properly constructed, a database will allow us to add and update metrics data and then extract it later as it is needed. Databases are quite easy to build using a proprietary Database Management System (DBMS) which supports SQL (Standard Query language). In fact a properly constructed database can process quite complex *queries*. For example, we might wish to output all the coverage measures for those modules implemented in Pascal or the names of those systems for which a portability checklist scored more than 5. Databases can be easily backed up so data can be properly archived.

At this point we should make a distinction between the database described in this chapter which is a *Software Engineering Database* used to store metrics data and a *Certification Database* described in Chapter 10. The latter stores information about the entire assessment process and subsumes the software engineering data. We also distinguish between the *database proper* which is where the data is actually deposited and the *database system* which also includes all the tools associated with moving data in and out of the database. These tools are likely to be distributed at a number of different sites.

8.2   REQUIREMENTS FOR THE DATABASE SYSTEM

Although the database system was built specifically to support the activities of the SCOPE project, there are many aspects of the requirements that will apply to other types of metrics schemes. Since the SCOPE case studies were geographically distributed throughout Europe we required a simple and effective way of transferring all the relevant data to a central site. A large (perhaps multinational) company setting up a company-wide metrics programme would be faced with a similar situation.

As we have taken great pains to point out, we wish to avoid any kind of paper-based system. We also need to bear in mind the quantity and complexity of the data that we are collecting. The database system should therefore have the following properties:

1. The transfer procedure should be automated and require minimal human interaction; this will make the system cheap to use and less prone to error.
2. The system should be adaptable to incorporate many of the tools used in applying assessment techniques.
3. The system should be reliable in that the chance of data being corrupted or lost is minimized.
4. The system should be platform-independent (e.g. hardware, operating system) to be generally usable.

We now describe how the database and its associated tools were designed and constructed. In doing so we address many of the important issues that will affect any data-collection scheme. Any metrics scheme for a large organization or group of organizations that wished to collect fine-granularity metrics would encounter many of the problems described in this chapter. Although the exact details will vary with the types of metrics and tools used, many of the general themes will reoccur. We should finally note that the reason why we need to pay such attention to the database system is because of the quantity and nature of the data we are collecting. If we only collected a few metrics at a coarse level of granularity then such a system would clearly be overkill.

8.3   ARCHITECTURE OF THE DATABASE SYSTEM

The SCOPE database did not contain absolutely all of the data collected from the assessment techniques but did include a large proportion of it. We specifically geared the database to those metrics collected over a number of projects. Some techniques were used in only one case study and so the storage of this data was given a lower priority. Nevertheless, to extend the database to contain all the data would not require a substantial enhancement.

In addition to the database proper with its input and output routines, the database system includes transfer tools that are specific to certain sources of data. Additional features may also be desirable such as the ability to encrypt certain data to preserve confidentiality. The various parts of the database described here are as follows:

1. The database proper consisting of tables and relations between them
2. The input routines (CMFI)
3. The output routines (CMFO)
4. Data-transfer tools
5. Encryption tools

Figure 8.2 shows how the metrics tools and the database system fit together.

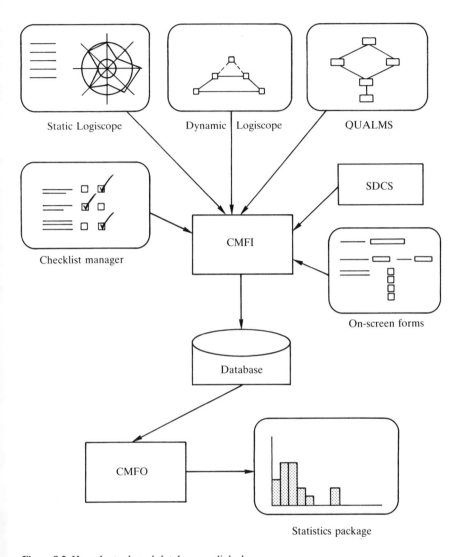

Figure 8.2 How the tools and database are linked.

8.4 THE DATABASE PROPER

Underlying the database is a data model similar to our product model described in Chapter 4 and illustrated in Fig. 4.1. Figure 8.3 shows the structure of the data model used for the database. The data model in Fig. 8.3 is similar but not identical to that of Fig. 4.1. Note that the executable

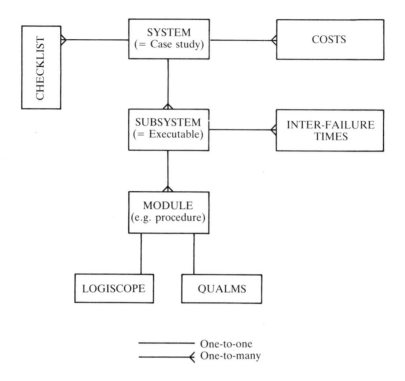

Figure 8.3 Structure of the database.

system and the non-executable components are all represented by a single entity because there was no need to have separate tables for this data. All the checklists used in SCOPE were defined at the system level (this in general need not be the case) and so to each software product system there are linked a number of checklist scores. We found that there was no information to store at the compound-module level and so this entity did not feature. The QUALMS and Logiscope *static data* are stored in separate tables purely for reasons of space efficiency. In principle these could all have been put in a single-module table. However, there are quite a lot of metrics from these tools and they take up a lot of space. Since some case studies did not collect metrics from one or both of these tools, including the metrics in a single table would result in a large amount of wasted space.

The product metrics stored as of February 1993 were:

All the QUALMS flowgraph metrics (7401 modules from 12 case studies)
All the static Logiscope metrics defined at the module and subsystem level (3529 modules, 9 case studies)
Test-coverage metrics from Logiscope (73 modules, 3 case studies)

Checklist scores (but not replies to each question) from the checklist manager (309 checklists, 12 case studies); these can be derived from inspection or black-box testing
Failure data from the SDCS (1340 failures, 2 case studies)
Language of implementation (e.g. Pascal, C, etc.); this information is generated by the static analysers
Readability indices from style
Cost data (21 case studies)

It would have been straightforward to add metrics from other tools, and in particular we could have added results of anomaly checkers (e.g. lint) and metrics from TEFAX. Process data too can be represented within this model. Faults and effort (of construction) data can be stored against a particular component.

If the data described above were the only data stored in the database, the database would consist of nothing other that metric values. We would not know what the metric values referred to. The following classes of data therefore had to be added to make the metrics analysable. These were:

Naming data Names of components such as subsystems and modules, etc.
Configuration data The version and date of the components
Component-structure data This links modules to their respective subsystem and subsystems to their respective system
Project data Information about the application domain and development style

Naming and configuration data are necessary so that we can query the database and extract metrics related to particular components or sets of components. Naming and configuration data have to be present when data is transferred to the database, otherwise we will not know what the metric values refer to.

Component-structure data allows us to aggregate metrics and determine which modules and subsystems belong to which products. This information is generated by program analysers such as Logiscope and QUALMS.

The project data gives background information about the software product such as the application domain, the criticality of the product and high-level information about the process. This enables us to make comparisons across application domains and development styles. The project data is entered by means of a specially constructed tool called the *on-screen forms*. This is a set of electronic forms that have to be filled in at the case-study site. The tool then generates a text file so that the information can be sent to the database. The on-screen forms have certain advantages over paper forms in that they can run simple consistency checks on the information that has been added. For example, we can check that all the fields are completed and that fields are within a valid range of values. Our version was implemented on a PC using a run-time version of dBase IV. The tool is so simple it could be reimplemented on almost any platform at quite a low cost.

The database itself was implemented in Oracle. Oracle is available on a number of platforms; we used a Sun workstation. The query routines described later were implemented in C with embedded SQL.

8.5 DATA TRANSFER

The SCOPE case studies were run by 12 different partners. In most cases the software products under examination were provided by separate organizations. Therefore, in total, we were dealing with about 35 different organizations at different sites. It is inevitable that they will use different hardware and operating systems. It would have been impossible to insist that all the organizations should use the same platforms just as it would be impossible to insist that they all followed the same development process or used the same programming languages. It was a problem that our metrics scheme had to be able to cope with. There was also the added complication of different versions of metrics tools being used within the project at any one time.

8.5.1 Transferring data as text

The one common feature in all current computer systems is that they support text files, usually represented as ASCII. It is usually possible to transfer text files between different platforms by means of tools such as Ftp or Kermit. These tools are widely used and are often in the public domain. We can transfer text data between different sites by standard floppy disks, tapes and, of course, electronic mail.

We have to ensure that the metrics tools used in assessment do produce their metrics in text files in an agreed format. For tools built by SCOPE, namely SDCS, the checklist manager and the on-screen forms, the facility for outputting text files was part of the specification. For QUALMS, we had access to the source code, so QUALMS was modified to output its metrics in an agreed format. However, those tools which were proprietary such as Logiscope and style posed more of a problem since in these cases we could not modify the tool itself. In both cases we had to build file conversion tools. These tools are simple to build and can be rapidly generated from code generators such as yacc and lex. The approach to extracting the data was different in the two cases.

Static Logiscope displays its metric results in tables and as graphs on the screen. However, it does provide a facility to export metrics data as a text file. This facility was originally intended to provide data for statistics packages but we used it in a quite different way. We constructed a text-file conversion tool to convert the files produced by Logiscope into the agreed text-file format. Dynamic Logiscope unfortunately does not output a metrics file. We therefore had to extract the coverage metrics from files generated within the Logiscope system. This approach was far less straightforward. As a result, one SCOPE partner, IST, took about three person-months to build the conversion tool.

The style tool produces its results on the standard output. It is possible to redirect this output into another simple file-conversion tool which generated the required text file. In the case of both Static Logiscope and style, the conversion tools took a matter of hours to build.

Of course, there is a class of tools for which this approach is not applicable. If the metrics tool is window-based and the metrics values are only displayed on the screen with no text-output feature then clearly the data cannot be captured and transferred to the database in an electronic way. The only long-term solution to this general problem is to persuade the tool makers to produce metrics data in some agreed format perhaps conforming to an international standard. This might be based on the CMF which is described in the next section.

8.5.2   The Common metrics format (CMF)

In the first part of the SCOPE project, the text files used for transfer were in fact flat files. The fundamental problem with flat files is knowing which metric each of the columns of the table represents. The whole meaning of the data is determined by an (arbitrary) ordering of the set of metrics in the file. This problem is compounded when several different versions of a tool have been used within the project. It is natural for tool makers to periodically enhance their products. In the case of metrics tools this often means including new metrics. The flat file approach cannot cope well with this addition of metrics since it means that the number of columns in the table will have to change. A further problem is the corruption of data. Since the flat file contains little redundancy of information, if the text file becomes corrupted during transfer (as sometimes happens) there is usually no way of finding this out; the metric values just get changed. Also since flat files are difficult for humans to read, testing the data-transfer mechanisms becomes all the more difficult.

The way around these problems was to define the *common metrics format* (CMF). This is a defined file syntax which is used to express the metrics data output by tools in a text file. The syntax is easily readable (by humans and parsers alike) and the language is sufficiently flexible to allow new metrics to be added or old metrics to be removed. Figure 8.4 gives an example of a CMF file. A full definition has been given by Kirkwood.[96] Note that this text can easily be read and checked by a human (for testing the transfer

```
*METRIC_SET = qualms_flowgraph_metrics;
*DATA;
name = "main";
version = "1";
language = "C";
file_name = "program.c.for";
date = "19900423";
nodes = 8;
length = 7;
mccabe = 1;
dstruct = 1;
biggest_prime = 2;
d0 = 0;
d1 = 0;
d2 = 0;
d3 = 0;
d4 = 0;
12 = 0;
cn = 0;
nesting = 0;
prather = 7;
lambda = 7.00;
yam = 1.40;
basili = 7.00;
s_vinap = 7;
p_vinap = 7;
e_vinap = 7;
statement = 1;
branch = 1;
```

Figure 8.4 An example of a CMF file.

mechanisms) and the names of the metrics are clearly specified in the file. Another important feature is that if two or more CMF files are concatenated they produce another valid CMF file. This is true even if the CMF files come from different data sources or case studies. This is useful because it is usually easier to transfer a small number of large files between machines than a large number of small ones.

8.5.3   Inputting data to the database

There is only one way of adding data to the SCOPE database, namely by means of CMF files. The database input routines (known as CMFI) read in the CMF files and check that the syntax is correct. At this point any corruption of the data is likely to be recognized, and there is sufficient information in them to place the data in the right part of the database. CMFI does perform some consistency checking such as the validity of ranges of metrics and provides warnings to the user if inconsistencies are found in the data. Apart from this, there is virtually no interaction with the user and inputting data is a routine and mechanistic process.

Since all the relevant information should be present in the CMF file, CMFI has no difficulty in processing a file that contains metrics from different cases studies or sources. If the data refers to a new case study then CMFI will automatically create new entries in the tables to accommodate this.

8.5.4 Outputting data

Data can be extracted from the database by using SQL (structured query language) and the data can be output in any format required, including the common metrics format. For this reason the output routines are known as CMFO. The most used format for outputting the data is a flat-file format so that the data can be read in by statistics packages.

8.6 NAMING CONVENTIONS

In a relational database certain fields of data are *key fields*, that is, they are used to link tables together. In the case of product metrics data, the key fields are the names of the components. When data comes from a number of different sources we must ensure that the names are consistent or else the database will not be able to link the tables correctly. For example, suppose that for a software product called 'Quasar', we have applied Static Logiscope and checklists, and in the latter case the name was mistakenly typed as 'Quazar'. When the data is transferred to the database, CMFI will treat these as separate systems. As far as the database is concerned there will be two products, one with no Logiscope data and one with no checklist scores. It is therefore important to ensure that the names are used consistently.

In SCOPE, some providers did not want their name or the name of their product revealed and so we used coded names; this does not cause a problem if the coded names are used consistently. The greatest problem with naming conventions occurs with module names.

8.6.1 Module naming

If we look at the source code we will see that each module (i.e. function, procedure, etc.) has an identifier to reference it. We call this identifier the *naïve name.* In a language such as FORTRAN the naïve names are unique within each subsystem. But with many other languages, especially the Algol languages, the naïve names will not be unique. For example, in C there are two types of module, static functions and extern functions. Extern functions always have unique naïve names, but for static functions the name only has to be unique within a particular source-code file. If a subsystem comprises two or more source-code files, we may have several modules with exactly the same name, each residing in a different file. This provides no problem for the C compiler since a static function can only be called by other functions in that source-code file. It does, however, create a problem for the database. One solution is to give a full name for static functions such as <filename>/<naïve name>. The full name of extern functions is precisely the naïve name. In this way all the names will be unique.

In a language such as Pascal, modules may be defined within other modules, and so we might have several identically named modules in one file. This again does not cause any ambiguity in the language because of the scope* rules. Ada permits modules to have identical naïve names but a differing type of the returned value and/or parameters. Again, it is quite easy to think up naming conventions to ensure that the full names are always unique within a subsystem.

The same problem occurs with program analysers where the naming conventions have been hard-programmed into the tool. Any naming conventions is as good as any other, but if we use two tools with different conventions, the resulting data cannot be linked in the database. If the same module were measured by two different tools and was given a different name by each, then these would appear as separate entries in the database.

The SCOPE solution was a pragmatic fix as follows:

1. Adopt the Logiscope conventions.
2. Alter the QUALMS front end to make it compliant.
3. Ensure that the Logiscope convention was used elsewhere in the case studies.

Clearly this was only possible because we could change the QUALMS source code. The only permanent solution would be to standardize the naming conventions for all tools.

Our experience from the case studies is that duplicate naïve names do occur quite often. Some readers wishing to implement a metrics scheme in their own organization might be tempted to think they can prevent duplicate names occurring in the first place, perhaps by issuing instructions to their programmers. First, if the programmers are following the principles of

---

* This has nothing to do with the SCOPE project *per se* but refers to the parts of a program where definitions are valid.

object-oriented design and information hiding, using duplicate names is quite natural. Secondly, even if attempts were made to eliminate duplicate names, then there is no guarantee that they would succeed without specially built tools to police the code.

8.6.2 Encryption

Many providers within SCOPE were understandably concerned about confidentiality of their data. Usually they do not mind data being stored in the database as long as neither they nor their product can be identified. It is certainly not possible to determine either of these facts from the metric values themselves and, as we said before, the product names can easily be coded. The problem lies with subsystem and module names. For example, if a product had modules with names like *shut_down_reactor* and *lower_fuel_rods* it would certainly not be difficult to guess what kind of software it was. However, we cannot remove the module names totally because they are needed to link the data. It would not be practical to alter all the names by hand if there were thousands of them. The solution is to use encryption. An encryption algorithm will render the module names meaningless but will still allow the database to link the data.

One feature of the CMF is that certain fields are qualified as '*ENCRYPTABLE'. These and only these fields can be encrypted. For example, we certainly would not want the metric values to be encrypted since this would render the data useless. An encryption tool can therefore work on any CMF file and encrypt those fields where it is necessary. Such a tool would search through the CMF file for those fields which were encryptable and would code these accordingly.

8.7 DATA STANDARDIZATION

As we stressed in Chapter 4, for us to be able to make comparisons across products, the metrics must have standard definitions. If a particular tool is used then this will enforce a metric definition and remove any subjective interpretation. Problems arise when two separate tools claim to generate the same metric. The one instance of this which occurred on the SCOPE project concerned certain flowgraph metrics produced by both QUALMS and Logiscope. There are three so-called common metrics which were not common at all.

Number of Nodes Logiscope represents any number of sequential statements as a flowgraph node whereas QUALMS produces one node per statement. As a result the number of nodes in the flowgraph will differ markedly.

Levels/depth of nesting These measure basically the same attribute for well-structured code but usually they differ by a value of 1. For unstructured code they differ markedly.

McCabe's metric QUALMS allows only one stop node for any flowgraph whereas Logiscope can have any number of stopnodes. As a result the flowgraphs and, by implication, metric values are often different.

This is an illustration of a general problem. Many software metrics are not precisely defined or else are defined on models which are themselves ambiguous. (In the case of Halstead metrics, there are no fixed definitions of operator and operand.) Tool makers often interpret a definition in a way which is easy to implement. This problem will become worse as the number of metrics tools increases.

We adopted the following fix for the problem. We treated metrics from different tools as separate metrics and stored them separately in the database. But ultimately we should look towards standard definitions of the metrics.

SUMMARY

The SCOPE data repository was a simple relational database with tools to transfer metrics data as text files. Many of the problems encountered when constructing the database system were ones of standardization, that is, adopting conventions to ensure that data integrity was preserved. Once these were agreed, we were able to modify the metrics tools either because we had access to the source code or else because the tools provided ways to intercept data. Many of the small conversion tools had to be built because we were using many of the tools in a way which had not been intended.

Ultimately the way forward is through defining standards for the respective tools. After all, the physical measurement systems we all use (such as the SI system) are all defined by international standards. The three areas where standardization is most needed is in defining the metrics, the naming conventions and the tool interfaces.

9

CASE-STUDY EXPERIENCES

Chapters 5 and 6 showed how software metrics could be collected and analysed and Chapters 7 and 8 described how the tools and database system support these activities. We now see the results of actually performing assessments. The SCOPE metrics scheme was used within the project itself but also outside the project where SCOPE partners had other research or commercial activities. It has therefore been widely tested. In this chapter we detail some of the results of performing the assessment particularly where the data gave rise to interesting conclusions.

9.1 OVERVIEW OF THE CASE STUDIES

The SCOPE case studies had three main purposes:

1. To show that the SCOPE assessment and certification model could be used in practice
2. To demonstrate that the techniques used to instantiate this model were feasible and cost-effective
3. To expose the providers to the assessment techniques and so gain publicity and acceptance in the software community

They succeeded in these objectives as well as providing a set of metrics data in the database which will be used well after the end of SCOPE.

We do not propose to give a description of each of the case studies since this would have little interest outside the SCOPE project and would certainly breach undertakings to preserve confidentiality. However Table

9.1 summarizes information about some of the case studies from the second phase of SCOPE. The table shows the languages and the required level of assessment for each characteristic on an ordinal scale A–D (A being the highest).

We will highlight the interesting results from the case studies and cite specific data where it illustrates such a result. By showing how metrics can be used we provide paradigms that can be followed by those using metrics in their own organizations.

We also draw on experiences outside SCOPE. It is a sign of the success of the approach that other projects wanted to use parts of the SCOPE method for their own purposes such as internal QA or third-party evaluation; these external case studies are also mentioned where the results are relevant.

As we stated before, many providers are understandably anxious about the source of their data being known and for this reason we have not usually identified the actual case study from which the data comes. Nor have we stated whether it was an actual SCOPE case study or data from another source.

The main results and experiences we describe here are:

1. The variation in structural metrics between case studies; this could be explained by other information we knew about each project.
2. In one case study two people applied checklists to the same case study to judge the objectivity of the approach.
3. In two quite different cases, failure data was collected and we show how this was analysed.
4. We uncovered a relationship between test-coverage metrics and structural metrics indicating that structure does affect ease of testing.
5. Four partners have used assessment methods developed by SCOPE for commercial assessment and consultancy and we describe these experiences.

9.2 STATIC ANALYSIS OF CASE STUDIES

Structural metrics can be used to assess how maintainable the code is. Since much maintenance activity is at the source-code level, this will greatly influence the maintainability of the whole product. The metrics in fact quantify attributes which related to what is widely accepted as good software engineering practice. By examining the metrics across a number of case studies which used different development styles, we can see how these help to identify the use of accepted software engineering practice:

Modularity It is accepted that a subsystem should be divided into a number of modules of reasonable size. Therefore the distribution of module sizes measured by, say, the QUALMS *number of nodes* measure can be used to

Table 9.1 Summary of SCOPE case studies

No.	Language	Characteristics					
		Functionality	Efficiency	Reliability	Usability	Maintainability	Portability
1	RULER	C	–	–	–	C	–
2	ANSI C	D	–	–	–	C	C
3	†	C	–	C	–	C	–
4	Pascal + Assembler	C	D	–	–	–	–
5	ABAP	D	–	–	–	C	B
6	C	B	–	B	–	C	–
7	COBOL	B	–	–	C	A	–
8	†	B	D	B	D	D	D
9	C	C	–	–	D	C	–
10	Pascal	C	–	–	C	C	D
11	ANSI C	D	D	D	D	C	–
12	C	–	–	–	–	–	–
13	Clipper	D	–	D	D	–	–
14	Pascal	–	–	–	A	A	–
15	Ada	C	C	–	–	–	–
16	C + Assembler	B	C	D	–	D	–

† Confidential.

judge this attribute. We are interested not only in the typical values but also in the outliers. A single outlier that is very large may be a maintenance black spot.

Conformance to structured programming The *is-D-structured* metric tells us whether a given module is written according to the rules of structured programming or not. Typically we are interested in the proportion of modules that are D-structured. When we know that some modules are unstructured we look at the values of the biggest prime metric. Large values for modules (say over 10) indicate spaghetti-like code.

Depth of nesting High levels of nesting are considered bad practice because it means that control structure becomes difficult to follow. Depth of nesting greater than six or seven is perhaps excessive.

Occurrences of control constructs QUALMS can determine the proportions of different types of construct such as IF-THEN, IF-THEN-ELSE, WHILE loops, etc. Although not directly related to maintainability, it does indicate different styles of programming.

9.2.1 Factors affecting the metrics

As we shall see in this section, the distribution of metric values varies markedly with different case studies. We examine some of the factors which might affect them.

Choice of language We would expect the programming language to have an influence on the structure and by implication the metric values.

Development style Information about the way the code was written may explain the particular values for the metrics.

Use of metrics and tools The fact that metrics were collected and used on the project will also have an influence.

9.2.2 Size of modules

As we can see from Fig. 9.1 the distribution of module sizes varies between the different case studies. There are three basic patterns:

1. A large number of small modules and an upper limit of about 90 (case studies A, B and D)
2. As 1 but with a number of outliers between 90 and 250 (case studies E, F, G and H)
3. A multi-modal distribution (many peaks) with a high proportion of larger modules (C only)

It is worth noting that case studies B and D used a static analyser during development and therefore the programmers consciously limited the size of the modules. In the case of D there were both an upper bound and a lower

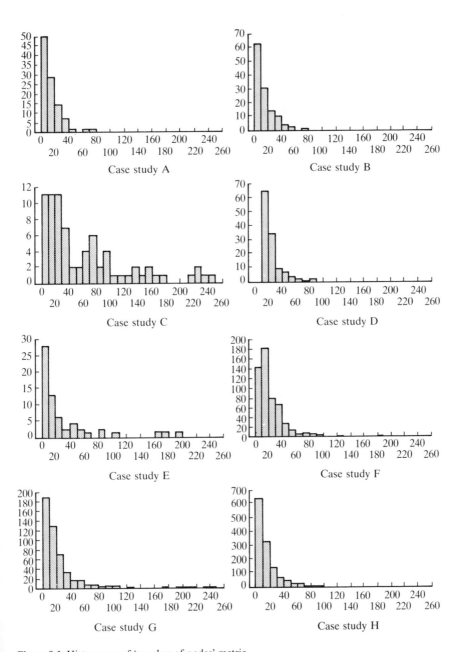

Figure 9.1 Histograms of 'number of nodes' metric.

bound for module sizes and these were enforced as a part of the quality assurance regime. Case study A was written in a fourth-generation language called RULER which is mentioned in Chapter 7. This language by its very nature tends to discourage large modules. The pattern in C is somewhat unique to this particular case study as this pattern has not been repeated elsewhere. It seems that the programmers on the project preferred different module sizes and this would explain the multi-modal distribution. All the other case studies show pattern 2 where there are a few outliers. In fact these outliers can actually make up quite a large amount of the total code even if there are only a few of them. Note that case study C had a module of over 800 nodes; case study G had one module of over 500 nodes. These are not shown on the histogram.

We have used number of nodes (from QUALMS) as the measure of size here. Note that *lines of code*, or the count of operators and operands (N) would have given a very similar result.

9.2.3 Well-structuredness

The idea that unrestricted use of unconditional jumps was bad was first proposed by Dijkstra in his famous 'GOTO considered harmful' letter.[58] Structured programming is the practice of using only simple one-entry one-exit control structures and is now taught on many programming courses. There is a large body of opinion which advocates it. Nevertheless the pie charts in Fig. 9.2 show that unstructured code is all too common. Note that any module that gets a value 0 is in some respect not written to the rules of structured programming. This can vary from a CASE statement (which most people would not object to) to a total spaghetti-like mess. There are really three views of structured programming:

The purist's view where only the simple structured constructs should be used; some in this category view even REPEAT-UNTIL loops with suspicion
Pragmatic exceptions where in most cases structured programming is used but occasional exceptions are allowed for clarity or efficiency, e.g. a two-exit loop is often more efficient for searching algorithms
No restrictions where any control flow structure will do

We can see from the case studies in Fig. 9.2 that there is only one case study with 100 per cent structured programming. This was written in RULER which prevents any unstructured constructs. For example, there is no GOTO statement. The next are B (with a few multi-exit loops) and D (with four modules having CASE statements). In other cases there is a large proportion of unstructured modules. If we look at the frequency histograms of biggest prime metric in Fig. 9.3 it becomes clear that the instances of

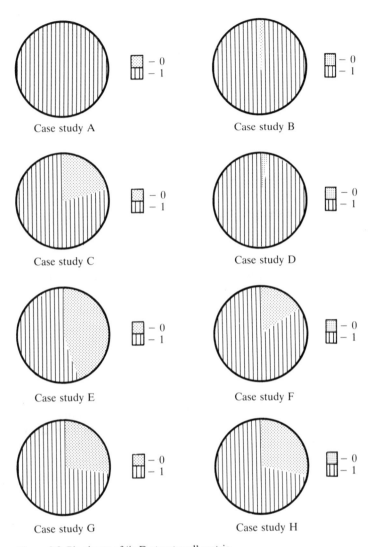

Figure 9.2 Pie charts of 'is-D-structured' metric.

unstructured programming are in some cases spaghetti-like structures with primes of 20 or more.

One factor which might influence structuredness of the code is the choice of language. One of the motivations for inventing the Algol-based languages was to encourage structured programming. The languages used in the case studies are shown in Table 9.2. C, Pascal, CORAL 66 and BCPL are all Algol-based languages with a block structure. These languages were supposed to encourage structured programming, but this does not seem to

Table 9.2 Languages used by case studies

Case Study	Language
A	Ruler
B	C
C	FORTRAN and CORAL 66
D	PASCAL
E	BCPL
F	BCPL
G	FORTRAN
H	C

be the case. In fact, in case study C, the FORTRAN modules were generally better structured than those written in CORAL 66. This leads us to the question: did five of the eight case studies not use structured programming deliberately? In fact, in one of the five a quality-assurance staff member told us that structured programming was part of their normal practice and, since unstructured code never occurred, using a static analyser was a waste of time. In other cases structured programming was prescribed in written guidelines. It seems that none of the QA staff had any idea what the code was really like.

9.2.4 Nesting

Figure 9.4 shows the frequency histograms for the depth-of-nesting metric. What is of most interest is the outlier values, that is, modules with nesting of seven or more. These modules are likely to be difficult to understand and as a result difficult to maintain. Seven of the eight case studies have such anomalous modules. Even the RULER code can have high levels of nesting.

9.2.5 Controlflow constructs

In Fig. 9.5 we can see that in all case studies the primes D0 and D1 occur frequently. This means that the most common control operations are IF-THEN and IF-THEN-ELSE. WHILE loops (D2) are also quite common. What is interesting is that programmers vary in whether they use REPEAT-UNTIL constructs (D3), middle-exit loops (D4), and CASE statements (Cn). Furthermore it does not seem to depend much on the language. However, we could find no relationship with anything other than programmer style.

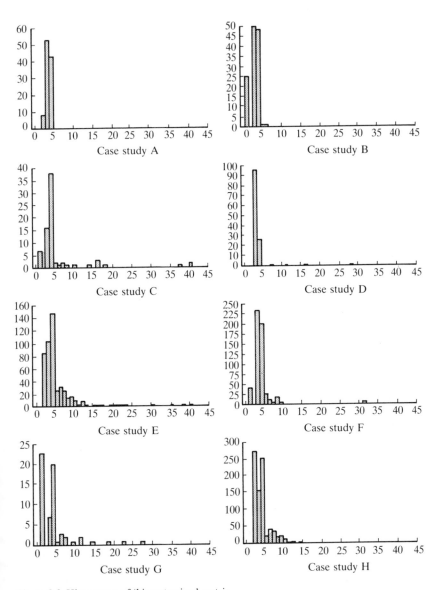

Figure 9.3 Histograms of 'biggest prime' metric.

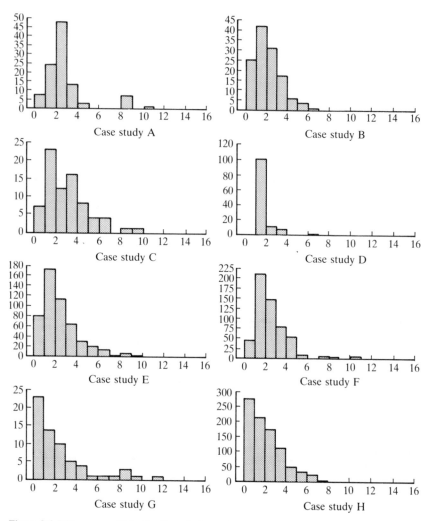

Figure 9.4 Histograms of 'depth of nesting' metric.

9.2.6 Multivariate analysis of static metrics

Multivariate analysis of the SCOPE case-study data was performed by Martin Neil using principal components analysis. From the QUALMS and Logiscope (static) metrics five or so principal components were identified. He then developed a number of techniques for identifying outliers and defining pass/fail criteria in n-dimensional space. The interested reader is referred to Neil's work[13,127] and in particular to his PhD thesis.[126]

It is worth noting that in order to prepare the data for multivariate analysis, we needed to query the database to extract all the static metrics in a

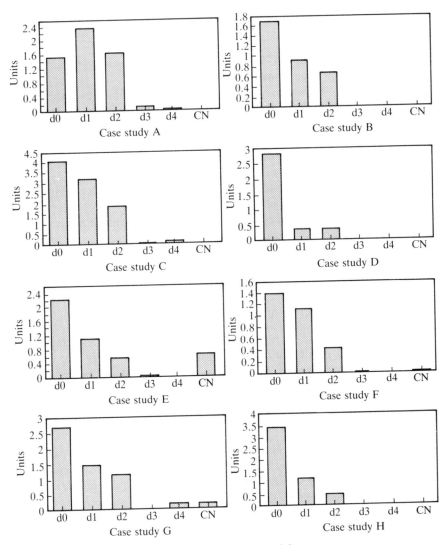

Figure 9.5 Bar graphs of mean prime occurrences per module.

flat-file format to be fed into a statistics package. To do this without a database is very difficult indeed.

9.2.7   Conclusions

Many of the providers were surprised and often a little shocked when we presented the results of structural analysis to them. The case studies we have looked at (and this includes those which were not described in this section but are detailed elsewhere[21]) show that all is not well with the internal structure of software. Specifically:

1. Systems often contain a few modules that are excessive in terms of nesting, size, or large primes.
2. Using an Algol-based language offers no great advantage over the older languages such as FORTRAN. The programming style is more a matter of 'culture' than of language.
3. If a static analyser is used during development and the programmers are aware of the 'acceptable bounds' for metrics then the size and structure will be better.
4. With respect to code structure, internal standards documents and exhortations from managers are usually ignored.
5. Use of particular control constructs seems to be a result of programmer style rather than any obvious factor like language.

9.3 REPRODUCIBILITY OF CHECKLISTS

OLE ANDERSEN AND HANS KYSTER

One major disadvantage of checklists is the loss of objectivity resulting from basing assessment results on questions for which the answers rely on the judgement of a single person. Of course a good checklist will be one where partial objectivity has been introduced by carefully formulating the questions so they can be answered unambiguously. However, in all checklists, problems still remain where the answers rely on the judgement of the assessor.

Given that there will be some variability, the questions we should ask are how much will this variability be, will it be random noise or show bias in the case of different assessors, and is this degree of variability acceptable. In one case study, two researchers separately applied the same checklists to the same components in a similar environment in order to assess the variability.

9.3.1 Conducting the experiment

In total, 50 checklists were applied to the case study in question. However, the experiment of applying the same checklists twice was only done for 9 of the 50. In any experiment we should attempt to hold as many factors constant as possible. In addition to using the same checklists on the same product, the assessment was performed in a similar way within the same organization with assessors who were colleagues and had worked together for a number of years. Both had had some input to the writing of the checklists although they were not themselves the authors. There was also some discussion between the two assessors on the product under assessment.

If we cannot achieve similar scores in these circumstances then it is doubtful whether checklists have any value at all.

The two components under assessment were the *requirements specification* and the *system specification.*

The requirement specification was in the approved version containing 75 pages. It was assessed using three checklists with special emphasis on the following features:

- Self-descriptiveness (C1)
- Conciseness (C2)
- Consistency (C3)

The second document was the system specification (D2) in a late draft version containing 70 pages. It was assessed using six checklists with special emphasis on the following features:

- Simplicity (C4)
- Modularity (C5)
- Instrumentation (C6)
- Self-descriptiveness (C7)
- Conciseness (C8)
- Consistency (C9)

The nine checklists applied contained a total of 115 questions, ranging from 5 to 27 questions per checklist.

9.3.2 Results

The raw data consist of one answer for each question on each checklist. The scale is such that 0, 1 or 2 points are given, or it is decided that the question is not applicable (N/A). Note that 2 points indicates that a (desirable) feature is present. When 0 points are given, this implies the absence of a desired feature. For each checklist a score is calculated by counting the number of points given, and the total number of points that the product could have received when excluding the N/A questions. The ratio of these two numbers is taken and multiplied by 10, to arrive at a final score for a checklist between 0 and 10, independent of the number of questions in the list.

A summary of the scores for each checklist is shown in Table 9.3 for the two assessors A1 and A2. We see a variation in both the median score and the mean score totalled over all the checklists treating all questions from all checklists as belonging to one checklist using the scoring algorithm indicated above. This is done to avoid the influence from the variation in the number of questions for each checklist.

Table 9.4 shows the number of questions that each assessor answered by giving 0, 1 or 2 points respectively, together with the mean value of the

Table 9.3 Checklist scores from each assessor

Checklist	A1 score	A2 score
C1	6.0	5.5
C2	7.4	7.6
C3	6.7	8.4
C4	1.5	5.4
C5	0.0	0.8
C6	1.3	3.0
C7	5.0	4.2
C8	3.0	3.3
C9	5.4	5.4
Median score of checklists	5.0	5.4
Mean score, all questions	5.0	5.8

answers for each assessor. This value is calculated as a weighted average using the points as weights. An analysis is made of the detailed variation in the assessors' answers to individual questions.

Table 9.5 uses the difference N in the answer between the two assessors (N = A2−A1) for each question. For each checklist a count is made of the number of questions with N equal to −2, −1, 0, 1, 2, and these numbers are given in the table. In doing so, answers assigned N/A have been treated as if the values were 0, since this would be the appropriate value if the possibility of using the N/A assignment was not available. The column marked 'sum' contains a projection of the nine checklist columns on to the N-axis, which gives the distribution of the variation of answers to

Table 9.4 Total number of answers from all checklists with the values 0, 1 and 2

Answer	0	1	2	Mean
Assessor 1	38	36	37	0.96
Assessor 2	28	39	45	1.12

Table 9.5 Number of questions with the deviation N (A2 answer − A1 answer)

N	C1	C2	C3	C4	C5	C6	C7	C8	C9	Sum
+2			2	4			1		1	8
+1	1	5	5	4	1	2	1	2	1	22
0	7	18	11	3	5	3	7	6	7	67
−1	2	4	1	2			3	2	3	17
−2							1			1

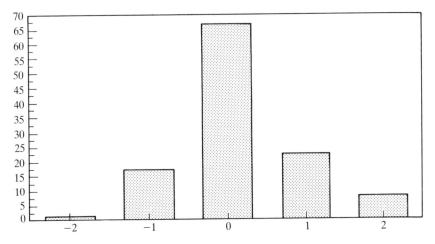

Figure 9.6 Histogram of deviation in answers to checklist questions.

all questions. Figure 9.6 shows a histogram of this data. Note that the distribution is skewed, showing some bias.

9.3.3   Discussion of the results

The simple analysis results presented above allow us to investigate the reproducibility of the scores of each checklist, assess the systematic variation in the assignment of points, and analyse the variation in the individual answers.

From Table 9.3 we can see that there is a significant discrepancy in the scores for three checklists (C3, C4, C6), while the scores are consistent for the six other checklists. Of the three checklists with large variations, the differences are expected to impact pass/fail decisions for two of them (C3 and C4), while it is not to be expected that a pass/fail threshold will be found between scores of 1.3 and 3.0 as is relevant for C6. The latter is a very short checklist with only five questions, and the difference is caused by A2 giving two points more than A1, and A1 judging one of the questions to be N/A.

It is apparent from Table 9.5 that the difference between the assessors is particularly pronounced for C4 where four questions show a difference of $N = 2$. Three of these are concerned with the same feature of the document D2, namely that of the description of the data structures. The same different interpretation by A1 and A2 of the description of the data structures has led to a deviation in all three questions. One circumstance which was contributing to the different interpretation, and in general to the relatively low scores for D2, is that it became apparent during the assessment that D2 is not a design document, but one which partially contains a detailing of the functional requirements, and partially the first approach to high-level design. The relatively low score is therefore an indication of the sensitivity of the checklist to variation in document content, but it does not imply that the experimental results are invalid.

A comparison of the median value of scores and the histogram in Fig. 9.6 definitely shows a systematic variation of the results. A2 is on average more positive towards the product than A1, but it is not a consistent difference, since A2 has a higher score than A1 for only six of the nine checklists. This bias is borne out in the mean score based on all the questions, shown in Table 9.3, or the mean answer value in Table 9.4. In this connection it should be noted that even with this systematic error caused by subjectivity, of the order of 15–20 per cent, the results above showed that only in two cases would the assessors have a possibility of arriving at different pass/fail judgements based on single checklists. This indicates a certain robustness of the checklist approach against systematic differences.

Table 9.5 shows that for 9 out of 115 questions the differences in the two assessors' answers were as large as they could get (± 2). Three of the cases were caused by the same entity, and in two cases the reason is that assessor 2 when reading a question disagreed with the formulation (finding the question irrelevant with the formulation used), and answered as if the formulation had been slightly different. In both cases assessor 1 had answered the question as it had been formulated. It is suggested that the ± 2 variation can be used to identify the checklists that are in need of modification. Using the presence of two questions where the answers deviate with ± 2 as indicative of checklists in need of modification results in C3, C4 and C7 as candidates for changes. It should be noted that C3 and C4 were the two checklists where the differences in scores between the two assessors could lead to different pass/fail decisions.

A restriction of the analysis to those questions where the assessors agree on the answers, or were within ± 1, focuses mainly on the randomly subjective element. It is seen in Table 9.3 that a systematic variation is still present (22 answers with $N = 1$ and 17 with $N = -1$), and that there was agreement for 63 per cent of the questions in this group of 106 questions. When interpreting this distribution, it should be noted that for a normal-shaped distribution approximately 65 per cent of the area is found within one standard deviation of the mean. The similarity of the fractions suggests that the ± 1 variation is mainly due to the random subjective element. A systematic difference which could affect the ± 1 variation, and thereby the conclusion that it is mainly due to random effects, would be if one assessor had a significantly higher or lower tendency to use the *middle* answer which would result in variations being non-random. Table 9.4 shows that assessor 1 uses the middle answer for 32 per cent of the questions, while the same fraction for assessor 2 is 35 per cent. This difference is so small that there is no indication of such a systematic variation in the use of the scale.

From the discussion above, a number of observations can be made. It seems a reasonable assumption that an update of the checklists will significantly reduce the number of ± 2 deviations. This will directly reduce the systematic variation seen in the answers, and remove most of the problems of checklists where the pass/fail result is uncertain. A further reduction of the subjectivity will result if the filling in of checklists were supported by an assessment handbook, which for each question in each checklist gave half a page of description. This should give an explanation of the background for the question, interpret the requirements in various situations, and exemplify significant features to take into account when deciding on an answer. Such a handbook would further reduce the bias (the systematic element of subjectivity) and the small variations in the answers (the random element of subjectivity).

Another important issue is to avoid very short checklists. It seems reasonable to require each checklist to contain, at least, a number of questions equal to the first-order resolution of the scoring scale, i.e. ten questions. This may be achieved by extending the very short checklists, or by merging a number of very short ones, even though this runs counter to the attempt to systematize, structure and modularize the checklists into independent units.

9.3.4 Conclusions

The main conclusions to be drawn from the results are:

- The checklists must be modified to correct mistakes and reduce the cause for variations in the interpretation of the questions.
- Very short checklists must be avoided, and a minimum length of the checklists, e.g. ten questions, must be introduced.
- An assessment handbook ought to be supplied with half a page of information for each question, to support the common interpretation of questions, and choice of answers.

It is an important result of the experiment that the two assessors disagreed on the answers to 40 per cent of the questions on the checklists. Most of the disagreement has been seen to be stochastic in nature, thereby reducing the uncertainty of scores based on mean values calculated from a number of answers.

This experiment should not be considered as the final word on reproducibility of checklist assessments. As was pointed out, the results will rather be an indication of the minimum variation to expect, due to the fact that it involved two assessors who had worked together for several years, that some cross-talk had occurred, and that both had to some extent been involved in the development of the checklists.

9.4 COLLECTION AND ANALYSIS OF FAILURE DATA

In two case studies we managed to collect inter-failure times to enable us to attempt reliability prediction. The cases were very different and illustrate some of the problems in collecting this kind of data. Failure data is one of the most useful kinds of data to collect, but is also one of the most difficult.

9.4.1 Example I

The case study was a program analyser being developed for a research project at Institut für Sicherheitstechnologie (IST). The software read in code in Occam II and output files containing information about the control flow and calling structure. This is the first time we know of this kind of analysis being applied to Occam. It was a small development lasting about 1 person-month. The software was developed in yacc, lex and C on a Unix workstation.

We were able to install the internal instrumentation SDCS for the testing phase of the development. To make use of the failure data for reliability estimation, we have to do operational testing. In this instance we used examples of Occam II source code developed on another project as the test data. In all, 34 failures were recorded.

The SDCS allows the user to classify failures by class and severity. Since the software under development was for experimentation the severity was not recorded, since it would in all cases be low. The failure classes recorded were:

Syntax error where the software flags a syntax error in the Occam code where one does not actually exist. This is a failure of the parser.
Crash where the program returns unexpectedly to the operating system.
Graph error where the control flow or call graph produced was not the right graph.
Bad message where error messages produced by the software (except syntax error) were incorrect or failed to appear (this never occurred).
Other anything not covered above.

In fact the vast majority of the failures were due to syntax errors.

Figure 9.7 shows the CPU time between failures plotted against the number of failures. It is clear that reliability is growing after failure number 13. We then used the SRM package to estimate the expected time to failure. Some of the models can only estimate the *median* time to failure because the mean time is infinite. Of the eight models that were applied, three gave

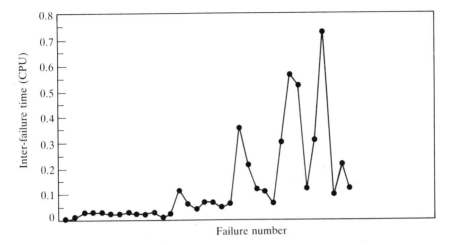

Figure 9.7 Time to failure plotted against failure number.

nonsensical answers, the other five gave realistic responses. Table 9.6 summarizes the results. Note that the values of 10^{30} means that the statistic does not exist.

There were not enough points to determine which of the models fitted the data best, this would have required more than 34 failures. However, it does seem clear that the time to failure was too low and testing should not have stopped. As it was, the tool had by this time served its original purpose in analysing a specific product. Nevertheless, we would know from this data that if the tool were used again we should expect a lot more failures.

For this small data set it is possible to produce reliability estimates, but it is not really possible to show which of the models fits the data best. As a result we are faced with a number of varying estimates of mean (or median) time to failure.

Table 9.6 Results of the SRM package

Growth model	Expected time to failure	
	Median	Mean
Bayesian Jelinski–Moranda	1.12	—
Duane	Infinite	—
Goel–Okumoto	0.99	—
Jelinski–Moranda	10^{30}	10^{30}
Keiller–Littlewood	0.12	0.28
Littlewood	0.081	10^{30}
Littlewood NHPP	0.024	—
Littlewood–Verrall	0.16	0.24

9.4.2 Example II

The second example concerns a commercial software product that was composed of more than 1600 KLOC (LOC = lines of code), and was a subsystem of an even bigger product. When we started to assess the software we were very pleased to discover a large quantity of high-quality failure data stored in a carefully handled automatic fault-log system. This was something developed by the provider and not one of our SDCSs. We had at our disposal several thousand failures registered in more than ten years of operation of numerous releases. Each failure was described by a number of data fields including date of registration, severity, component affected, version affected and phase of discovery. This was really a dream-come-true for failure data.

However, we found that applying the reliability growth models was not a trivial matter.[24] Through a number of trial-and-error experiments we finally came to an analysis strategy that was found to be effective, as summarized in Fig. 9.8.

First of all, a decision had to be taken about which failures were to be taken into account. We did not want to consider all of them if some were inaccurate and possibly meaningless. We had to take into account which classes of failures could be trusted as objectively and consistently registered and of the granularity at which reliability was to be measured (system, subsystem, etc.). In our case we decided to focus our attention on a specific release and its corrective sub-releases since that was the most recent period for which we had a significant amount of failure data both for the testing phase and for actual operation. This included some phases of the development process but excluded the earliest steps of internal testing. We also restricted ourselves to the most serious classes of severity since they were more likely to be accurately monitored. This reduced the data set to about 400 failures. Of course, this meant that we could only measure expected time to next serious failure.

Then we had to deal with systematic errors in registering the failures. Since they were recorded by means of electronic forms, with automatic registration of the date, we had to consider human factors like the fact that failures were registered once a week, that the meeting with the customer had some impact on the fault log and that some periods seemed to be error-free (August, Christmas, Easter and the like). This brought us to a redistribution of failures based on assumptions agreed with the software developer.

Then we had to solve another problem, namely shifting from calendar time to processor time. This was not that difficult, due to the nature of the software product which runs 24 hours a day, each day of the year. In adherence to verified methods[123,124,156] we simply had to multiply inter-failure times based on calendar dates by the number of plants running the product at these dates. This involved the analysis of the issuing strategy

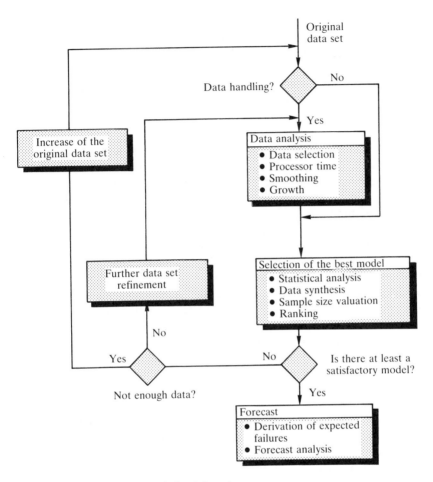

Figure 9.8 An algorithm for analysing failure data.

followed for installation of the product at the final sites since it was not possible to install several hundred complex systems in a couple of days.

At this stage we were ready to compute the inter-failure times. We did it by transferring the failure data to a database, computing the inter-failure times, and then outputting these in a format suitable for the reliability modelling packages to read in. Before applying complex growth models we had to apply some simple statistical test in order to verify that there was a growth in reliability; this led to the deletion of the very early failures from the data set. After a lot of work we were then ready to apply reliability models. We know that there is no model that is best for every data set; rather, the adequacy of the models has to be checked for the specific data set. It should be noted that there was not one model that was best for all phases: some were good for testing, others better during the acceptance phases, and other still were better during operation. So we applied a strategy taking into account the following selection criteria: accuracy (prequential likelihood), deviation (y-plot) and noise (ROCOF (rate of occurrence of failure) standard deviation).[151] We did this by submitting a subset of the inter-failure times to the SRM package in order to estimate the best model from a set of nine that it supports. All models were calculated for the various phases of the testing and operational processes. For the system-testing phase the Duane model was best, whereas Keiller–Littlewood performed well for the beta-test phase, and Littlewood NHPP was best for the operational period. Such a choice was possible because we based the decision on the empirical evidence rather than by trying to match up the theoretical assumptions.

We investigated how many data points we had to use to obtain a good estimation of the model parameters and how many we should use to judge the predictive accuracy of the model. We did not succeed in deriving any scientific rules but a rule of thumb was that about half of the data was necessary for a good estimation of the model. At this point we had chosen a model and the values of its relevant parameters. We then tried to verify its predictive capability. This means that we calculated the failure date foreseen by the model and compared it with the one really experienced. Results were encouraging in that the predictions differed from the real failures by a small amount: 5 per cent for system testing, 10 per cent for beta-testing and only 1 per cent for operation. This was comparable with other published work[41] and was one of the most important results of the experience, since it proved the pragmatic applicability and the usefulness of such a technique.

Finally we tried to link several stages of the development and maintenance cycle together, deriving quantitative values for the failure-rate compression factors needed for this. This is important because what we really need is to predict reliability in the field once we know the failures experienced during testing. The error rate here was found to be about 3 per cent, which is very encouraging. The overall scheme was then applied to data sets selected in accordance with varying selection criteria, in order to fine-tune both how representative the data set was and how accurate the predictions were.

The results of the experience were twofold. From the process side, the analysis of software failures led to a refinement of their classification, an improvement of the registration process, suggestions for improvement to the tool supporting their handling, and the beginning of an activity of root-cause analysis for each failure.* From the product point of view, we were able to make a Pareto analysis of the distribution of failures and so it was possible to specify and check quantitative targets for reliability.

* This is what the Japanese call the *naze-naze* or why-why approach.

Furthermore, we investigated how to combine this approach with an existing reliability estimation model based on indicators from management metrics.

We also tried to relate failures to structural aspects of the code but no strong correlation emerged, perhaps due to a sparse data set; this is consistent with other experiences[105] and is not at all surprising. If structural metrics purport to measure maintainability aspects, why should they be related to reliability?

Another issue arose; while reliability growth modelling is very important to estimate future reliability, simpler techniques might be used for assessing reliability as it is at the time when evaluation occurs (what we call current reliability). That is to say that a reliability growth model should be used when assessing a product in parallel with its development and test, whereas other techniques[17] might be used when assessment take place on a single version of a delivered software product.

A very simple tool was built to automate all the steps of applying reliability models and not just the selection of the best model. This kind of tool has proven to be very cost-effective as reported by other experiences.[108]

9.4.3 Conclusions

The first example shows that the SDCS can be used in practice and does record inter-failure time in an accurate and effective way. Many of the problems encountered in the second example would have been mitigated if an SDCS or something like it had been present at each of the users' sites.

The analysis of the data shows that we need a large number of points before reliability models become accurate. It is ironic that we can only predict the reliability accurately if the software has failed a large number of times. So good reliability estimates required unreliable software.

9.5 TEST COVERAGE AND STRUCTURE

Although for the purposes of assessment we are more interested in linking the internal metrics with external ones, in one case we discovered a relationship between two internal attributes, the (static) structural metrics and the (dynamic) test coverage. Since this result was very interesting and confirmed what many people had suspected for a long time, we include it here.

9.5.1 Theory linking structure and coverage

One of the arguments for writing well-structured code (D-structured, small module sizes and limits on factors such as nesting) is that it makes the code easier to test. Code which is poorly structured, so it is argued, will be tested less well or else will take longer to test. We have a number of well-understood measures of structure but we do not have ready access to data on difficulty of testing. There are of course the *testability metrics*, but these are themselves structural metrics and do not measure the actual difficulty of testing.

Test coverage gauges the effectiveness of a particular campaign of testing. If the coverage measures are available during the testing phase, then development staff can deliberately choose test cases to execute those paths which have not yet been exercised. Therefore, the actual level of coverage will depend largely on how thoroughly the code was tested and not on how difficult the code was to test in the first place. If, however, the test data was derived without reference to coverage metrics, the actual level of coverage attained would indicate the ease of testing. In other words, if the testing is done in a purely *black-box* fashion, and coverage measures are derived only after testing has finished, we would expect the badly structured parts of the code to have a low rate of coverage.

9.5.2 Conducting the experiment

In two case studies (here known as X and Y) we had both the test-coverage measures (from Logiscope) and the structural metrics (from QUALMS). In both cases the test data was available and had been derived without any reference to dynamic analysers. The test cases had to be re-executed after the source code had been instrumented. We were therefore able to test the hypothesis that structural metrics do affect the level of coverage. The structural metrics used were McCabe's metric, biggest prime and depth of nesting. Surprisingly enough we did not use the testability metrics. This is because these metrics can only be calculated for D-structured modules and many of the modules did not satisfy this requirement. The measure of coverage was DDP coverage.

Since DDP coverage is an ordinal measure (and we do not suppose that any relationship is linear anyway) we cannot use Pearson's linear correlation. We have to use Spearman's rank correlation coefficient instead, and that is non-parametric. The biggest prime metric, incidentally, is ordinal as well as giving us even more justification if that were needed. Table 9.7 gives the Spearman correlation coefficients.

For case study X, correlation is significant at the 99 per cent level of confidence for the first three metrics which capture structural attributes. For case study Y, the coefficients seem very low but they are in fact significant at the 95 per cent level due to a large data set (95 points). McCabe's metric and biggest prime are significant at the 99 per cent level.

Number of nodes, which is a size metric, correlates less well in X but quite well in Y. The badly structured modules are usually the larger ones, so it is

Table 9.7 Correlation of structural metrics with DDP coverage

	Correlation with DDP	
Structural metric	Case study X	Case study Y
McCabe's metric	−0.780	−0.276
Depth of nesting	−0.690	−0.207
Biggest prime	−0.721	−0.272
Number of nodes	−0.486	−0.246

possible that the correlation with size is due to this indirect effect. It would be possible to have a large module consisting of a number of sequential statements with no branching. Such a module would only need one execution to attain 100 per cent coverage (for all strategies).

9.5.3 Conclusions

We do not propose that structural metrics should be used in any way to predict the level of coverage during (black-box) testing. The significance of these results is more subtle. What we have done is indirectly link structural metrics to the external attribute testability which is a sub-characteristic of maintainability.

9.6 RESULTS FROM THE CASE STUDIES

If we leave aside the publicity and political aspects of the case studies (which are certainly important) we can see the following overall benefits.

1. We identified which techniques would work.
2. We provided documented instances of the techniques being applied.
3. Validation of theories was conducted.
4. A large pool of metrics data was collected.

Documented case studies are important in the industrialization of any emerging technology, and so we consider how the results of the SCOPE case studies could be extended to other case studies.

At the beginning of the SCOPE project, we conducted a wide-ranging review of the state of the art in software assessment. Although there were a large number of techniques which we might use, only a minority of these were actually used in the end. In Chapter 5 we explained and justified the ones that were used, rather than giving a wish-list of all the things we might try to do. This does not mean that these other techniques can never be useful, it is just that we have no experience to recount. It is worth looking at the reasons why the rejected techniques were not used.

No tools support SCOPE had limited access to metrics tools for the simple reason that we had a finite budget and so not all possible tools and metrics were tried (e.g. other static and dynamic analysers). There are other areas where no tools exist at all (or at least are not available to us at any price). One example is tools to conduct very stringent test strategies like path testing.

No available opportunity In some cases there was not one case study on which a technique could be applied. For example, we wanted to perform static analysis of a formal specification, but alas no case study had one.

Not relevant to assessment Any technique used in assessment must yield a metric value and relate to some quality characteristic. There are several techniques in software engineering which do neither. Of course, this does not mean that they are not useful for systems construction or enhancement, e.g. re-engineering and reverse engineering.

Not mature enough Some techniques may be usable for assessment in the future but are not ready now. For example, data-flow analysis could be used for assessment if a set of well-defined metrics had been developed and linked to quality characteristics.

These problems are likely to be encountered by anyone establishing a metrics scheme. Of course, things will have changed since we did our survey, and readers should be on the look-out for emerging techniques. But this does underline the need for a quality model and well-defined measures into which the chosen techniques can fit. It also underlines the need for the necessary tools.

It is particularly important to be sure that a technique works before serious resources are committed. It would take a brave manager to use technology which was not tried and tested. This is where research projects and plot studies are useful. If we know how a technique was used on one or more occasions, we can try to emulate the experience and adapt where necessary to a new environment. For example, someone wanting to measure reliability may want to collect failure data and use reliability models. We have documented how it can be done and where the pitfalls are likely to be. They might decide to use an SDCS and thus save considerable time and money through not using manual collection.

In the case studies we formally attempted to validate two theories, concerning test coverage and reliability.* We informally attempted to validate the relationship between structural metrics and other factors. (The repeatability of checklists was not validation of a theory, but of the

---

* If a reliability model fits a data set it implies that future reliability can be predicted from past failures.

measurement process.) Building up an experience base of validated theories is an important part in developing a mature software-assessment disclipine.

One of the lasting results of the case studies is the SCOPE database. It is not that easy to collect such an amount of data and it does represent a valuable resource for researchers. This is why the project decided to exploit the data and make it available to the community at large. At the end of the project, nearly all the providers agreed that data could remain in the database after the end of SCOPE as long as anonymity was guaranteed. This means that we have a useful resource for the software engineering community—a collection of metrics from a variety of different products that can be used to set norms or explore interrelationships between the metrics.

The data can be released at a nominal fee provided that no commercial use is made of it and the source of the data (i.e. the SCOPE project with no further qualification) is acknowledged. At the time of writing, the SMARTIE project (a UK DTI funded project which is investigating the impact of standards on software quality) was planning to use the SCOPE database and contribute its data to the database.

9.7 SOFTWARE PRODUCT ASSESSMENT IN THE INDUSTRIAL DOMAIN

Up to now we have focused on experiences in the research domain. The reader might be tempted to think that these methods are not yet used in the real world. This is certainly not the case, since several SCOPE partners have performed numerous assessments in the industrial domain and been paid for doing so. We shall describe some of the experiences in this section, to underline the commercial potential of the work.

9.7.1 The product check-up service

Etnoteam SpA is an independent Italian software firm with a long-standing tradition in software engineering. This has made the company particularly suited for third-party software product assessment. In particular, three schemes have been successfully devised in the last five years, these are the maintainability spot-check, product check-up and *ad hoc* assessment.

Maintainability spot-check refers to a fast-turnround service in which a software developer submits a piece of software (say a couple of thousand LOC) and this is automatically processed by static analysers in order to derive textual and structural metrics. These are compared with threshold values based on reference values and from previous assessments to give an evaluation of the maintainability of the product. This service of software source-code assessment is based on the automatic use of the tool Logiscope, which means that it is very quick and quite cheap. Up to now it has been performed on about 50 products coded in various implementation languages and dialects, for different industrial software-producing units covering many different application domains.

An *ad-hoc assessment* is normally performed on medium-to-large products for which we need both to identify the quality requirements and to assess them. We rely on a black-box testing approach guided by a well-tried method and supported by the tool TEFAX. Assessment activities based on functional testing have been applied to management information systems, telecommunications switching systems, transmission protocols, military systems, real-time kernels, banking applications, medical instruments and productivity packages.

The *product check-up* scheme is the one that most closely follows the assessment scheme proposed in this book. Indeed it has evolved over recent years in order to incorporate many of the SCOPE ideas. Looking at Fig. 9.7 (page 167) the reader will notice that it consists of an assessment process sandwiched between two additional activities, one at the beginning and the other at the end of the procedure. The first one is a presentation of the method and its instantiation to the specific problem. This is necessary to get agreement on the way the work will be carried out and on the nature of the relationship between the sponsor and the assessor. The last step represents reporting of the recommendations for improvement to the product; this step is scarcely dealt with in any assessment process and would be deliberately avoided in any certification scheme. However, it is of great importance for a third-party assessment and is often the main reason for seeking such a service. It enables the sponsor to take well-informed decisions about the evolution of the software product. So, after the assessment of the relevant characteristics, critical aspects of the product are identified, and this leads to risk analysis and a technically detailed action plan. This can actually be the most difficult part of the overall work, but also the most engaging one.

A typical check-up takes from two to five months of elapsed time and concentrates on product functions, system architecture, data structures, source code, technical documentation, user documentation, user interface, distribution of failures. Techniques and tools applied are just those described in Chapters 5 and 7: static analysers, CASE tools extracting measures, a checklist manager, testing tools (test-derivation assistants, automatic execution systems, coverage analysers), anomaly checkers, reliability modelling tools, performance monitors and diagnostic tools, capacity analysers, profiling performance tools, simulation tools.

In Table 9.8 some of the products assessed are summarized. The size of the software-producing unit (SPU) is classified as follows:

Table 9.8 Some of the products submitted for the check-up service

SPU size	Application domain	Product size	Language	Characteristic levels	Reason for check-up	Combined with
Medium	Data processing	Medium	Pascal	Maint—B Rel—D	Maintenance problems	Quality system
Medium	Data processing	Medium	COBOL	Funct—D Maint—D	Guide to evolution	
Large	Support system	Large	C	Effic—C Rel—C	Operational problems	
Small	Off-the-shelf	Small	COBOL, C	Maint—C Usab. B Port—C	Guide to evolution	Testing
Small	MIS	Large	COBOL	Maint—C Funct—D Effic—D	Comparison with competitor	Process assessment
Small	MIS	Medium	4GL	Maint—C Funct—D Effic—D	Comparison with competitor	Process assessment
Small	MIS	Large	RPG	Maint—D Funct—D Effic—D	Operational problem	Process assessment

Small: less than 20 people
Medium: from 20 to 100 people
Large: more than 100 people

The size of the product is classified as follows:

Small: less than 20 KLOC
Medium: from 20 to 200 KLOC
Large: more than 200 KLOC

We think that is worth considering the reason that sponsors ask for an assessment and the activities with which the assessment was combined. First of all, it is clear that an assessment can take place for one of the three following reasons:

- To try to understand the technical reasons for bad aspects of the product that can manifest themselves through operational problems or maintenance problems
- To compare the product with another one (even if indirectly)
- To formulate an action plan of how to make the software product evolve

This means that an assessment is normally requested during hectic activity or when a strategic decision has to be taken. The work of the assessor and his technical advice therefore come at a critical time.

Secondly, usually the product assessment is combined with an evaluation of the development process. This is not surprising since most IT organizations believe that the two are highly interrelated. In Chapter 11 we present data from a Europe-wide survey concerning this topic.

A good process is a necessary precondition for a good product but process assessment is not sufficient to determine the final quality of the software products since this is influenced by so many environmental, organizational and technical aspects. So both types of assessment are useful. In particular the assessment of a software product at a high level of confidence involves the checking of aspects related to the application at the project level of the quality system principles, for instance: configuration management and version control (affecting maintainability), organization of the test log and procedures for change control (affecting reliability), internal testing and review process (affecting many characteristics including functionality) and so on. This ultimately means that the advice originating from product assessment can also touch on many process issues, from organizational through methodological to technical ones. This is also the reason why it is very important for those companies offering consultancy services to possess knowledge of several areas of technology and application domains.

9.7.2 Assessment of programmable electronic systems

MARTIN BREWER

SRD, the independent safety and reliability consultants of AEA Technology has offered to industry for several years a service to assess programmable electronics systems (PES), based on the UK Health and Safety Executive (HSE) guidelines for PES in safety-related applications.[77]

SRD has a background of over 30 years' experience as independent advisers and assessors on the safety of nuclear plants operated by its parent body AEA Technology, and by the Ministry of Defence (MoD) for the UK's nuclear submarine fleet. In fact, no British nuclear submarine goes to sea after a major refit without a safety case which has been reviewed by SRD. The experience in nuclear and non-nuclear industries has made SRD a major consultant to the UK HSE for research and development to support major hazard-risk assessment. This collaboration between SRD and the HSE led to the production of the HSE PES guidelines which were published in 1987.

The aim of the PES guidelines is to provide advice for those who manufacture, design, supply, apply, program and use PES in applications which affect safety. The PES guidelines also provide a method for assessing the safety integrity of a PES including the hardware and software, and it is this assessment method which has been exploited by SRD and successfully applied to a wide range of software applications throughout the world.

The method of assessment is based on the use of sets of checklists. The checklists are divided into two sections: Section A is applicable to all systems and Section B is applicable only to redundancy configurations. Within each section the checklists are organized so that one checklist relates to one of the 16 life-cycle phases (as defined by the HSE), and of these life-cycle phases only seven apply to software. Of the seven software checklists, five cover the specification, design, coding, testing and maintenance of the software, and apply to the production of software for a system requiring a large element of original design. The remaining checklists apply when use is made of a proprietary design of programmable electronics in which the manufacturer provides a large element of the software necessary to carry out a general type of task (usually referred to as embedded software), and the application software is developed by the user.

In utilizing the PES guidelines as a methodology for performing a software assessment, SRD has identified several weaknesses within the approach. The major weakness of the PES guidelines is that they only address the software development process and have little reference to the quality of the final product. Within the remainder of the PES guidelines very detailed approaches are defined for the assessment of hardware, e.g. fault-tree analysis. The need to expand current software assessments, particularly to concentrate on the final software product, has led SRD to develop an enlarged version of the PES guidelines which also include other related aspects, such as the use of formal methods and hazard analysis. The SCOPE assessment methods will therefore also be directly usable within the SRD assessment framework to provide a total assessment of the software component with a PES.

9.7.3 The MicroScope Service

The MicroScope service is a software product assessment scheme applied by ElektronikCentralen, an independent Danish test laboratory that has been conducting commercial evaluation activities on safety-critical products of medium criticality for 10 years. At the beginning, the method was based on questionnaires (seven checklists with a total of 60 questions) focused on the avoidance of faults and their consequences. The method was applied in a total of about 30 assessments with an effort ranging from 5 to 60 person-days. ElektronikCentralen then entered SCOPE with the aim of bettering and extending the approach; this actually resulted in an enhanced method that applies the SCOPE approach and it is based on some SCOPE assessment modules. MicroScope is a subset of SCOPE, in which the assessment is level-oriented, depending on the techniques applied: from a checklist looking at the 'workmanship' of the product (level D), to safety issues (level C), to the execution of functional tests (level B) and, ultimately, application of formal methods (level A). On each level, domain-specific checks are used, based on specific standards such as those for fire detection, gas burners, as appropriate for the application and the needs of the client. The overall scheme relies on more than 50 evaluation modules and several hundreds of check-points.

It is interesting to observe that the assessment is focused on specific application domains that involve safety issues. This is typical for testing laboratories that have a long tradition in certifying electrical devices. For them it is quite natural to have to deal first of all with software embedded in particular devices. For instance, in the USA one of the biggest test laboratories has started dealing with software where it is embedded in larger systems. Those who are faced with similar problems will find many interesting hints on the guidelines of assessment of this kind of software.[152]

Results from MicroScope are reported using a standard format including a statement that declares whether the quality is deemed to be sufficient. The cost in the 5–10 assessments using the MicroScope approach is of the same order of magnitude as the previous pre-SCOPE assessment and is based on fixed-price and delivery-deadline constraints. Expectations are that with a well-introduced scheme, the price will settle at a level of about twice the old approach.

9.7.4 Assessment of software products for local public administration

We now describe the experiences of software assessment by the Information Technology Department of ICT (Institut Catala de Tecnologia, Barcelona, Spain). The story is interesting more from a historical perspective than from a technical one, since it shows the evolution of the need of product assessment from a sector that is not high-tech: a corporation of about 200 town councils. In 1988, ICT began to assess local public administration software against a checklist of 10–12 items covering very general aspects mainly based on configuration aspects (such as memory requirements and printers needed). The method was obviously just a first attempt, limited and not very objective. This is the reason why in 1990 a new questionnaire was devised including about 70 check-points, focused on functionality, efficiency and usability from the user's point of view. The aim was to have an evaluation from final users as to whether the products met the expectations. In order to cover all relevant aspects, seven people (four auditors in local administration and three computer experts) proposed their check-points independently and the proposals were then cross-checked and merged to form the *official* check-list. Since then, 10 accounting products by the most important software developers for municipal government have been assessed, and the results published. The contact with the SCOPE project represented a further step in that it brought forward the assessment of other software characteristics and greatly increased the precision of check-points and advice, thus increasing the quality of software products in this area. The results of this work were very important for ICT because it was a bridgehead that led to more than 200 pieces of consultancy for Spanish local councils.

9.7.5 Towards a network of evaluation facilities

As we have seen, the absence of both rigorous standards and political pressure prevents software certification being applied extensively in the short term. This is certainly not the case for the evaluation services offered by various companies in Europe. For this reason, interest is growing in setting up a network of evaluation facilities.[25] Such a service would be beneficial to a range of organizations:

Developers who would use the results to identify corrective actions and determine evolution strategies
Vendors for using quality as a marketing ploy
Buyers as a substitute for their own acceptance testing and to evaluate competing products
Users who will have greater confidence in the product
The software community at large as a way of deriving and validating the assessment methods as well as giving the techniques a 'track record' which would increase their credibility in a legal context

Test labs for developing a consistent approach and maximizing cost-effectiveness

In order to establish such a network, work has been going on to determine the rules of operation, specifically:

Membership rules Accreditation of facilities, acceptance of new participants, evaluating the evaluators

Administrative rules Harmonization of operation, management structures, mutual recognition, central register, confidentiality issues

Technical aspects Quality model, evaluation process, format of evaluation reports, technical procedures, data collection, keeping records, reassessment, tools, etc.

Commercial aspects How the service will be marketed and priced

We envisage that the network would start as a loose association of organizations and progress to the eventual establishment of an EOTC agreement group if conditions will allow.

SUMMARY

We have shown that the techniques and tools proposed in earlier chapters have been used both for experimentation, which helps us refine and validate the techniques, and for commercial services. Validation is not a one-off activity, and no one experiment can be treated as demonstrating incontrovertible truth. Each successful validation attempt builds up the level of confidence in the technique. We have shown this with structural metrics, reliability models and checklists. We have also given examples of how statistics should be used to interpret software metrics.

The commercial applications of this work should be obvious and we have given but four examples. Both authors certainly intend to be involved in the commercial exploitation of this work in future years.

10

A WORKBENCH FOR SOFTWARE ASSESSMENT

In Chapters 7 and 8 we saw how we could build a data collection scheme from a set of loosely coupled tools. For a collaborative research project like SCOPE that could not undertake an extensive tool-building programme this was sufficient for our purposes. But, as we move towards establishing certification facilities with their associated test laboratories, we will need a more closely linked set of tools as proposed in the assessor's workbench described in this chapter.

At the time of writing, a full assessor's workbench had not been constructed although prototype versions had been developed by SCOPE partners. So this chapter really looks to the future of tools development for software assessment and sets out the requirements and design issues that building such a workbench would entail.

10.1 REQUIREMENTS FOR AN ASSESSOR'S WORKBENCH

In order to attain an assessment and certification method which is both unbiased and cost-effective, we need to automate it as much as possible. This means not only automating the assessment techniques but also the methodological aspects of assessment (the evaluation process). Furthermore, these component parts need to be integrated.

So far we have looked at tools which collect, analyse, store and transfer data. These are important functions that must be performed within any assessor's workbench. But attention must also be paid to the evaluation process itself. Since assessment can be undertaken by a number of test laboratories, we also need any method to be repeatable and reproducible. It is crucial to the success of any recognized scheme that application of the assessment method by any test laboratory produces consistent results. To this end, the assessment process must be regulated and this can be done by means of tools. Another necessary feature is the ability to estimate and then record the cost of the assessment process. This will determine the price charged to the sponsor of the assessment (usually the developer) and may determine whether the assessment is cost-effective to the sponsor before the actual assessment starts.

The assessor's workbench is the name we give to an integration platform for all the different categories of tools used for product assessment and certification, such as:

- Technique support tools
- Evaluation-process support tools
- History support tools
- Data-management and communication tools

The assessor's workbench is not intended to replace existing tools but to integrate them in order to build one system supporting the entire evaluation process.

In this chapter the subject is developed in terms of:

1. The functions that the workbench should provide
2. General design of such a workbench and tools that might be incorporated into it
3. Database technology
4. Experiences gained in developing prototypes
5. Examples based on current state-of-the-art technology

10.2 FUNCTIONS OF AN ASSESSOR'S WORKBENCH

The assessor's workbench is intended to fully assist the assessors during their activities. Hence, the product needs to be independent and self-contained. It must be noted, however, that the product is mainly intended to be an integration platform and, as a consequence, it must take into account existing tools and state-of-the-art technology. Before describing the functions of an assessor's workbench we single out the major constraints that will influence the design.

1. The workbench must be flexible, expandable, independent of tool suppliers and use standard integration technology, such as PCTE.[46,60]
2. The product is intended to handle a large amount of changing data, thus it requires configuration and version management capabilities.

3. The data will be accessed by several users, possibly from different locations; it follows that the product must assure data views and data distribution and handle concurrent access.
4. The data stored is often confidential. For the sake of security, access to data must be strictly controlled.
5. The workbench will hopefully be used very intensively. This is the reason why usability must be considered.
6. Users can be at different levels of skills. Learning facilities are expected to be added to train would-be assessors.
7. The product will be used in different countries. Although the first version might be developed in English, language must be considered as a parameter.
8. The product must be independent of existing tools but at the same time it must take into account current technology. Attention must be paid to portability, interoperability and the definition of adequate encapsulation techniques.

The functions of the assessor's workbench can be represented as a system that transforms inputs into outputs as shown in the SADT[115] diagram in Fig. 10.1.

Inputs processed by the assessor's workbench are the product to be assessed (together with elements of process evidence) and the requirements of the sponsor of the assessment activity. The assessor's workbench must be able to support the assessors in their work and to produce all items needed for a sound decision. Therefore the outputs provided are the information on the assessment activity performed on the product together with detailed evaluation data.

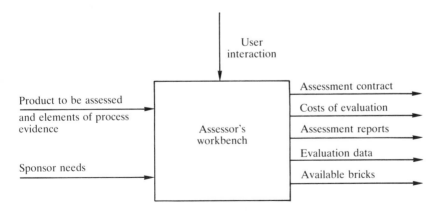

Figure 10.1 SADT context diagram of the assessor's workbench.

The purpose of the assessor's workbench is to apply an assessment method such as the one defined by the SCOPE project. This incorporates the assessment techniques, the methods of data analysis and a procedural framework for carrying out these activities. It follows that the three main functions that must be supported are:

Execution of the evaluation method which supports the assessment activities. The definition of this function is in accordance with the SCOPE assessment procedure.

Provision of services which includes functions related to the *use* of the Workbench (access control), to the *management* of the product to be evaluated (configuration information), and to the *submission* of the product which is the first stage of the assessment method.

Configuration of the workbench which deals with the integration with and the removal of tools from the assessor's workbench.

For more details the reader is referred to the software requirements specification.[20]

10.3 DESIGN OF AN ASSESSOR'S WORKBENCH

RICCARDO BRIGLIADORI

Figure 10.2 gives, by means of the so-called 'toaster' model, the general idea of the architecture of an assessor's workbench. The services that surround the tools provide an open environment, a uniform user interface, independence from the operating system, message passing, data storage and data integration. Within the environment two classes of tools are integrated and constitute the *core* of the assessor's workbench:

Technique support tools These are tools supporting the application of specific techniques during the assessment (for instance, static analysers, anomaly checkers).

Assessment process support tools These are tools supporting the overall evaluation procedure (for instance, documentation facilities, product analysis facilities, cost estimation, planning, statistical packages).

In the next section we will discuss which tools should be included. Here we briefly deal with some issues concerning data and tools integration.

First of all, configuration facilities are needed. The workbench should not be seen as static but must be flexible to conform to the needs of specific assessments. Furthermore, from time to time the tools which live within the workbench will be changed either because existing tools are upgraded or because new tools become available. Therefore we need to be able to include or remove specific tools, manage the data produced by such tools, handle

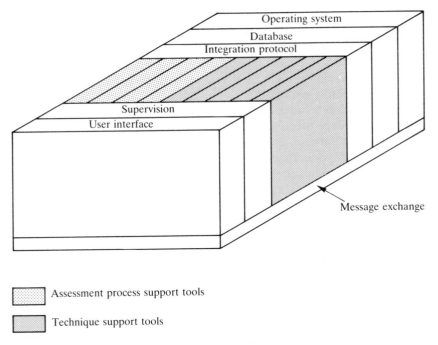

Assessment process support tools

Technique support tools

Figure 10.2 High-level design of the assessor's workbench.

the assessment procedures that comprise the evaluation process, and carefully define and check users' authority to access data. The problem becomes more complicated when the tools are to some extent interconnected. Tools may overlap: for example, a static analyser may share its front end with a coverage analyser. Some tools may require the outputs produced by other tools. Therefore we need to consider how message exchange, data integration, execution supervision and person–machine interface will affect this.

For more technical details about the design of such an assessor's workbench, the reader is referred to the general design description.[18]

10.3.1 Message exchange

This allows different tools to exchange messages among themselves during operation. If included, message exchange allows a strong integration of tools. The basic idea is as follows: part of a given tool is executed in order to perform a function, during its execution the routine sends some information, such as a numeric value or a string in a predefined format, about the status of its process. At this point the module responsible for message exchange interprets the information received and performs the proper actions. For instance, if an error occurred, then an error handler is called; if some service is required, then another tool needs to be called. The possibility to exchange messages between different tools can occur only if the tools are designed in such a way that they provide the possibility of their output being intercepted and interpreted. If existing tools are implemented without this capability, such as if output is displayed in windows, then strong integration is not possible.

Communication between tools can occur by means of a utility that is able to perform message broadcast functions or by means of a set of functions defined for that purpose. For instance, the PCTE (Portable Common Tools Environment) provides functions that can fully support inter-tool exchange messages, but these functions need to be embedded in the source code of the tools to be integrated.

10.3.2 Data integration

The fact that the assessor's workbench is composed of several tools affects the management of data. Usually each tool will have been designed to produce data in its own format and to store it in its own database or data files. The minimum requirement for tools integration is that the data must be shared. It follows that data produced by various tools must be stored in a central database. One way this can be done is by using a common file format such as the CMF described in Chapter 8. A more direct method is if the tools can directly query the database, but again this requires a much stronger kind of integration. Different approaches can be adopted to implement this, for instance: a relational DBMS with SQL as query language, or the PCTE Object Management System with its related functions.

10.3.3 Execution supervision

This service is needed to help the user to work with the assessor's workbench as if it were a single coherent system. When the user selects an option in a menu of the workbench, the supervisor is activated and becomes responsible for identifying and executing the proper tool or tools that perform the function requested by the user. The existence of such a component greatly improves the usability of the workbench rather than if the tools had to be invoked explicitly.

10.3.4 User interface

The user interface should ideally provide a uniform way of operating the workbench and the various tools that reside in it. The architecture of existing tools incorporated into the workbench can limit the availability of this feature, because few tools allow a complete redefinition of their user interface. However, at least two aspects ought to be assured: the usage of a windowing system, and the adoption of an object-action approach where the user first selects an object and then the operation to be performed on it. Examples of a menu bar and of an edit window, both following the style guides of most widespread graphical user interfaces, are shown in Figs 10.3 and 10.4 respectively.

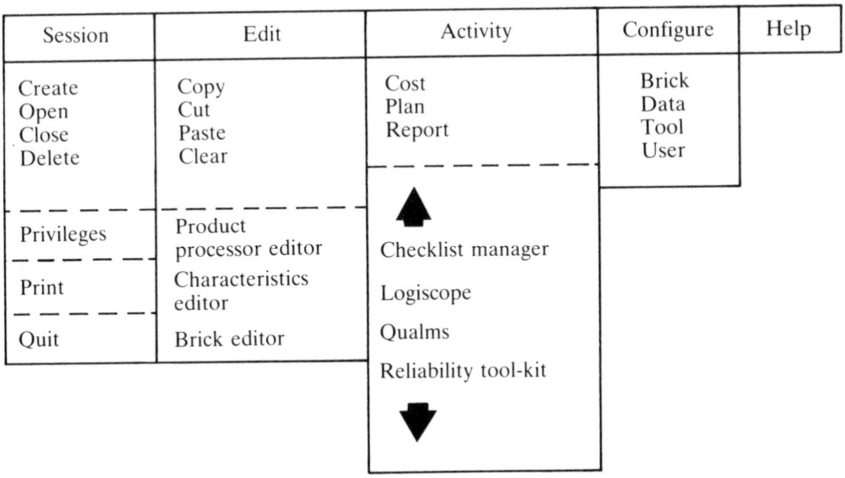

Session
Edit
Activity
Configure
Help
Create
Open
Close
Delete
Privileges
Print
Quit
Copy
Cut
Paste
Clear
Product processor editor
Characteristics editor
Brick editor
Cost
Plan
Report
Checklist manager
Logiscope
Qualms
Reliability tool-kit
Brick
Data
Tool
User

Figure 10.3 Example of a menu bar of an assessor's workbench.

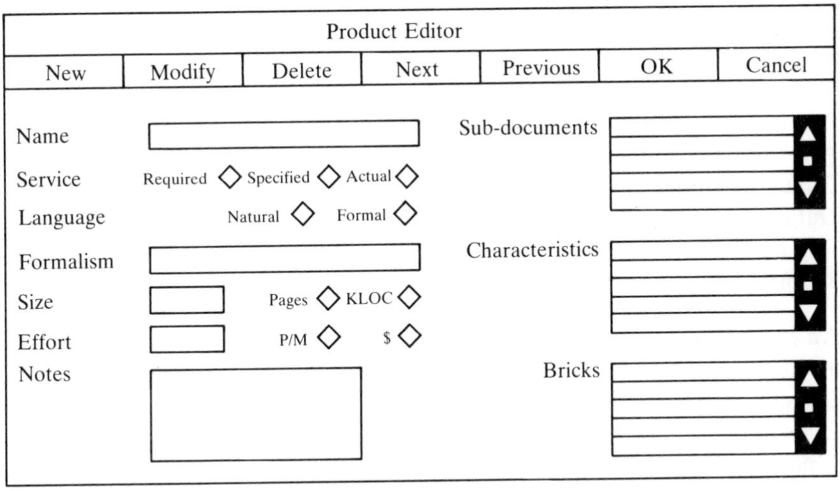

Product Editor
New
Modify
Delete
Next
Previous
OK
Cancel
Name
Service
Required
Specified
Actual
Language
Natural
Formal
Formalism
Size
Pages
KLOC
Effort
P/M
$
Notes
Sub-documents
Characteristics
Bricks

Figure 10.4 Example of an edit window of an assessor's workbench.

10.3.5   Adaptability of the tools

All the above facilities can be achieved at different levels of sophistication depending on how the tools were originally built. We can have strong or weak integration. In weak integration, a tool is seen as a black box that provides one single function to the other tools, and integration can be managed with shared data. In strong integration, a tool is seen as a set of functions that are accessible to other tools. For instance, a planning tool is weakly integrated if it allows only activation from another tool and the reading of its stored data about plans. On the other hand it is strongly integrated if it allows another tool to perform functions such as adding a new activity in a plan or delaying a deadline. For an assessor's workbench, requirements of integration among technique support tools are weak, since these tools can be considered as *data producers* and do not need to read data produced by other tools or to perform intensive inter-tool communication.

10.3.6   Candidate tools for inclusion

As we have seen, tools can be subdivided into those which support the techniques and those which support the assessment method. The main functions that are required to be supported from the method support tools are:

Product submission
Assessment requirements definition
Cost estimation (of the assessment, not of the whole software)
Product analysis
Derivation of assessment goals
Assessment specification production
Selection of the assessment procedures
Assessment planning
Assessment costing
Data collection
Data integration
Report production
Tutorial sessions for beginners

An example of a tool covering some of these functions has been developed as part of the TASQUE project,[104] and it is described later.

As far as technique support tools are concerned we can draw from the list given at the beginning of Chapter 7. There are, in addition, other techniques which we have not included so far but may in the future be used in a workbench. Examples are theorem provers and proof checkers for formal methods, and symbolic executors.

10.4 DATABASE TECHNOLOGY

In Chapter 8 we described a software engineering database which can store the metrics collected during assessment. The assessor's workbench will itself need a database to store and retrieve data created during assessment. However, this data will be considerably more complex than that described in Chapter 8. Certification data includes software engineering data but also includes the quality model, assessment procedure, cost analysis and the actual results of assessment. We give a description of the underlying data model that would be used to design such a database and then describe a tool for automatically generating the database from a description of the model.

10.4.1 Certification data model

If we view the evaluation process as a black box we have as inputs the software product, the characteristics and the software measures (that is, the definitions, not the data). To be completely general we can add process evidence as well as the products. Any assessment will produce reports which in particular will indicate whether the product has passed or failed. Figure 10.5 shows the highest-level data model where an assessment is related to characteristics, products/processes, measures and reports. The relationships are shown as many-to-many to be as general as possible. The data model needs to be general so that it does not specify any particular quality model

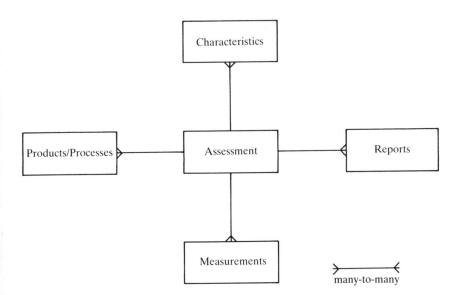

Figure 10.5 High-level certification data model.

or set of metrics. As new techniques and metrics are developed and as the mapping from characteristics evolves, the precise relationship will alter.

A *package* submitted for assessment will have a number of *documents*; each of these documents will have to be classified (e.g. source code, design document, etc.) and it will have size metrics such as number of pages which is used for cost estimation. Furthermore, documents can be parts of other documents and they can describe other documents (in that a functional specification describes one subsystem).

In a similar way to this the characteristics to metrics mapping can be expressed as a data model. So the certification data model will include in addition to the software engineering model, the product, the process model and the quality model. For a full description of the certification data model produced for SCOPE the reader is referred elsewhere.[3] It is obvious that the resultant database would have a great many tables and relations and be difficult to implement by hand.

10.4.2   The BUILD tool

Many metrics projects have needed databases to store data collected on software projects. Two examples which we cited earlier are SWDL and REQUEST. Therefore the construction of a database is a feature common to many such projects. Furthermore, for each of these databases, the requirements, although broadly similar, bear a number of subtle differences. It would not be possible to re-use the same database in all cases, and yet reconstructing the database each time from scratch would be a waste of time and effort.

The solution to this problem is the BUILD tool which has evolved from a number of years of research at AEA Technology. The BUILD tool automatically generates database code from a description of the data model. It was originally developed in the REQUEST project to generate new metrics databases as the data model was altered. The BUILD tool reads in a description of the database, known as the *meta-database* and produces SQL which creates the database and handles interfacing with the database. There is also a comprehensive set of library functions that can be used to access the database.

10.5   EXPERIENCES IN THE DERIVATION OF THE ASSESSMENT

There have been several instances of building prototypes of parts of the assessor's workbench dealing with the assessment method. This has led to two results:

1. Development of tools integration techniques for use in product assessment
2. Better understanding of the assessment procedure

Here we concentrate on the second aspect, that is to say enhancements and refinements of our approach obtained as results of the development and trial usage of the assessment process support tools.

The first step in any assessment is to decide to what level the software will be assessed. Even if it is the right of the sponsor to decide the assessment boundaries (characteristics and levels), the test lab can refuse to perform the assessment if it is thought that the request clearly does not conform with the product profile or its intended usage. There is always the risk of issuing accurate but irrelevant certificates that would devalue any evaluation scheme. Let us imagine that a software producer had its product assessed and certified. It can then be stamped with the quality mark. Any software buyer will therefore tend to think that they can place trust in the product (functionality, usability, and the like) even if it was only assessed regarding portability at level D! Of course the assessment report will clearly state what actually has been evaluated but it is unlikely for such a document to be exhibited in every retail outlet. The worth of assessment, especially in the voluntary area, is largely based on the credibility of the test labs. Therefore it is counter-productive to perform assessments that are clearly nonsensical.

There are several different solutions to this problem:

1. The quality stamp must give evidence of characteristics assessed and their levels
2. The assessment report must be included in full in the user's manual of product
3. Assessment criteria must be defined for different application domains depending on the product and user profiles

Even if the first two solutions are straightforward to apply, the third way will probably be needed if product assessment is to become widespread and widely accepted. In other words we cannot accept that a spreadsheet is not checked against usability or that security is not taken into account when assessing a stock-exchange management system.

A method[69] and a tool for deriving the quality characteristics and sub-characteristics of interest for a software product has therefore been developed as part of the assessor's workbench. In order to master all the possible relationships, a knowledge-based system has been adopted in order to automatically derive from users' replies to selected questions the characteristics that are relevant for the product.

The approach has proven to be useful, not only for assessment but also for the planning of quality assurance activities in large projects.[113] In this case the method can be used to establish a constructive approach to software quality. This extends not only to the derivation of characteristics but also to the determination of technical documents to be produced during the project, of reviews to be conducted, and of tests to be performed. To set up and calibrate this tool, we conducted an extensive survey with major Italian companies using a Delphi approach, deriving risk classes[114] which depended on the usage characteristics, the usage environment, and possible damages in case of failure. Then for each class we determined the quality profile.

Table 10.1 summarizes the basic approach and gives some hints on how to select the ISO characteristics; for each characteristic relevant issues to be considered are listed together with their values affecting the choice of the right assessment level.

When deciding the assessment characteristics and levels, one should consider the various issues and, for each characteristic, choose the level corresponding to the maximum one derived from the values assigned to the enumeration of cases for various issues. Furthermore, we should note that all characteristics have a minimum value meaning *not relevant*. It follows that we might have situations in which a characteristic is deemed to be not important.

For example, a mature, non-critical, company-wide management information system will need to be assessed against the characteristics in Table 10.2. What we want to stress is that the tool produced was a prototype and it should not be seen as a definitive version. But such a table (probably specialized by application domains) should exist in a certification scheme, since it is important in guiding both the sponsor and the assessor during the first steps of the assessment process.

10.6 EXAMPLES BASED ON STATE-OF-THE-ART TECHNOLOGY

We now describe the implementation of integration platforms and assessment-method support tools aiding the assessors in carrying out their duties. Although the assessor's workbench as designed by SCOPE had not been built (at the time of writing) there are in existence two tools which incorporate many of the ideas of the workbench.

10.6.1 Argo

Argo[112] is an environment developed by Etnoteam SpA to organize the software development and assessment process. This IPSE (Integrated Project Support Environment) is therefore useful most of all when carrying out assessment in parallel with the software development. The basic idea

Table 10.1 Guidelines for selecting characteristics and associated levels

Characteristic	Not relevant	Level D	Level C	Level B	Level A
Functionality					
Safety risk	No risk	Recoverable environmental damage	Irrecoverable environmental damage	Physical harm to people	Threat to human life
Economic risk	No risk	Negligible economic loss	Significant economic loss (company affected)	Large economic loss (company endangered)	Financial disaster (company will not survive)
Security constraints	No constraint, ITSEC classes E0, E1	ITSEC class E2	ITSEC class E3	ITSEC class E4	ITSEC classes E5, E6
Reliability					
Service availability	Seldom, on-the-spot request	Working days, usage on request	Working days, 8 hours a day continuously	Every day, 12 hours a day	Every day, 24 hours a day
Robustness	No tolerance to any fault	Robustness to users' errors	Data integrity in case of failures	Robustness to s/w faults	Robustness to h/w failures
Replaceability	By a copy of the software product	By other automatic procedures	By organizational solutions	By organizational solutions, with severe problems	Impossible to replace
Usability					
Interaction style	Command-driven	Menu-driven	Subset of graphical user interface	GUI, with usage of pointing devices	Multimedia
Users	Technicians	Experts of the application domain	Trained people	Anyone, limited to a country	Anyone, all over the world
Efficiency					
Turnround/throughput	Non-interactive systems	Interactive systems	Fast-response interactive systems	Real-time	Strict real-time (within milliseconds)
Resources used	Negligible	Significant data volume (> 5 Mb)	Big data volume (> 20 Mb); communication lines	Huge data volume (> 1 Mb); dedicated communication lines	Multi-processor
Usage	Single user, randomly	Dedicated user	Multi-users	Multi-users with high peaks	Geographically distributed, with high peaks
Maintainability					
Lifetime	Less than 2 years	2–4 years	4–7 years	8–10 years	Greater than 10 years
Evolution style	By release, less frequently than once a year	By release, once a year	By release, twice a year	Three to six releases per year	Continuous maintenance
Correction deadline	Up to the producer	Next release	One month's time	One week's time	Immediate
Portability					
Adaptability	Product designed for a unique hw/sw platform	Unique but adaptable hw/sw platform	Few similar hw/sw platforms	Several similar hw/sw platforms	Utterly different hw/sw platforms

Table 10.2 Characteristics for a management information system

Characteristic	Level	Reason
Functionality	C	Economic risk
Reliability	C	Service availability, replaceability
Usability	D	All issues
Efficiency	C	All issues
Maintainability	B	Correction deadline
Portability	—	Not relevant

behind Argo is to have a tool-set for the development and assessment process to perform QA automatically and shadow all the bureaucracy related to inspections and control. The environment can be customized to a particular development process and this will in turn be followed by the tool-kit. The main aim is to integrate several tools into a uniform environment that characterizes the software development and assessment. This can then be regulated by the specific organization of the software-producing unit or of the test lab.

Data integration, inter-tool communication, a common user interface and access control are provided, together with active handling of the environment. Preconditions to activities are automatically checked and possible actions are automatically started when all preconditions are satisfied. As the reader will notice, assessment is just a part of the general software-process that is supported by such an integration platform.

In terms of the implementation, we note the two following points:

1. At the present time the environment is Unix-based and includes, together with other tools dedicated to the various phases of the development life cycle, the following tools useful for software product assessment: record keeping and configuration management facilities, a static and dynamic analyser (Logiscope), a tool supporting test cross-referencing (TEFAX), a utility for anomaly checking (lint), a CASE tool extracting software metrics (AGE).
2. Tool encapsulation and intercommunication have been implemented, adopting a commercial tool-kit (HP Encapsulator[78]), that allows us to integrate tools and that does not require that tools be modified in order to be integrated.

The intention is to further exploit the environment, enforcing tools integration and adding several modules: self-tuning facilities, decision-support-making procedures, statistical packages and an extended evaluation tool-set (including a checklist manager, reliability support tools and automated verification systems).

Argo can work on heterogeneous networks (i.e. different types of hardware and operating system) and is based on X11 client/server architecture. The Argo user interface is built using HYPERFACE, a hypertextual GUI built by Etnoteam.

10.6.2   IQUAL

DANIELA PINA AND PAOLO SALVANESCHI

IQUAL[142] is a tool developed by ISMES SpA (Bergamo, Italy) to support the assessor during software quality evaluation. It automates an evaluation process based on:

1. The use of quality characteristics and sub-characteristics related to the standard ISO 9126
2. The view of the product as a set of documents
3. The use of a set of metrics and checklists in order to measure quality sub-characteristics on software documents

The evaluation process supported by the tool (defined inside the Eureka Project TASQUE, EU 240) is executed through the following main steps:

Specification of the assessment requirement This step allows the assessor to tailor the measurement environment on each specific product to be evaluated. Each component of the environment can be specified: the quality characteristics and sub-characteristics, the related links and weights, the identification of the available product parts, the set of metrics, the checklists and the related interpretations.

Generation of the assessment plan This step allows the assessor to insert the quality characteristics goals, obtained by interviewing the end-user, to select the documents to be analysed, and to choose the quality operators in order to propagate the quality characteristics goal down to the model. This step provides the assessor with a report organized on the basis of the available documents, which contains all the checklists and metrics requested for the product quality evaluation.

Assessment and evaluation This last step allows the assessor to interactively answer metrics and checklists of the measurement plan, showing all the possible answers defined during the measurement environment tailoring. After giving all the requested answers and defining the quality operators, this step rates the quality scores and provides a report describing the quality profile of the software product. By comparing the desired values against the measured ones, the assessor will be able to evaluate the quality of the product. If requested, the tool can give an explanation of the results obtained.

The use of the tool provides the following main benefits:

1. Very easy management of the most important steps of the evaluation procedure;
2. The possibility of re-using metrics and checklists and the related interpretation functions. This may be useful in defining specific measurement environments for target product classes;
3. A comprehensive set of reports;
4. Interactive management of the measurement plan;
5. The availability of explanations about the quality profile. This function helps the assessor in identifying the changes required to improve the quality;
6. Support for choosing the most suitable techniques (e.g. type of tools) for metrics collection or checklists answering.

IQUAL can be used in different situations, for various purposes and by different users. A first context is to use the tool during the software production process, both by the developer and by the customer in order to evaluate the technical documentation. Moreover the tool can be used before final delivery of the product, to evaluate its quality. Finally it can be used to evaluate the quality of a product already in use.

At present IQUAL uses about 200 questions and metrics, runs on a PC and does not require any particular configuration.

10.6.3 TASQUE-TüV

UWE ANDERS AND RICHARD FLOR

The TASQUE-TüV tool was developed by TüV Nord e.V. (Hamburg). Its aim is to provide an easy-to-use way to:

1. Define quality attributes from the user's point of view derived from the requirements of risk-based standards and special project needs
2. Translate and refine these quality attributes to attributes relevant to the programmer's and quality engineer's point of view (change external attibutes to internal ones)
3. Propose and manage metrics for the different steps of the life cycle
4. Transform metric values (including checklist scores) to quality attribute scores and also generate reports

The main development work on this tool was based on the definition work done within the EUREKA project EU 240 (the German part was funded by the German Ministry of Research and Technology, BMFT).

The evaluation procedure consists of a derivation phase and an integration phase. The whole procedure can be divided into the following steps:

Definition of quality goals from the user's point of view (capabilities) The main emphasis of the tool is to support and help the engineer take into account the safety-relevant standards and rules. The engineer can thus navigate through the different risk-class groups, risk classes and risk parameters to achieve the capability goal profile based on risks. In addition the capability goal profile can be tuned, based on the project's needs. These two goal profiles are merged and filtered.

Translation and refinement of quality attributes into 'properties' and 'features' In the next step the resulting capability goal profile is transformed into a property goal profile which describes the quality requirements from the programmer's point of view. Besides this, an addition goal profile is derived directly from the chosen standards and standard parameters. The needs of the project lead to a further property goal profile. These three profiles are merged and filtered. Then the resulting property goal profile is transformed into a feature goal profile which describes the quality requirements directly in terms of the respective software items. From this information, a qualification process plan is generated.

Proposal of metrics and checklists In the final step of the derivation phase, the tool proposes the metrics to be collected and the checklists to be answered. Depending on the proposed metrics, TASQUE-TüV suggests the appropriate measurement tools.

Transformation of metric values and checklist answers It is the user's task to complete the checklists, evaluate the other metrics, and enter the data into the tool. After formatting the data, the tool transforms the metric values into feature, property and capability scores which can be compared with the goal profiles mentioned above. The integration path is finished by generation of a report.

The information which is necessary to run the derivation and integration path is defined in a quality model. The model consists of:

1. A set of capabilities, properties, features and metrics (including checklists)
2. Link intensities between them
3. The risk-class groups, risk classes and risk parameters
4. Requirements of different standards with respect to the capabilities and properties

TASQUE-TüV is able to run with different quality models. Up to now only the models based on the TASQUE definition phase and ISO 9126 have been used. It is, however, possible to tailor these models according to the needs of the company.

Some utilities support interaction with the user in TASQUE-TüV. A graphics utility shows the goal and score profiles and gives information about the link intensity between the capabilities, properties, features and metrics; a help facility is also part of the tool. The graphical user interface is very simple to use and easy to learn.

Currently TASQUE-TüV is a prototype running on VMS workstations using OSF/Motif.

SUMMARY

As we move towards the setting up of test labs and specialist QA departments for product assessment, we will need integrated sets of tools. Although no fully integrated set has been produced which supports the whole assessment process, we do have the key technology in place and a number of (partial) prototypes. It is therefore reasonable to assume that building an assessor's workbench is desirable and feasible and would not create any great technical problems.

11

MANAGEMENT ISSUES

The aim of this chapter is to give some ideas about aspects of assessment that are of interest both to those submitting their own product evaluation and those setting up evaluation facilities and/or certification services. Therefore we think that the main target audience for this chapter is management rather than technical staff. Of course technical staff will have an interest in these matters as well.

11.1 MANAGING SOFTWARE ASSESSMENT

Management encompasses a wide range of functions from motivating staff to controlling budgets. Here we look at those aspects which are specifically different for software assessment. These are:

1. Costing assessment and certification
2. The needs and expectations of customers
3. The politics of software assessment
4. Moving from assessment to certification

We illustrate these areas with data and examples collected within and outside the SCOPE project.

11.2   COST OF THE EVALUATION PROCEDURE

The people paying for evaluation or certification seem to be very keen to have quantitative replies to the following questions about product assessment:

Q1 How much does it cost overall?
Q2 Which are the most expensive steps of the evaluation process?
Q3 Which factors do affect costs?
Q4 What additional effort is requested from the sponsor?
Q5 How much time is needed to evaluate a product?

We obviously cannot blame them for their curiosity. Rather, we should try to give them quantitative replies. These questions can be answered by the collection and analysis of historic data about:

1. Cost of the evaluation process
2. Breakdown of costs by phase of the evaluation process
3. Relationships among costs and peculiarities of the evaluations
4. Effort put in by the sponsor of the evaluation
5. Elapsed time for the evaluation

We will briefly summarize some of these results in this section. For more details and raw data the reader is referred elsewhere.[21]

Before looking at the figures, it is important to understand clearly what was counted as the cost of assessment and what was not. The following data has been collected and analysed:

1. Cost of the evaluation in person-days, broken down by each stage
2. Elapsed time in calendar days allocated to each stage
3. Product size
4. Criticality
5. Application domain, assessor's understanding of application domain
6. Characteristics evaluated (with details of level)

These costs include all the activities that might be offered by a fully operating independent test lab, provided that it already had the know-how in terms of methodology, techniques, tools and experience. These costs do not correspond to the total effort spent on the SCOPE case studies. There were certain tasks done by the case studies which would not normally be included in an assessment, such as enhancement of evaluation procedures, project-related activities (feedback reporting to other tasks of the project, travelling and meeting, review of other case studies, deliverables), tool-related activities (setting up particular tool-kits, customizing tools) and promotion of the project at conferences, etc. We therefore had to remove these costs from the total. Cost figures from several case studies, both from the first and the second phases of the project, were analysed.

11.2.1   Cost of the evaluation process

In Fig. 11.1 we show the effort in person-days spent on product assessment by the selected case studies. In the histogram the global effort figure is broken down into the 10 steps of the assessment method. The 10-step method was proposed as the procedure for conducting evaluations and was used on several case studies. The 10 steps were later reduced to five steps as we shall see later in the chapter. The 10 steps are as follows:

1. Submitting the software for evaluation
2. Agreeing the assessment requirement
3. Agreeing an initial estimate of cost
4. Analysis of the product
5. Producing an assessment specification
6. Selecting assessment procedures (bricks) according to assessment objectives
7. Producing the assessment plan
8. Estimating the cost
9. Performing the assessment
10. Reporting the results and recommendations

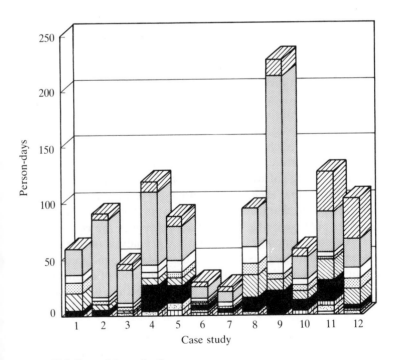

Figure 11.1 Cost of the evaluation process.

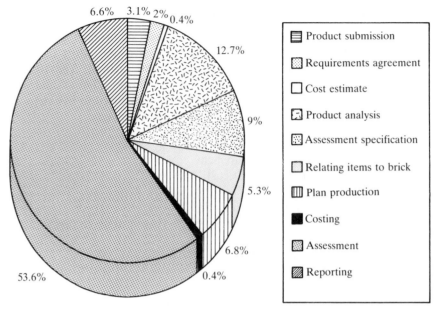

Figure 11.2 Cost distribution across the ten steps.

At first sight it is possible to see that the average effort is about 90 person-days and that seven assessments out of 10 fall within 40–120 person-days. The pie chart in Fig. 11.2 shows the percentage distribution of costs across the steps of the assessment method. It is to be noted that more than half of the effort is spent in the assessment implementation. The product-analysis phase is also quite time-consuming. We can also see that relating product parts to evaluation modules is a low-effort task and that the documentation effort does not consume much effort either.

Any evaluation or certification service will have to apply standard procedures when assessing software. With SCOPE we developed a number of these standard procedures each of which used one technique and assessed one of the six ISO 9126 characteristics; these were known as *bricks** or *assessment modules*. We were able to analyse thoroughly the cost of using two classes of assessment modules, based on static analysis (structural and textual measurement) and checklists. Indeed these were the most commonly used throughout the case studies. In the first case, the cost of application of an assessment module on a software component is less than 0.1 person-day which assumes that all the tool support exists. Of course this figure will be

---

* At any early SCOPE meeting after a very long discussion on what the procedures should be called we decided to use the temporary name 'brick' to avoid wasting any more time. The name stuck.

higher if we need to build a new front end. Even this is normally cost-effective for a single evaluation exercise.

As far as checklist-based techniques are concerned, we experienced the following:

- Costs are quite low (average effort: 0.4 person-day).
- Effort is minimized when bricks are applied by the people who designed them, although the level is still acceptable when applied by third parties.
- Source code is more time-consuming to assess than higher-level documentation.
- Usage of a checklist manager does not substantially decrease the assessment effort. It does have a major influence on the reporting stage where effort is decreased by more than 50 per cent.

Two of the SCOPE case studies attempted to use the GGS approach as the particular assessment technique subsumed within the scheme. The cost of the overall evaluations did not differ greatly from other techniques; in one case it consumed 90 person-days and in the other about 110 person-days. Within the SCOPE scheme the application of the GGS techniques implied the assessment of functionality at level D and (partially) usability at level D.

In addition to the assessor, the software producer also has to contribute effort. For example, the producer may need to do some reverse engineering to provide documentation, follow the activities, and discuss evaluation results. In our experience this effort ranges from 5 to 25 per cent. Therefore it can be considered a small but not trivial contribution to the total effort.

We should stress that the effort put in by the producer is generally independent of the assessor's understanding of the application domain. The producer does not have to contribute extra effort to areas the assessor cannot cover. Rather it depends on the involvement and interest of the developer in the evaluation activity. For this reason the results derived from the SCOPE project might be biased (too high), since the main motivation of a case-study provider was to get know-how. The situation might in fact be quite different when talking about third-party certification.

11.2.2 Relationship with costs and product profile

The evaluation of software products cannot be a fixed-price activity. It would be very strange if the cost of assessing the software from a nuclear power station were the same as for a spreadsheet package. This means that we should provide some ideas about how to give a rough estimate of the effort needed, given the characteristics for the software under evaluation and information about the product.

The most important factors affecting costs are the number of characteristics to evaluate and the level of stringency of assessment. Functionality implies a geometric growth in effort which becomes extremely high for the assessment level 'A'. This is due to the fact that we shift from a checklist-driven assessment to testing the application for functional coverage. This means that the assessment can grow to 30 per cent of the development effort. This would be higher still if even more costly techniques such as formal proof were applied. The story is much the same for efficiency and reliability but with a less dramatic increase in costs. On the other hand, the assessments of maintainability, portability and usability show a low increase of the effort with the assessment level. This is due to the fact that the analysis is based on techniques supported by tools and, most of the time, on an application of the same evaluation modules with increasingly stringent levels for the pass–fail criteria.

The second important factor is *size*, which has been shown to be linearly correlated with the effort needed for assessment. In particular, a full assessment of all six quality characteristics at a medium level of stringency costs around 10–15 per cent of the development effort. This is based on the assumption that the evaluation is being made in parallel with the development and can thus directly use all the information arising from the project team and, if necessary, even impose some guidance and constraints on the project itself. When we looked at what had been reported on experiences of other large-scale projects we found figures that seemed to be comparable. It has been stated[103] that the inspection of documents and the collection and analysis of static analysis data related to maintainability issues has resulted in 18 per cent of the overall development effort for a 200 KLOC telecommunication subsystem. We think that this figure can be reduced by an approach in which the assessment methodology is sound, standardized evaluation modules are available, and tools can be used to automate as much as possible data collection, integration and analysis. From our experience we also notice that when the product is large, the assessment planning is more time-consuming than normal. On the other hand, when the product is small the product analysis is very time-consuming as a percentage of the total cost of the assessment. This fact might be explained by a psychological phenomenon: when the product is small the assessor is convinced of the fact that he can fully master it and for this reason he spends more time gaining knowledge of the product. One of the most important things we noticed in the analysis of costs is that they do not seem to be related to the assessor's knowledge of the application domain. This is very important since it shows that assessment techniques are mature enough to provide a sound evaluation in totally different product areas. We do not need to have an expert assessor for each application domain. If we do have a domain expert then we should try to benefit from their technical skill but this is not necessary for the successful completion of the evaluation.

11.3 NEEDS AND EXPECTATIONS OF PRODUCT ASSESSMENT AND CERTIFICATION

Too often research workers live in ivory towers and produce concepts and theories that are of little interest or relevance to the software community. This was the reason we decided to ask selected people about their interests and needs in software product assessment and certification. A questionnaire was developed to elicit the positions and views of key IT representatives. The analysis of the questionnaire results had the following objectives:

1. To evaluate the current situation with respect to software product assessment and certification and, more generally, about the impact of software quality problems
2. To single out the needs and demands of key IT representatives for software product assessment
3. To understand which factors can influence assessment and certification
4. To have a clear picture of the expected relationship between product and process certification for software
5. To investigate the level of knowledge of assessment-related issues
6. To get an impression of how potential users would expect an assessment service to be carried out
7. To monitor the changes in the awareness about these issues, by comparing the results with those collected five years before in a similar analysis

11.3.1 Data collected

Two surveys were carried out and compared, the first in 1987 and the second in 1992. The survey conducted in 1987[63] by Etnoteam and Nomos did not focus only on software assessment; rather it was a general overview of current practices and needs in software quality control (QC). The data that related to software product certification was collected by means of face-to-face interviews with a sample of 105 Italian companies selected because of their interest in the topic from a larger set of about 400 companies contacted and screened by telephone. The interviewed people were typically heads of development or quality control/assurance departments. The survey conducted in 1992 was quite different in that it was solely focused on software product assessment. The data was collected by means of a questionnaire distributed during public tutorials about the SCOPE project. The returned questionnaires totalled 73. Interviewees were typically heads of development departments or senior academics. Table 11.1 summarizes the application domains covered by the surveys.

Table 11.1 Application domains for the 1987 and 1992 surveys

Application domain	1987	1992
Management information systems	28	9
Off-the-shelf packages	25	15
Process control	15	12
Banking and insurance	10	8
Computer integrated manufacturing	10	6
Embedded systems	10	6
Telecommunications	5	14
Avionics and military	2	3

As far as the 1992 survey is concerned, the sample is limited in number and when interpreting the results this must be taken into consideration. However, the companies that cooperated are representative from a geographical point of view: we have companies from southern (Italy and Spain), central (UK and Denmark) and northern Europe (Finland and Sweden). The same applies to the application domains (as detailed above) and the size: 10 companies are small (less than 100 employees), twelve are medium-sized (from 100 to 1000 employees) and the remaining eleven are large companies. Differing relationships with IT are also represented: both developers (either for selling or for internal usage) and users (either of off-the-shelf packages or bespoke systems) are there.

The main results of the 1992 survey are presented in accordance with the defined objectives; when possible, comments will be substantiated by comparison with results obtained from the earlier analysis. A detailed analysis and the complete list of questions and answers is available separately.[22]

11.3.2   Assessment and certification: current practice

From our point of view, the first prerequisite for a company to undergo software product assessment is that the IT managers realize that an independent verification and validation (IV&V) is necessary to guarantee the quality of the product. This can be monitored by the percentage of companies that declare the presence of an internal separate quality-control department. More than 56 per cent of interviewed people declared the existence in their company of a quality control/assurance department for software, separated from development. Table 11.2 shows the breakdown within regions. This result is encouraging, especially when compared with the equivalent statistics for five years before: the Italian survey in 1987 showed that less than 24 per cent of companies were in this situation. This means that the usage of independent V&V is good and has more than

Table 11.2 Presence of independent V&V and interest in evaluation

Region	Independent V&V	Evaluation
Northern Europe	75%	45%
Central Europe	63%	43%
Southern Europe	43%	27%

doubled in five years. The amount of money spent for testing (as an average: 20 per cent of the overall development effort) demonstrates the fact that testing is interpreted in its true meaning (not, for instance, simple debugging), and that there is scope for investment in the application of a software evaluation scheme. The number of companies that had their software products assessed by an external body in the last year is encouraging too, see Fig. 11.3. About one-third of the companies have already undergone or thought of product assessment. From the geographical point of view, interest decreases from north to south and confirms our hypothesis of correlation of evaluation with independent V&V as shown in Table 11.2.

We should consider that five years before 70 per cent of those interviewed had declared that in three years' time they expected official certification performed by a recognized body to be available. Despite this not happening, companies have not stood still but have moved into the market trying to have their products assessed independently. So it seems that, despite the absence of official certification bodies and services, there is now a need for

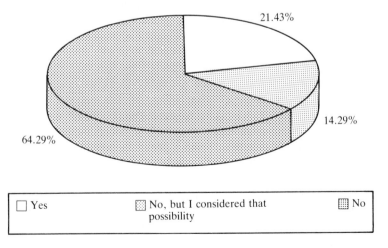

Figure 11.3 Assessments performed or planned.

software product evaluation. This is confirmed by the reasons given for having a software product assessed. The three main reasons were:

1. Marketing purposes
2. Planning the evolution of the product
3. Imposition by the user or an authority

Among the reasons for not having yet submitted a product to external assessment, the most important one is the lack of awareness that such a service exists. Another reason is the belief that quality control carried out by internal independent V&V is enough. This view will clearly have to change. It is evident that evaluating a product against the six ISO 9126 characteristics (or indeed any other set) requires a great deal of know-how and expertise. This is not always present in QC departments, which are usually restricted to black-box testing.

11.3.3   Certification needs and demands

Let us come to the central point: is assessment a friend or a foe? Do IT people need product certification or do they fear it as a possible external imposition? The first thing to notice is that no one saw software product certification as a road to tighter regulation in the IT area. In very few cases did customers' complaints bring developers to a law court and even software users do not believe that certification can exempt the producer from liability. Rather, they expect from a certificate a trusted declaration that assures them that the product is adhering to the declared functionality. This is one of the strongest points of convergence: the same answers are given irrespective of role, application domain and nationality. Moreover, users think that a product with a quality stamp on it must be more reliable and/or efficient; we tend to think that the term *reliability* is used here in a very comprehensive way, as a synonym for quality.

We shall now look at the advantages expected by software producers from a quality certificate. Producers see a quality mark as essentially a marketing leverage, giving them a better image in the market and an advantage over competitors. If we group together the producers who have already undergone software assessment, they believe a certificate can give access to specific markets rather than being a general guarantee of quality. On the other hand, those who have not considered software assessment see the certificate as a matter of competition and image, but do not think that it can be a discriminating factor for software sales.

Turning our attention to the characteristics of ISO 9126, we notice that the six can be grouped into pairs: functionality and reliability are essential, maintainability and usability are considered quite important, efficiency and portability are given a lower priority. If we look at Table 11.3 we can see

Table 11.3 Relevance of ISO characteristics from surveys in 1987 and 1992

ISO characteristic	1987 score	1992 score			
		Total	Italy	Finland	UK
Functionality	9	9	8	10	8
Reliability	7	9	9	10	9.5
Maintainability	8	8	8	8	8
Usability	7	8	7	8	9.5
Efficiency	6	7	7	8	6
Portability	6	5	5	5	6

which of the characteristics are given the greatest importance. The rating (0–10) is on an ordinal scale and so we should consider the median values.

It is interesting to see whether the importance of software characteristics has changed with time. Table 11.3 compares the results of the two surveys and shows an overall stability of the priorities. We do, however, notice a lower priority for maintainability and a growth of interest for reliability.

A thorough analysis of data would tell us that:

- Scores are higher in industry and market-driven software-producing units: where quality is a matter of competition, requirements are higher
- The highest score 10 is assigned to functionality by software users
- The lowest score 5 is assigned to portability in northern and southern Europe
- In the UK usability has been promoted as the most important characteristic (score: 9.5), while functionality has been demoted to the third ranking
- Maintainability is of paramount importance for captive SPUs (second factor in importance, with a score of 8)
- The Finns are extremely concerned about the reliability of software products (score: 10)

11.3.4 Factors influencing assessment and certification

A first conclusion is that people need confidence in the quality of their software, but there are some factors that work against product evaluation; among these are the lack of mutual recognition or official acknowledgement and concern about excessive cost.

Costs certainly cannot be considered a trivial matter. People seem to be willing to spend about 10 per cent more of the overall development effort (see Fig. 11.4) in order to obtain a quality mark; this is a considerable amount of money and is well in line with the findings of the SCOPE case studies (see Sec. 11.1), and with the pragmatic experience of assessments in

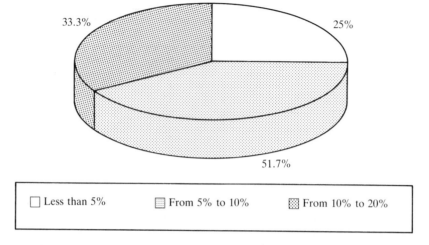

Figure 11.4 Acceptable costs for getting quality certificate (percentage of the development effort).

the industrial world. This means that assessors can provide a service at a price that sponsors are willing to pay. For the time being, this applies to an assessment in which all characteristics are checked at a medium level of stringency (the C level).

If we distinguish people that have experienced assessment from those who have not, we discover that costs were not considered a barrier for those who have put assessment and certification into practice. This could mean that they found that the return on investment was justified and the overall experience cost-effective.

This is one of the most important results of the survey in that it shows the pragmatic feasibility from an economic point of view of software product evaluation in the short term.

If we now look at factors that are likely to influence costs, those interviewed saw several important *variables*, with product-related factors (*product criticality, size*) given greater weight than evaluation-related factors (*lack of techniques, assessor's knowledge of the application domain*).

11.3.5 Relationship between product and process certification

The relationship between product and process assessment is very delicate and controversial.[23] Which is best? Are both necessary? Is one the precondition for the other? IT people proved to have quite clear ideas:

- Process certification is not sufficient to guarantee the quality of a specific software product.

• Software product assessment is better if accompanied by an evaluation of the software development process.

This perception is heavily underlined when ISO 9001 certification was considered; a very low percentage declared that such certification can give any guarantee of the quality of the ultimate software product. That means that, from the user's point of view, product and process are closely linked and cannot be separated when quality is analysed. This is confirmed by the replies of those who consider process certification not enough; a majority (about 62 per cent) asked for a coupled certification.

11.3.6 Awareness of assessment-related issues

We need to know the level of awareness of assessment- and certification-related issues to evaluate the success of information dissemination activities and to design the advertising and commercial strategies for setting up an assessment and certification service. First of all, people seem to know quite a lot about ISO 9126, despite the fact that it is a very recent standard. About 60 per cent of the interviewed people had at least heard of it, with a peak of 70 per cent in southern Europe. By contrast, we must remember that in 1987 only 8 per cent of IT representatives knew about AQAP-13, which was the most important standard at that time. However, it is a matter of concern that *none* of the IT users knew about ISO 9126. The situation is a little less clear with respect to certification bodies. Several of the interviewed people claimed to know of some certification bodies, but a great deal of confusion exists in this field. Some of the so-called certification bodies named by the interviewees were not exactly what they thought. For instance, certification bodies concerned with process assessment and quality system certification were thought to perform software product assessment and certification.

11.3.7 Expectations of an assessment service

It is important to determine how producers would like the assessment service to be carried out. First of all, the survey showed that software product assessment was acceptable to producers in one of the two following ways: either in parallel with the development of the product or before its release, provided that the activity does not take longer than three months (see Fig. 11.5).

The demand for 'concurrent' assessment is interesting for two aspects:

1. Software producers do not want delays caused by the evaluation process.
2. The concurrent assessment implies that assessors evaluate the product phase-by-phase, as the internal quality control does: sponsors would know immediately if the product does not satisfy the required level of

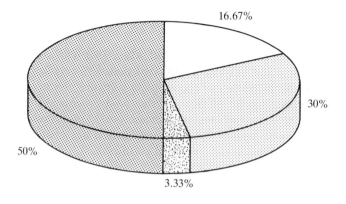

16.67%

30%

50%

3.33%

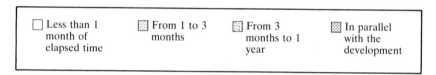

| ☐ Less than 1 month of elapsed time | ▦ From 1 to 3 months | ▦ From 3 months to 1 year | ▦ In parallel with the development |

Figure 11.5 Time constraints for assessment.

quality. As a consequence, actions might be started as soon as quality deficiencies are detected, thus allowing them to implement a constructive approach to quality and avoid assessment as an additional step at the end of the software development, with a limited set of feedbacks for software quality development.

Finally, the assessment was expected to report a lot of information, including:

• The methodology used (this implies the need to have a common method as has been defined in SCOPE)
• The goals of the assessment
• The pass/fail decisions (people need a justification of results)
• The summary of results

It is worth noting that nobody asked for any additional information other than that already contained in the SCOPE template for the assessment report as described in Sec. 11.5.

11.4 THE POLITICS OF DATA COLLECTION

When assessment is performed as a means to certification, then the certification bodies will define procedures for the assessors and producers to follow. Their relationship will be formalized. The sponsor of an assessment (who will usually be the producer) will have to face the consequences if the product fails and the economic loss that would bring. When the relationship between the assessor and producer is less formal, then we need to be more careful about how information is presented, particularly when it contains criticism, implied or otherwise. This specifically applies in the situation of in-house QA or (unofficial) evaluation and consultancy services.

11.4.1 Breaking the bad news

During the SCOPE case studies, we approached a number of companies with a view to their becoming case-study providers. They often seemed to be under the impression that we would make some measurements, and then pat them on the back and tell them what a good job they were doing.

Product-based assessment usually exposes a number of previously-unknown problems with the software. Many of the problems seemed obvious, such as huge unstructured modules, poor or non-existent comments, meaningless variable names, etc. It is therefore surprising that they were not discovered before. Before the analysis, we have been told that looking for unstructured code was a waste of time because we would not find any. Nothing could have been further from the truth.

Managers are surprised that the software should be so bad. If you are the person presenting unwelcome news, then it has to be done with tact without diminishing any of the necessary impact. Naturally people are defensive because they feel loyalty to their organization or department. One common reaction is to reject the metrics as unimportant, e.g. 'I don't really care about the GOTO and ×1, ×2, ×3 are really good variable names.' Another is to say that it will be better next time, but take no steps whatsoever to remedy the underlying problems in their processes.

We therefore propose the following approach:

1. Before any analysis starts, get the producer to agree what constitutes good software. Make sure they agree, e.g., that a high level of test coverage or commented code is a good thing.
2. Warn them that the first stage of any improvement is to identify the problems, no matter how unpleasant they might be.
3. Present the results is an objective way, identifying numerical scores and particular examples rather than general views and opinions. Subjective views can be dismissed as 'it's only your opinion'.
4. Point out that although their software is bad, so is everyone else's.
5. Identify clear steps that can prevent or mitigate the problems.

11.4.2 Unrealistic expectations

Many people are still sceptical about metrics; this is partly because they have expectations which cannot possibly be fulfilled. People often take the attitude that because metrics are not a panacea, they cannot be any use. In fact, this search for the silver bullet has been a very negative influence throughout the history of software engineering. Many people have made inflated claims about metrics just as they have done in other areas like formal methods, cost prediction and process certification. As we stressed in Chapter 5 we cannot usually make accurate predictions about the software. The first thing is not to exaggerate what can be done. If the clients seem disappointed, then draw analogies with other fields. The MOT test in Chapter 4 is a useful example.

11.5 FROM ASSESSMENT TO CERTIFICATION

When shifting from assessment to certification (awarding of a quality mark on the basis of the assessment results) we tend to create commercial leverage (a quality mark can be used for advertising purposes) and, ultimately, trade barriers (if the evaluation process has high costs, this could prevent small software-producing units from obtaining it).

The following four principles[128] are of paramount importance as far as assessment for certification is concerned:

Repeatability repeated assessments of the same product against the same assessment specification by the same testing laboratory should give the same result.

Reproducibility repeated assessments of the same product against the same assessment specification by different testing laboratories should give the same result.

Impartiality evaluation must be free from unfair bias towards achieving any particular result.

Objectivity the assessment result is obtained with the minimum of subjective judgement.

In this section we shall try to address the matter of assessment for certification, taking into account organizational and technical issues that try to guarantee compliance with these principles. In any case, it is clear that no agreed world-wide product certification will be possible until a reference standard exists. This is the reason why standardization should continue towards the agreement of generic technical requirements for software, paving the way to certification.

11.5.1   The context for setting up a certification scheme

Since we want to demonstrate the technical soundness and pragmatic feasibility of software assessment and certification, we need to be compatible with the activities of standardization and certification bodies,[143] at both national and international levels. In this field, an important series of standards has been adopted at European level, the EN 45000 series, which deals with the testing and certification process and is therefore very relevant. The aim of the standards is to facilitate the mutual recognition of test reports and certificates throughout Europe. The series includes the following standards which relate to testing, certification and accreditation in any industrial sector (standards which appear to have most relevance to software product assessment/certification have been marked with a †):

1. EN 45001 General criteria for the operation of testing laboratories†
2. EN 45002 General criteria for the assessment of testing laboratories†
3. EN 45003 General criteria for laboratory accreditation bodies
4. EN 45011 General criteria for certification bodies operating product certification†
5. EN 45012 General criteria for certification bodies operating quality system certification
6. EN 45013 General criteria for certification bodies operating certification of personnel
7. EN 45014 General criteria for suppliers' declaration of conformity

It is likely that any European software-product certification scheme will have to be created in accordance with these standards and in the framework set up by EOTC. The standards EN 45001, 45002 and 45011 will be briefly summarized, paying attention to their implications to the topics of major interest to us.

EN 45001 General criteria for the operation of testing laboratories

This standard (intended to be used by test laboratories and accreditation authorities) specifies the requirements of a testing laboratory in the following areas of operation:

Legal identity
Impartiality, independence and integrity
Management and organization
Personnel (numbers, skills, qualifications and training)
Premises and equipment
Test methods and procedures
Quality assurance of assessments made
Content of test reports
Records to be kept

Identification and handling of test samples
Confidentiality and security
Use of subcontractors

This standard has several implications for a general software-product certification scheme since it allows situations in which there is neither standardized test procedure for a product characteristic nor standardized measurement. In this case an agreement between the client and the test lab should be documented. This is exactly the purpose of the assessment specifications which were developed within SCOPE to determine what characteristics would be assessed at what level. Moreover, it clearly shows the need for a central database of *certification instances* as a basis for inter-laboratory comparisons and validation of techniques. It is very prescriptive on the minimum contents of the test report to be issued. In particular it is stressed that the report should not include any advice or recommendations arising from the test results. This is a notable distinction when shifting from assessment to certification.

The ECITC (European Committee for IT&T Testing and Certification) has produced an interpretation of EN 45001 specifically for the software and communications sectors, addressing specific issues such as: repeatability, guidance on selection and validation of test cases, criteria to make accept/reject decisions, validation of tools, reassessment of software that has undergone to minor changes, etc.

EN 45002 General criteria for the assessment of testing laboratories

This standard specifies the general criteria for the procedures to be used in the accreditation of test laboratories, in terms of:

• Criteria to be used in accreditation
• Procedures to be used by a laboratory when applying for accreditation
• Information required for the assessment of the laboratory
• How to assess a test laboratory
• Monitoring and renewal of accreditation, etc.

We should note that a test laboratory can only be accredited to a prespecified list of tests or to a prespecified range of product types. Thus a test lab that proposes to assess an undeclared set of characteristics of undeclared product types using undeclared assessment methods is unlikely to be accredited. This introduces an interesting topic: in accordance with the rules applied by some accreditation body (for instance in Italy, CIMECO— Centro Italiano Metodologie di Controllo—the Italian member of the European Certification System), a testing laboratory can be registered or accredited. *Registration* is the statement of the accreditation body about the technical capability and organizing ability of the lab to carry out conformance tests in the IT field, without reference to specific products.

Laboratory accreditation on the other hand is the statement of the accreditation body about the availability of the lab to carry out conformance tests on specific products. The accreditation is issued only to those labs which have already attained registration and will nominate specific products. For every product there shall be a specific regulation issued by the European System and by implication a precise standard and a well-defined testing method. Since general product certification is not carried on with respect to an agreed European standard, labs will just need to be registered.

EN 45011 General criteria for certification bodies operating product certification

This standard specifies general criteria that a certification body operating product certification must meet if it is to be recognized at national or European level. It addresses organizational and operational issues of a certifying body such as:

Organizational structure
Qualifications of personnel
Documentation and change control of certificates issued
Records to be kept
Confidentiality
Mandatory periodic publications
Prevention of misuse of certificates
Handling of complaints
Withdrawal and cancellation of certificates and so forth

With reference to data collection and analysis this standard emphasizes the fact that 'records shall demonstrate the way in which each certification procedure was applied including test and inspection reports'.

11.5.2 The SCOPE evaluation method

JØRGEN BOEGH

The evaluation method developed by the SCOPE project fits well into the work currently going on within ISO. Here Working Group Six under Subcommittee Seven is concerned with providing guidelines for the practical interpretation of the standard ISO 9126; in fact the SCOPE approach has been accepted as the starting-point for ISO 9126, and furthermore the SCOPE approach has been accepted as the starting-point for ISO. The evaluation method is described in the evaluator's guide.[29]

The intended use of the evaluator's guide is for third-party evaluation. Therefore we need to distinguish two actors in the evaluation process: the evaluator and the client. The evaluator could be the software producer, the system manufacturer, the distributor, the buyer, the user, or an independent party like an insurance company or a government agency. The client is the one who negotiates the requirements of the evaluation and signs the contracts with the evaluator.

The method described in the evaluator's guide is a stepwise approach to software-product evaluation. It consists of four main steps: requirements of the evaluation, specification of the evaluation, design of the evaluation plan, and conduct of the evaluation. The results of these activities are collected in an evaluation report. Figure 11.6 gives an overview of the evaluation procedure.

The first step in the evaluation procedure is concerned with deciding the requirements of the evaluation. This is primarily the responsibility of the client seeking the evaluation, but it is important to notice that an agreement between the client and the evaluator must be reached. The reason is that the evaluator must ensure that the evaluation be stringent enough to provide real confidence in the quality of the product in question. Furthermore it must be ensured that all relevant laws and regulations are taken into account.

The evaluation requirements include the selection of quality character-istics to be evaluated. The quality characteristics considered here are those

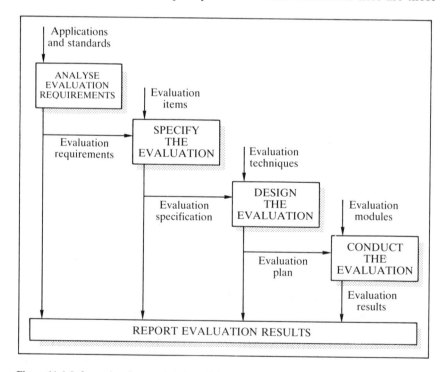

Figure 11.6 Information flow and main activities of the evaluation.

defined in ISO 9126.[89] They are described in detail in Chapter 3. All six characteristics may not be equally relevant for all applications. For example, as stated in ISO 9126, reliability is most important for a mission-critical system, efficiency is most important for a time-critical, real-time system, and usability is most important for interactive end-user software. For most applications the functionality and maintainability characteristics will need to be addressed.

All the selected characteristics need not be evaluated with the same degree of thoroughness for all types of applications. Obviously nobody would expect the same effort to be allocated to the evaluation of a railway signal system, a computer game and an office automation system. To ensure this flexibility the evaluation is level-oriented. There are four levels, named A, B, C and D. The levels define the depth or throughness of the evaluation. The levels constitute a hierarchy with A as the highest level and D as the lowest. Evaluation at different levels gives different degrees of confidence in the quality of the software product. At level A the most stringent evaluation techniques are applied to give the highest confidence. Going down to level D gradually, less stringent methods are used and consequently less effort is devoted to the evaluation.

It must be noted that the evaluation level can be chosen independently for each quality characteristic. Also in some cases the evaluation level for each software characteristic can change for different components of a product, e.g. if critical components of a program with high reliability requirements are kept separated from other components. Some guidance for selecting the relevant evaluation level is given in Table 11.4. When the evaluation requirements have been agreed by the client and the evaluator, the evaluation must be specified in detail. This is done by the evaluator based on the evaluation requirements and the information made available for the evaluation. This information is said to be made up of evaluation items. At

Table 11.4 Guidelines for selecting the relevant evaluation level

Level	Environmental	Personal	Economic	Application
D	Small damage to property	No risk to people	Negligible economic loss	Household entertainment
C	Damage to property	Few people injured	Significant economic loss	Fire alarm, process control
B	Recoverable environmental damage	Threat to human lives	Large economic loss	Medical systems, financial systems
A	Irrecoverable environmental damage	Many people killed	Financial disaster	Railway systems, nuclear systems

the start the received evaluation items must be identified and classified. The identification is a formal record of which items have been received. This includes document identifier, special characteristics of items and legal implications of handling evaluation items, such as confidentiality requirements requested by the software producer.

Evaluation items are then classified according to the information they contain. For this purpose an information model has been developed. The information model identifies all types of information which may be required for an evaluation. Three general types of evaluation information are considered: product information, process information and supportive information. Product information includes information such as software requirements specification, software design description, and source code. Process information is documentation of the development process like test plans and test reports. Supportive information is documentation of the development process like test plans and test reports; supportive information such as description of design methods, definition of programming languages and compiler manuals provides necessary background information for the evaluation.

The information model does not require a particular structure for the software documentation. The only requirement is that the different types of information can be extracted from the evaluation items and mapped into the information model.

When the classification of information has been completed, the evaluator is in a position to write down the detailed specification of the evaluation. The specification will often be based on the requirements specification of the software product, but other requirements may also be needed. It is important that the evaluation specification is detailed and complete since it constitutes part of the formal basis of the evaluation. The evaluation specification should be formulated as a combination of the following types of statement:

- An exact reference to statements in the software-requirements specification document, the user manual, or possibly other information, specifying program requirements that must be evaluated.
- Supplementary statements about the software product which is either not mentioned in the program specification or needs to be explained more carefully for the evaluation.
- An exact reference to statements in relevant standards and regulations documents where additional program requirements are given which should also be included in the evaluation specification.

The specification of the evaluation should be organized according to the quality characteristics of ISO 9126.

When the evaluation specification is ready it is time to produce an evaluation plan. Table 11.5 (on page 229) shows how to attach evaluation techniques to quality characteristics and evaluation levels.

Based on information in this table the evaluator can select evaluation modules from a library of modules. Evaluation modules are encapsulated descriptions of software metrics associated with evaluation techniques and evaluation levels. They include procedures for collecting data, use of supporting tools, threshold values for the related evaluation levels, and guidelines for reporting results. Evaluation models are discussed in more detail later in this section.

In the selection process technical constraints of the software product must be taken into account. This could, for example, be the programming language used as this puts some restrictions on the tools for static analysis. Taking such constraints into consideration a set of evaluation modules can be chosen to minimize the cost of the evaluation. Finally a plan for conducting the evaluation including schedule and resources can be developed.

Conducting the evaluation means applying the selected evaluation modules according to the evaluation plan. The results of applying the modules must be documented, both for the evaluation report and for the internal records of the evaluator. The reporting must conform to ISO Guide 25[92] as explained in the evaluator's guide. ISO Guide 25 is almost equivalent to EN 45001. The evaluation report represents the major deliverable to be supplied by the evaluator. The table of contents of the report closely reflects the steps of the evaluation procedure. Each of the four main activities is documented separately. The recommended table of contents is the following:

1. Preface—identification of producer and evaluator
2. Evaluation requirements—product overview, quality characteristics, evaluation level
3. Evaluation specification—identification and classification of items, detailed specification
4. Evaluation plan—selected evaluation modules, evaluation process planning
5. Evaluation results—results of applying the individual evaluation modules
6. Conclusion—evaluation result

Beside the technical aspects of a software product, evaluation, the evaluator's guide also develops a legal model for handling a third-party evaluation. The legal model defines a set of legal actions or contracts to be dealt with during the evaluation process. There is a close relationship between the legal model and the different technical steps of the evaluation. One advantage of integrating the legal view into the evaluation procedure is that a set of decision points can be defined where both the evaluator and the client must choose either to continue the process or to withdraw.

11.5.3   An experience

We shall now describe some lessons learnt in setting up an experimental certification scheme dealing with general product assessment. The scheme was set up in Italy by IMQ (Istituto Italiano del Marchio di Qualità),[87] in conformance with the SCOPE approach to software product assessment. IMQ is the most important Italian certification body, dealing with all kinds of products (from washing machines to electrical plugs) and with long-standing experience in information technology, namely in process assessment certification in line with ISO 9001. In all fields of information technology, certification involves the following players: the accreditation body (that registers and accredits test labs), the certification body (that issues the certificate) and the test lab (that is, the body that actually carries out the assessment and evaluation).

What is problematic about a certification service based on software quality is that no standards exist against which conformance can be tested. ISO 9126 is just a set of definitions and does not imply any specific technique nor does it give any quantitative thresholds. For this reason we decided to enlarge the usual organizational scheme for certification, adding a *technical commission*. This was created in order to guarantee the soundness of the technical approach and to review the evaluation results before giving the quality mark. The duty of the technical commission is twofold: first to periodically scrutinize the technical procedures to guide their evolution and secondly to evaluate the results (are they reproducible, repeatable, unbiased and objective?). This means that the certification is applied by IMQ but approval and policing of the procedures are assigned to the external technical commission. This is due to the fact that, since it is impossible to claim conformance to any standard, the credibility and soundness of the overall procedure must be confirmed by recognized experts. At the time of writing the technical commission was composed of representatives from the following: major Italian industrial companies, software development companies, public companies, universities, national standardization bodies and testing laboratories.

As already mentioned, test labs just need to be registered and, what is more, the certification scheme must be composed of three distinct parts: general certification rules, technical procedures and assessment techniques. The last part is necessary since no agreed standard exists. Therefore there is the need to specify the detailed assessment techniques against which certification is performed.

Of course, the certificate does not give any guarantee that the product is error-free nor that it is fit for its intended purpose. This reflects the approach of assessing the specified service, without any reference to the expected service. After all, if a health certificate does not assure that you will not suffer from headache in the next three years why should a software certificate assure that it is zero-defect? We can just content ourselves with knowing that this piece of software has a greater likelihood to be high-quality than it would otherwise have had.

From the organizational point of view, assessment can be performed either by IMQ or by an external lab, provided that the lab is registered or accredited. Fairness, independence, confidentiality and technical capability must be assured. Moreover, there is the statement to keep a public list of certified products. For practical reasons, the certification process (see Fig. 11.7) is structured in such a way that the sponsor can decide whether to continue or not after the first contacts and also after the preliminary phase, i.e. after the agreement of the assessment plan. Finally, in the area of certification, monitoring is a matter of great importance. Repetition of measures by sampling is done at least once a year. Inspectors must have access to the sponsor at the latter's headquarters at any time. The certification body can ensure that the product as sold corresponds to the one submitted for assessment. The maintenance process adopted by the producer must be declared. Conditions of usage of the mark are strictly controlled and revocation can occur if the software producer breaks the rules.

As far as technical aspects are concerned two issues are worth mentioning: the flexibility of the system and which techniques were selected.

It is clearly important that the service is flexible, in that we can select different characteristics for different levels. The decision was taken to let the sponsor select which characteristics were relevant and, for each of them, what level of stringency was required. The problem is that the sponsor might ask for a quality mark on grounds that were wholly inappropriate; for example, software for factory automation might be certified only for portability (level D). We looked at this problem in Chapter 10. Therefore, the choice must be agreed with the certification body in order to be sure that the certification is not misleading. Moreover, the quality stamp must give evidence of the characteristics certified and the associated levels, for instance by means of letters or indicators. To put this information on the certification report only is very dangerous because the user might never see it and just trust in the quality mark.

As far as techniques are concerned, almost all those listed in this book were adopted and handled by means of questionnaires. A questionnaire is designed for each sub-characteristic of ISO 9126 and each item in the questionnaire is detailed in terms of importance (optional or mandatory), document class in which it must be present, technique to be used, tool to be used (when applicable), and link to the detailed evaluation module (see

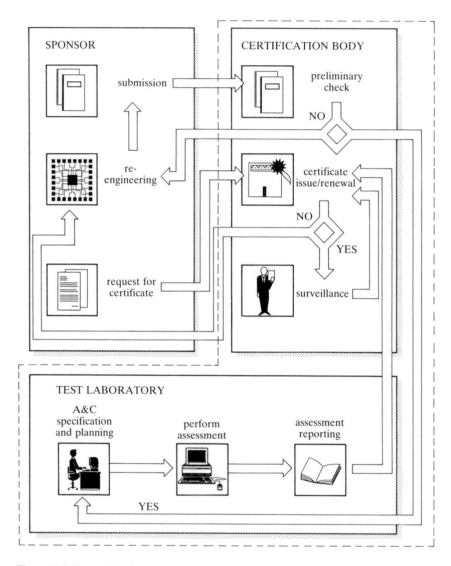

Figure 11.7 The certification process.

the next paragraph for a thorough discussion of this topic). The total number of check-points is a little less than 1000.

11.5.4 The evaluation modules

We feel that one of the most important ideas that matured within the project was the one to structure the evaluation around self-consistent and modular evaluation procedures, the so-called *bricks*. The advance of research in metrication and the new challenges presented by modern hardware and software technologies made us think that it would have been unwise to have a predefined set of metrics *set in concrete*. The software engineering community has been flooded by schemes proposing the ultimate metrics and thresholds for software product quality. These magic numbers have become obsolete in a couple of years or were not even applicable and meaningful outside the environment where they were devised. This is the reason why we think that it is better to have a library of evaluation modules that can be subjected to change in order to keep up with evolution.

These evaluation modules (bricks)[140] must be well structured and designed in order to be used consistently by several test laboratories. A first example is to be found in the *IEEE Standard Dictionary of Measures to Produce Reliable Software*.[84,85] From its analysis and from the experiences that matured within the project we think that an evaluation module should be made up of two parts with some optional annexes. The first part is what we call the *evaluation specifications*. Within it the following information must be given:

General and specific definitions
- Target characteristic (among the six proposed by ISO 9126) and optional refinement into sub-characteristics
- Evaluation technique to be used (inspection, execution analysis, static analysis or modelling)
- Documents required (i.e. the product parts needed, such as user's manual, source code, etc.)
- Details of the assessment method and of its underlying *theory*
- Identification of factors and metrics (unambiguous questions and formulae together with their target scales or units)
- Clear identification of the data to be collected
- Cost information
- Required structure and elements of the evaluation report
- References (to standards, recognized theoretical work, etc.)

A specification is necessary for performing the assessment but might not be enough; this is the reason why examples of interpretation are also needed as a second part. These examples should give guidelines on thresholds, score computation and anything related to the pass/fail decision process. Some evaluation modules might also have optional annexes needed for adaptation to specific environments in terms of definitions (that is to say, how the defined items translate or map given a particular product coded, for instance, in C++ and specified using SADT), data collection and tool selection. During the lifetime of the project more than 100 such evaluation modules were defined.[120] The most valuable dozen or so covering all the six ISO 9126 characteristics were refined and are now publicly available. A guide for developing software-evaluation modules is going to be produced and submitted at ISO standardization level to provide the scientific community with common guidelines to allow the incremental completion of the brick library.

11.5.5   Mapping characteristics, levels and techniques

While dealing with the various assessment techniques, we have already shown their relationship with the ISO 9126 characteristics. We include in Table 11.5 a suggested mapping of characteristics and levels to a set of techniques. It is in fact a superset of those we addressed in Chapter 5 and many of them have not been fully tried out. It should be noted that:

1. All the specific techniques fall into the classification technique described in Chapter 5. We have changed the terminology from the original SCOPE version to make the terminology consistent.
2. The mapping is not definitive and is given as an example.

When shifting to a higher level we have to apply all the techniques of lower levels as well, possibly with a greater level of stringency.

11.5.6   The assessment contract

The analysis of legal issues in various EC countries, together with practical experiences like the one presented in the previous chapter has led us to the definition of a template for a contract between a test laboratory and the sponsor of the evaluation.[107] Such a contract becomes essential when performing product certification. The contract ought to be structured in the following way.

*   Preliminary matters
    *   Identification of the parties
    *   Identification of the product
    *   Purpose of the agreement
*   The assessment plan
    *   The producer's obligations
    *   Provisions regarding delivery of software and associated information
    *   Cost of the assessment and method of payment

Table 11.5 A mapping of techniques to levels and characteristics

ISO characteristic	Level	Checks performed
Functionality	D	Inspection/walkthrough
	C	Traceability/ black-box testing
	B	Test coverage
	A	Formal proof
Reliability	D	Anomaly checking
		User survey
	C	Field experience/fault tolerance
	B	Reliability models
	A	Formal proof
Usability	D	Checklists applied to human–machine interface
	C	GUI standards/readability indices
	B	Laboratory test/user survey
	A	User mental models
Efficiency	D	Execution and measurements
	C	Benchmark testing
	B	Algorithmic complexity
	A	Profiling performance evaluation
Maintainability	D	Checklists
	C	Structural and textual metrics
	B	Programming rules
		checking
	A	Traceability/development process
Portability	D	Installation
	C	Anomaly checking
	B	Platform/environment assumptions
	A	Program design assessment

- The assessor's obligations
- Duration of assessment
- Form of assessment to be conducted
- Qualifications of assessment staff
- Conduct of the assessment
- Procedural matters
  - Presentation of the results and format of the assessment report
  - Dispute-resolution procedures
  - Use to which the report may be put
  - Resubmission of products and testing of new versions
- Legal issues
  - Confidentiality
  - Intellectual property issues
  - Exclusion/limitation clauses
  - Choirs of law/jurisdiction

SUMMARY

This chapter should have brought good news to IT managers who are interested in software product assessment. First of all, costs of assessment are not prohibitive and allow for a pragmatic application of the assessment techniques in the industrial market, now. Secondly, the results of a Europe-wide survey have shown that several software companies have already undergone software product assessment, that many factors can influence assessment, that process certification is felt as being not enough, and that software companies and end-users are looking for evaluation facilities and certification services.

12

CONCLUSIONS

12.1 MEETING OUR OBJECTIVES

In Chapter 1 we identified a number of reasons why metrics had not been more widely used in software. We now show how the approach and methods we have discussed can address these problems. The good news is that the problems identified in Chapter 1 are all solvable, and thus our conclusions are optimistic.

1. *Data collection often starts without a clear idea of the data requirements and how the data will be analysed* We have stressed the need for some underlying model to guide data collection and analysis. In the case of software assessment we need a quality model and ISO 9126 provides a good (but not perfect) example. These characteristics are external attributes, but we can usually only measure internal attributes. We therefore look for those internal metrics which will relate to our quality model.

2. *The definitions of the metrics are often not clear* It is important not only to have well-defined metrics and procedures for collecting them but also to know at what granularity the metrics should be collected. Using tools to collect metrics will enforce standard definitions, assuming of course that the same tools are used throughout. For inspection-based metrics the checklist becomes the definition of the metric.

3. *Metrics projects will often not survey the literature, or else reject existing work on spurious grounds* We have tried to present a broad set of metrics-based techniques, but of course we cannot provide an

exhaustive guide to metrics. The important point is to identify the type of metric first (e.g. checklist score, textual metric) and then look for well-defined metrics in that class which can in practice be collected.

4. *A consequence from point 3 is that metrics with no tools support may be applied* For the collection of many metrics at a fine granularity over many projects the use of tools cannot be stressed enough. However, we have seen that many tools are available and, where necessary, new tools can be built.

5. *Metrics projects collect only a very simple set of metrics at a very high level* Chapter 5 gives detailed descriptions of the types of metrics available. There is far more to metrics collection than a fault log and lines of code, and we have demonstrated this. There is a wide range of attributes which may be measured, but it is always important to be sure what is being measured.

6. *Metrics are collected on paper forms* We have shown that everything can be tools-based. Even that data which is best collected on a form should be supported by electronic forms so that we can run simple consistency checks and allow automatic transfer of the data.

7. *Any reasonably sized metrics scheme will have to cope with diverse hardware and different versions of operating systems* The problem is transferring data between machines and the lowest common denominator is usually text files. For this reason the SCOPE data-transfer mechanisms relied on text files.

8. *Data is often collected at the wrong level for the purposes that it is needed for* This is data granularity again. One reason that data is collected at a coarse level is that it means fewer data points. Without a database and appropriate transfer mechanisms, large data sets become unmanageable. However, with a database these problems are diminished.

9. *Often the data is considered sensitive by the provider* As well as keeping secret the name of the provider, certain steps can be taken to sanitize data such as encrypting the module names.

10. *The onus of data collection is often placed on the programmers* Tools-based collection actually requires little additional effort. In fact, in some cases, metrics could be collected with virtually no effort at all. Programmers should therefore not find metrics collection a significant burden.

11. *Programmers are often asked to make evaluations of their own or even a colleague's work* Many techniques such as structural metrics and test coverage require no human intervention at all. Even when we use checklists, strenuous efforts are made to be as objective as possible. Even so, interpretation of the metrics should be done independently.

12. *The Hawthorne effect should also be considered* In fact, this might work to our advantage, since programmers will subconsciously try to improve the metrics values. However, it is much better if attempts to

produce better software are conscious. We saw in Chapter 9 that the one thing that influenced structural metrics was having the information during coding. Thus if programmers are given the metrics as they are collected, they will be better able to control their own work.

13. *The data must be cross-referenced so that it can be related when it is stored* A database which contains no names or structure data would be almost useless. Therefore care must be taken that this data is collected and that it has high integrity.

14. *Inappropriate statistical techniques are often applied to software metrics data* Software metrics are in many ways different from classical physical data. We do not have normal distributions, and the data is often ordinal. Often outliers are very significant. There is a battery of statistical techniques which can be applied to this kind of data. We therefore have to bear these points in mind when we apply statistics.

15. *The central repository for storing the data is often not appropriate* For the data we have proposed, nothing less than a database can cope with the kinds of analysis we will want to perform.

The obstacles to using metrics are not trivial but nevertheless there are technical solutions to them.

12.2 WHAT A METRICS SCHEME SHOULD LOOK LIKE

We can now draw together all the ideas from the previous chapters and paint a picture of a metrics scheme for software assessment. Such a scheme might be used for QA, independent V&V, or certification. Nevertheless many features will be common to any such scheme.

First we need a quality model which splits our global notion of *quality* into a number of characteristics which can be set at different levels depending on the application domain and criticality. We have adopted the six characteristics from ISO 9126 but other models might be equally valid. To measure them, we then need assessment techniques (static analysis, execution analysis and inspection) to provide metrics for each of the characteristics. It would be foolish to use just one technique, so we should adopt as many as possible and often use several for any one characteristic.

All the techniques yield data which are software metrics. The concept of a metric or measure is sufficiently broad to encompass all the kinds of objective data we will produce. We need to ensure that the metrics are valid both in that they measure what is claimed and that there is some theory linking them to the characteristic. Here empirical evidence is a bonus.

The techniques should be supported by tools, and these tools should generate the metrics data in an electronic form such as a text file. We then can transfer this data to the central database which stores data from many previous projects. The database can be queried to support statistical analysis of the results. We can generate diagrams such as histograms and pie charts as well as more complicated statistics. We might well have one member of staff with a statistical background who can derive thresholds and norms based on the historical data.

The metrics tools, database and statistics packages are linked together so that data may be transferred electronically between them. This might be through a weakly integrated set of tools using CMF files or a more strongly integrated assessor's workbench.

12.3 HOW TO PROCEED FROM HERE

Readers may well now ask themselves how such ideas should be incorporated into their own organizations. How should they go about collecting metrics and using them for software assessment? We now briefly summarize the most important features; it is essentially the responsibility of managers to ensure that these things are in place.

It is now widely accepted that any metrics scheme should have the support of senior management. This is necessary but not sufficient. There must also be the support of technical staff and the necessary resources. Resources means equipment and tools, not just people.

There are three important features that should be present in any metrics scheme.

1. The set of models and theories that justify what you are doing—this should ideally be set out in a report or handbook that is periodically revised
2. The tools and database system that allows the metrics to be collected, stored and interpreted
3. A pool of data from past projects

The first of these is important but also has the danger of becoming a navel-examining exercise if it is conducted by a large committee. It is probably best left to one or two people to take a pragmatic view and base it on what tools are available. In any case there is no need to do all the planning at once. You can always start small with just one or two techniques and add to them later.

Building up the tools and database system is no trivial matter. You should ensure that any metrics tool you buy can export metrics either as a file or on the standard output. This is essential for electronic transfer of data, without which your scheme is likely to fail. If you can, get the vendor to make alterations to the tools to fit in with your system. You will also need to commission a database. This need not be very complicated, since it can always be enhanced later. However, the text files that go into the database should be separately archived; so if the database is ever totally redesigned, the data can be entered a second time.

A decent-sized pool of data will take time to collect. Some types of metrics such as static metrics or coverage measures can be extracted any time after the software has been produced, assuming that the software has been archived. Therefore you can use some of your old products (or even public-domain products) to quickly build up a common pool representing typical values long after these systems were developed. However, fault, failure and effort data must be captured as the events happen. Since fault and failure data are so useful, it is worth starting to collect them as soon as you can, even if the rest of the metrics scheme is not yet in place. Unlike static analysis and coverage data, they cannot be obtained later. Note that fault data is most useful when you collect information about the module in which the failure occurred.

A metrics scheme needs staff to be assigned to it. Clearly any scheme needs resources and a manager who is responsible for them, but other types of personnel are also important. The three types of people whom you should consider having are:

1. Someone with past experience of metrics
2. Someone with a background in statistics (e.g. at graduate level)
3. An experienced programmer (preferably a yacc and lex freak)

This key mixture of people in the tools and database tasks of SCOPE was an important factor in the success of our work.

You must be prepared to put the necessary investment into organizational infrastructure, development of methods and procedures, and metrics tools (off-the-shelf and bespoke) including the database and transfer tools. In the future we would expect a workbench of some sort to be available, for the time being we have to make do with loosely coupled tools.

It surprises us to see commercial organizations that are prepared to invest labour time by using employees to try to introduce metrics to their organization, but are not willing to spend a penny on the necessary tools. The result is either nothing at all or some paper-based system. This is not economically sensible. Labour is expensive and the tools are, by comparison, often much cheaper.

The SCOPE project was lucky in that we had access to several tools either free or at nominal cost. Had we not used these tools, there is little doubt that the case studies would have failed to produce anything and the database would be empty.

It has been said that a metrics scheme does not bring any results for two years. This is only true if you collect process metrics, since they cannot be collected retrospectively. For product metrics, results are available almost immediately. Three months after data starts to be collected should be enough time to yield some results.

12.4 PRODUCT AND PROCESS

Process certification already exists (ISO 9000 and the SEI method); product assessment can be done and by implication, certification is technically feasible. We will have to wait for the administrative structures to be created, but this is a commercial and political issue, not a technical one. The interesting question arises as to how product and process certification relate to one another. We can offer no definitive answer to this question; it is still a controversial area, and it would be true to say that the two authors have differing opinions. The fundamental difference between the approaches is that process certification applies to an organization (or part of one) and product certification applies to individual pieces of software. Therefore we do not see that they could be merged into a single approach. They can, however, be used together. To carry forward the debate, we set out a series of scenarios, without indicating any preference:

Product certification as an add-on Assuming that the present process certification schemes remain much the same, product certification would be a further and additional step to apply to software for organizations that have already attained process certification. So ISO 9000 certification would be a precondition to performing product certification.

Process absorbs product Product assessment is seen as an essential part of the development process, and so any certified process must assess the product. This would require that existing process schemes be enhanced by including more specific details of agreed product assessment procedures. There would be no explicit certificate of product assessment, but an implication that it had been done if the process was certified.

Competing approaches Process and product certification would be offered as separate services. Suppliers and customers can opt for either or both, but in some cases one would be used without the other.

Product replaces process Product certification is shown to be technically superior and eventually replaces process certification. Process assessment then becomes an issue internal to the software producer to ensure they produce products that pass the certification procedure.

12.5 FUTURE DIRECTIONS

Finally we should look to future areas of research that will be able to help us. It would be useful to have some more assessment techniques, and to have the existing ones enhanced. For example, data-flow analysis is an area where work needs to be done, as is metrics of black-box testing, and these will need to be supported by tools. However, the most important thing is to empirically test the theories on which assessment is based by means of experiments.

There is a problem here which is political and commercial rather than technical. Experiments can have a direct commercial benefit: for example, by showing which of two design methods produced the most easily maintainable code. Yet there is often reluctance to commit resources to this kind of activity since it is (wrongly) perceived not to add value or contribute to profits. Yet how else can we understand the factors that affect the production of good software? Even when a commercial organization does collect good data and results, there is a reluctance to publish them for fear that it might damage the reputation of the company. This is particularly true for fault and failure data.

Research which is not influenced by commercial pressures is usually done in universities. But except by using students, there is no way an experimental observation of software can be done there. Collaborative projects between academia and industry would be the ideal medium for such experiments with academics designing the experiments and industry providing the data. However, these collaborative projects are only partially funded by government and so industry needs to meet some of the costs and for this they would expect a return on their investment. We need to persuade companies to collect data and share the results, and that ultimately this is the only way we can be sure that better software will result.

If we had a greater amount of experimental evidence linking internal and external attributes we could not only assess software better but also develop processes to generate a higher-quality product.

GLOSSARY

Throughout the book we have defined and used a number of terms; we now provide a glossary to act as a reference point for the reader. There are many formal glossaries and in order not to conflict with them we have defined only those words which either are given a special meaning in this book or are new terms. However, the following are not included: ISO 9126 characteristics (to be found in Chapter 3), names of specific metrics (see Chapter 5) and names of specific statistical techniques (Chapter 6).

Anomaly checking   Identification of those features which might be faults, including non-portable features.

Assessment   An action of applying specific documented assessment criteria to a specific software module, package, or product for the purpose of determining the acceptance or release of the software module, package, or product.[89]

Assessor's workbench   An integrated set of tools which support the evaluation process and the assessment activities.

Back end   The part of a static or dynamic analyser which is language-independent and displays graphs and metrics.

Black-box analysis (also known as *closed-box*)   Analysis where we examine the relationship between the inputs and outputs and pay no attention to the internal workings.

Black-box testing   Testing where the executable components are tested against the functional specifications or user manuals using a checklist.

Certification   Issuing of a certificate by an official body to demonstrate that an evaluation has been performed successfully.

Change   A modification of one or more software components.

Checklist   A set of questions used to obtain measurements. Each question has a predefined number of answers each of which has an associated score.

Checklist manager   A tool used for applying checklists.

Common metrics format   A file syntax devised to transfer metrics data between different tools and machines.

Common pool   A set of metrics data from previous projects that is in some sense representative of the software in general.

Component   A part of a software system. A component may contain other components.

Compound module   A number of modules from the same subsystem which perform a common function.

Design document   A document that describes the design of the system or component.

Evaluation   The process of identifying quality targets, selecting product parts, choosing appropriate techniques and tools, performing the measurements and reporting the results.

Executable component   A software component that may be run, interpreted, or compiled.

Execution analysis (also called *dynamic analysis*)   Analysis which requires the software to be running.

External attribute (of a product, process, or resource)   An attribute which can only be measured with respect to how the product, process, or resource relates to its environment.[64]

Failure   An occasion when the software does not behave as it should.

Fault   The result of an error that has been made by someone constructing the software.

Flat file   A text file used to store data, where the data is represented as lists of numbers and symbols.

Front end   Part of a static or dynamic analyser which reads (and changes) the source code and is language-specific; also the part of an SDCS which is operating-system-specific.

Functional specification   A document that specifies the functions that a system or component must perform.

Glass-box analysis (also known as *white-box* or *open-box*)   Analysis where we examine the internal workings, that is, which statements, module variables, etc., are used while the program is being run.

Granularity   The level of component at which a metric is collected: e.g. system, subsystem, etc.

Incident   The perception by someone that the software is not performing as expected. This perception may be right or wrong.

Inspection   A technique that requires manual examination of the software products.

Internal attribute (of a product, process, or resource)   An attribute which can be measured purely in terms of the product, process, or resource itself.[64]

Metric   A measure used in the domain of software.

Modelling   Creating an abstraction of the software on which assessment may be performed.

Module   A single procedure, subroutine, or function from an executable component.

Naming convention   A set of rules for ensuring that modules are given unique names by program analysers.

Non-executable component   A software component that may not be run, compiled, or interpreted.

Norm   A value or range of values that programmers should aim for when building software.

Operational testing   Testing where the type and frequency of inputs corresponds to the expected software usage.

Outlier   A data point that is much larger or smaller than most of the population.

Reliability model   A statistical technique for estimating the time to failure from historic failure data.

SDCS   Session data collection system, a tool for collection failure data from operating systems.

Static analysis   Analysis that is automatic but does not require execution of the software.

Structural analysis   Analysis based on structural models such as flowgraphs or call graphs and metrics from these models.

Subsystem   A software component that corresponds to a single executable program.

System   A number of programs and files that perform a common function.

Test coverage   Measurement of the amount of source code executed during testing.

Test cross-referencing   A technique for obtaining measures of the functional coverage based on cross-referencing the test cases and functions of the software as described in the documentation.

Test document   A document that specifies the test inputs, execution conditions and predicted results for an item to be tested.

Testing   Where a subset of all the possible inputs is selected, and actual outputs produced by the software are compared with the expected results.

Textual measurement   Measurement based on the count of tokens or words or symbols in the document.

Threshold   A value such that if metrics are above (or sometimes below) this value, the component can fail the assessment.

User manual   A document that presents information necessary to use a system or component to obtain desired results.

BIBLIOGRAPHY

1. American Bar Association, *Universal Guidelines—Version 0.1*, ABA LTAC, 1987.
2. American Bar Association, *Word Processing Guidelines—Version 2.2*, ABA LTAC, 1987.
3. Adams, G., *Certification Data Model*, SCOPE Consortium, October 1992.
4. Agostoni, G., P. Caliman and D. Di Ventura, 'Assessing quality for business oriented software: an experience on an application supported by relational data base', in W. Ehrenberger (ed.), *Approving Software Products*, North-Holland, Amsterdam, 1990.
5. Agostoni, G., R. Lancellotti and M. Maiocchi, 'Towards software quality control automatic documentation and test case generation: a product based on SA specification methodology', *AICA* (Associazione Italiana per il Calcolo Automatico) *Annual Congress, Bari*, 1990.
6. Agostoni, G., G. Albinola, E. Fagnoni and M. Maiocchi, 'Software science: an extensive application to C language', *AICA* (Associazione Italiana per il Calcolo Automatico) *Annual Congress, Bari*, 1990.
7. *AMI Handbook*, AMI Consortium, 1992.
8. Arthur, L. J., 'Software quality measurement', *Datamation*, December 1984.
9. Arthur, L. J., *Measuring Programmer Quality*, Wiley, New York, 1985.
10. Azuma, M., 'Information Technology—Software Product Evaluation—Indicators and Metrics', Working draft, International Standards Organization, ISO/JTC1/SC7/WG6 Project 7.13.3, March 1993.
11. Bache, R. M., 'Graph models of software', PhD Thesis, South Bank Polytechnic, 1990.
12. Bache, R. M., *Specification of RULER Graph Modeller*, SCOPE Consortium, 1991.
13. Bache, R. M. and M. D. Neil, 'Validating technologies for certifying software products', in W. Ehrenberger (ed.), *Approving Software Products*, North-Holland, Amsterdam, 1991.
14. Baker, A. L. and S. H. Zweben, 'A comparison of measures of control flow complexity', *IEEE Transactions on Software Engineering*, **6** (11), November 1980.
15. Basili, V. and D. Weiss, 'A methodology for collecting valid software engineering data', *IEEE Transactions on Software Engineering*, **SE-10** (3), pp. 728–738, November 1984.
16. Bazzana, G., G. Borella, M. Maiocchi and F. Pescarolo, 'Software quality for real-time systems', *2nd European Conference on Software Quality Assurance, Oslo*, 1990.
17. Bazzana, G., K. Kirkwood, B. von Neumann and G. Rumi, 'Assessing the reliability of software products', *ESREL* (European Software Reliability) *93, Munich*, March 1993.

18. Bazzana, G., and R. Brigliadori (eds), *Certifier Workbench—General Design Description*, SCOPE Consortium, December 1992.

19. Bazzana, G., M. Maiocchi and G. Rumi, 'Software testing and verification for concurrent systems: practicable experiences', *AICA* (Associazione Italiana per il Calcolo Automatico) *Annual Congress, Turin*, 1992.

20. Bazzana, G., R. Brigliadori and F. Seigneur (eds), *Certifier Workbench—Software Requirements Specification*, SCOPE Consortium, 1992.

21. Bazzana, G., R. Brigliadori and P. Carson (eds), 'Data Analysis for the First Set of Case Studies,' July 1992.

22. Bazzana, G. and R. Brigliadori (eds), *Analysis of Users' Needs and Expectations about Software Product Assessment and Certification*, Version 3, SCOPE Consortium, January 1993.

23. Bazzana, G., R. Brigliadori, O. Andersen and T. Jokela, 'ISO 9000 and ISO 9126: friends or foes?', submitted to IEEE Software Engineering Standards Symposium, Brighton, October 1993.

24. Bazzana, G., G. Damele, M. Maiocchi and G. Zontini, 'Putting reliability models into practice: an experience report from industry', submitted to *IEEE ISSRE '93, 4th International Symposium on Software Reliability Engineering, Denver, November 1993*.

25. Bazzana, G. and P. Robert, *A Network for Software Product Evaluation Services*, SCOPE Consortium, 1993.

26. Bellcore–Bell Communication Research, *Reliability and Quality Measurements for Telecommunications Systems (RQMS)*, Technical Reference: TR-TSY-000929 Issue 1, June 1990.

27. Beizer, B., *Software Testing Techniques*, 2nd edition, Van Nostrand Reinholt, New York, 1990.

28. Bicego, A., M. Jacobone, M. Maiocchi and U. Poggi, 'Towards automation in software quality control: the case of products described by formal grammars', *IFIP Conference, Dublin*, Elsevier North-Holland, Amsterdam, 1986.

29. Boegh, J., H. L. Hausen and P. Robert, *Guide to Software Quality Evaluation: The Evaluator's Guide*, Committee draft, International Standards Organization ISO/IEG,JTC1/SC7/WG6, May 1993.

30. Boehm, B. W., *Software Engineering Economics*, Prentice-Hall, Englewood Cliffs, NJ, 1981.

31. Boehm, B. W., J. R. Brown, H. Kaspar, M. Lipow, G. J. MacLeod and M. J. Merritt, *Characteristics of Software Quality*, TRW Series of Software Technologies, Vol. 1, North-Holland, Amsterdam, 1978.

32. Bollinger, T. P. and C. McGowan, 'A critical look at software capability evaluations', *IEEE Software*, July 1991.

33. Bowen, T. P., G. B. Wigle and J. T. Tsai, *Specification of Software Quality Attributes*, Vols I, II and III, Rome Air Development Center—Air Force System Command RADC-TR-85-37, 1985.

34. Brocklehurst, S. and B. Littlewood, 'New ways to get accurate reliability measures', *IEEE Software*, July 1992.

35. BS 5750, British Standards Institution, 1987.

36. Carsana, L., R. Lancellotti and M. Maiocchi, 'Software metrics measurement and interpretation: definition and experimentation of a flexible technical environment', *Acts of Eurometrics 91*, March 1991.

37. Cachia, R. (ed.) *Bootstrap—Course and Demo Information Package for Middle Management* [public-with-restrictions] Bootstrap Consortium, 1992.

38. CEN/CENELEC, EN 45000 series standards, The Joint European Standards Institute, 1989.

39. Ceriani, M., A. Cicu and M. Maiocchi, 'A methodology for accurate test specification and auditing', in Ed. Chandrashekaran, *Computer Program Testing*, North-Holland, Amsterdam, 1982.
40. Cherry, L. L., *Writing Tools—The STYLE and DICTION programs*, Bell Laboratories, New Jersey, 1987.
41. Christenson, D. A., 'Using software reliability models to predict field failure rates in electronic swtiching systems', *Proceedings National Security Industrial Association Annual Joint Conference on Software Quality and Reliability*, Washington, 1988.
42. Coallier, F., N. Gammage and A. Graydon, *Trillium—Telecom Software Product Development Capability Assessment Model*, Draft v2.2, Bell Canada, 1992.
43. Coehn, L., 'Quality function deployment: an application perspective from Digital Equipment Corporation', *National Productivity Review*, pp. 197–208, Summer 1988.
44. Commission of the European Community, *Information Technology Security Evaluation Criteria (ITSEC)—Provisional Harmonised Criteria*, Version 1.2, June 1991.
45. Commission of the European Community, *Information Technology Security Evaluation Manual (ITSEM)*, Draft Version 0.2, 1992.
46. Commission of the European Community, *PCTE—A Basis for a Portable Common Tool Environment*, Functional Specification, Version 1.5 C, Vol. 1, 1988.
47. *Qualigraph—User's Guide*, Version 10.3, Computer Research and Innovation Centre, Budapest, 1986.
48. Conte, S. D., H. E. Dunsmore and V. Y. Shen, *Software Engineering Metrics and Models*, Benjamin/Cummings, Menlo Park, USA, 1986.
49. *Metropol—Introduction au Système*, Control et Prévention, Toulouse.
50. Curtis, B., S. B. Shepperd, P. Milliman, M. A. Borst and T. Love, 'Measuring the psychological complexity of software maintenance tasks with the Halstead and McCabe metrics', *IEEE Transactions on Software Engineering*, **5** (2), March 1979.
51. Darwin, I. F., *Checking C Progams with Lint*, O'Reilly & Associates Inc., 1988.
52. Department of Defense, *Trusted Computer Systems Evaluation Criteria*, DOD 5200.28-STD, December 1985.
53. Department of the US Air Force, *Software Maintainability Evaluation Guide*, AFOTEC Pamphlet 800-2, Vol. 3, HQ Air Force Operational Test and Evaluation Center, October 1989.
54. Department of the US Air Force, *Software Usability Evaluation Guide*, AFOTEC Pamphlet 800-2, Vol. 4, HQ Air Force Operational Test and Evaluation Center, November 1987.
55. De Millo, R. A., W. M. Cracken and J. F. Passafiume, *Software Testing and Evaluation*, Benjamin/Cummings, Menlo Park, USA, 1987.
56. Deutsch, M. S., *Software Verification and Validation*, Prentice-Hall, Englewood Cliffs, NJ, 1982.
57. Deutsch, M. S. and R. R. Willis, *Software Quality Engineering*, Prentice-Hall, Englewood Cliffs, NJ, 1988.
58. Dijkstra, E., 'GOTO considered harmful', *Comm. ACM*, **11**, p. 148, 1968.
59. DIN 66285, *Anwendersoftware—Güterbedingungen und Prüfbestimmungen*, Beuth, Berlin, 1989.
60. ECMA—European Computer Manufacturers Association, *Standard ECMA 149—Portable Common Tool Environment (PCTE)—Abstract Specification*, 1990.
61. Eva, M., *SSADM Version 4: A User's Guide*, McGraw-Hill, London, 1992.
62. Etnoteam SpA, *TEFAX—Guida Utente. Release 3.01*, 1991.
63. Etnoteam—Nomos, *Il mercato dei servizi per il controllo di qualità del software in Italia*, Etnoteam—Nomos Public Report, CQS, July 1987.
64. Fenton, N. E., *Software Metrics: A Rigorous Approach*, Chapman and Hall, London, 1991.

65. Ferrari, D., *Computer System Performance Evaluation*, Prentice-Hall, Englewood Cliffs, NJ, 1978.
66. Finkelstein, L., 'A review of the fundamental concepts of measurement', *Measurement*, **2** (1), 25–34, 1984.
67. Freedman, D. and G. Weinberg, *Handbook of Walkthroughs, Inspections and Technical Reviews*, Little, Brown and Co., Boston, 1982.
68. Forse, T., *Qualimetrie des systems complexes*, Les Editions d'Organisation, Paris, 1989.
69. Gabaglio, R., M. Maiocchi and M. Tentori, 'The production of quality in software development: the role of artificial intelligence', *3rd International Congress of Informatics Association, Rio de Janeiro*, 1990.
70. Gillies, A. C., *Software Quality—Theory and Management*, Chapman and Hall, London, 1993.
71. Grady, R. B. and D. L. Caswell, *Software Metrics: Establishing a Company-Wide Program*, Prentice-Hall, Englewood Cliffs, NJ, 1987.
72. Grady, R. B., *Practical Software Metrics for Project Management and Process Improvement*, Prentice-Hall, Englewood Cliffs, NJ, 1992.
73. Haase, V., R. Messnar and R. Cachia, 'Process improvement by measurement', *Klagenfurt Conference, 1992*, to be published by Springer.
74. Halstead, M. H., *Elements of Software Science*, North-Holland, Amsterdam, 1977.
75. Hausen, H. L., N. Cacutalua and D. Welzel, *A Method of Software Assessment and Certification*, Gesellschaft für Mathematik und Datenverarbeitung mbH, Bonn, 1991.
76. Hetzel, W., *The Complete Guide to Software Testing*, QED, Wellesley, Mass., 1984.
77. Health and Safety Executive (UK), *Programmable Electronic Systems in Safety Related Applications*, HMSO Books, 1987.
78. *HP Encapsulator: Integrating Applications into the HP Softbench Platform*, Hewlett-Packard, 1989.
79. *HP-UX Documentation*, Hewlett-Packard, 1989.
80. Humphrey, W. S., *Managing the Software Process*, Addison-Wesley, Wokingham, 1989.
81. Humphrey, W. S., T. R. Snyder, and R. R. Willis, 'Software process improvement at Hughes Aircraft', *IEEE Software*, July 1991.
82. IBM, *Systems Applications Architecture—Common User Access*: Vol. 1, *Basic Interface Design Guide*, SC26-4583-0; Vol. 2, *Advanced Interface Design Guide*, SC26-4582-0, IBM, December 1989.
83. IEEE, *Standard for a Software Quality Metrics Methodology*, Unapproved draft published for comment only, April 1990.
84. *IEEE Standard 982.1-1988—Standard Dictionary of Measures to Produce Reliable Software*, The Institute of Electrical and Electronic Engineers Inc., 1988.
85. *IEEE Standard 982.2-1988—Guide for the Use of Standard Dictionary of Measures to Produce Reliable Software*, The Institute of Electrical and Electronic Engineers Inc., 1988.
86. ANSI/IEEE Std 729—1983, *IEEE Standard Glossary of Software Engineering Terminology*, The Institute of Electrical and Electronic Engineers Inc., 1983.
87. Istituto Italiano del Marchio di Qualità, *Regolamento per il rilascio di certificati di qualità IMQ per prodotti software—Servizio Sperimentale*, Version 3.1, January 1993.
88. International Standard ISO/DIS 9000-3, *Quality Management and Quality Assurance Standards—Part 3: Guidelines for the Application of ISO 9001 to the Development, Supply and Maintenance of Software*, ISO, September 1990.
89. International Standard 9126, *Information Technology—Software Evaluation. Quality Characteristics and Guidelines for their Use*, ISO, December 1991.
90. International Standard 9241, *ISO 9241 Working Draft: Ergonomic Requirements for Office Work with Visual Display Terminals (VDTs)*, ISO/TC159/SC4/WG5, Working Draft, 1992.

91. Interim Def. Stan. 00-55 (Part 1), *The Procurement of Safety Critical Software in Defence Equipment*, HMSO.
92. ISO/IEC Guide 25, *General Requirements for Competence of Calibration and Testing Laboratories*, International Standards Organization, 1990.
93. Johnson, S. C., 'Lint, a C Program Checker', *USENIX UNIX Supplementary documents*, Bell Labs, November 1986.
94. Kada, S., *Requirements Specification Documentation for Tool: Data analyser*, SCOPE Consortium, 1992.
95. Kirakowski, J., M. Porteous and M. Corbett, 'How to use software usability measurement inventory: the user's view of software quality', *3rd European Conference on SW Quality, Madrid*, 1992.
96. Kirkwood, K. B. (ed.) *Definition of the Common Metrics Format*, SCOPE Consortium, 1991.
97. Kirkwood, K. and G. Bazzana, 'A software reliability tool-kit', *CSR Conference, Luxemburg*, 1992.
98. Kitchenham, B. A., 'Towards a constructive quality model, part 1: Software quality modelling, measurement and prediction', *Software Engineering Journal*, **4**, pp. 105–113, 1987.
99. Kitchenham, B. A. and L. A. Pickard, 'Towards a constructive quality model, part 2: Statistical techniques for modelling quality in the ESPRIT REQUEST project', *Software Engineering Journal*, **4**, pp. 114–126, 1987.
100. Knorr, G., 'The Gütergemeinschaft Software—A major concept in the Certification of Software Quality' in W. Ehrenberger (ed.), *Approving Software Product*, North-Holland, Amsterdam, 1990.
101. Kyster, H. (ed.), *Brick: Safety*, SCOPE Consortium, 1992.
102. Kyster, H. (ed.), *Brick: Workmanship*, SCOPE Consortium, 1992.
103. Legall, G., M. F. Adam, H. Dierrenic, C. Lassudrie, J. P. Lucas and N. Valette, 'Controle de la qualité lors d'un development de logiciel', *3rd European Conference on Software Quality, Madrid*, November 1992.
104. Lemaitre, P., P. Nguyen-Duc and E. Azoune, 'TASQUE: a tool for assisting software quality evaluation', *Acts of Eurometrics*, pp. 305–314, 1992.
105. Lennselius, B. and L. Rydstrom, 'Software fault content and reliability estimation for telecommunication systems,' in 'Telecommunications Software Quality and Productivity', *IEEE Journal on Selected Areas in Communications*, **8** (2), February 1990.
106. Littlewood, B. and L. Strigini, 'Validation of ultra-high dependability for software-based systems', to appear in *Comm. ACM.*
107. Lloyd, I. J. and M. J. Simpson (eds), *Fourth Report on the Legal Aspects of SCOPE*, SCOPE Consortium, February 1992.
108. Lyu, M. R. and A. Nikora, 'Applying reliability models more effectively', *IEEE Software*, July 1992.
109. MacLeod, M., *An Introduction to Usability Evaluation*, NPL Report DITC 102, UK National Physics Laboratory, Teddington, 1992.
110. Maiocchi, M., *Il Controllo di Qualità del Software*, F. Angeli, New York, 1988.
111. Maiocchi, M., A. Mazzetti and M. Villa, 'TEFAX: an automated test factory for functional quality control of software projects', *2eme Colloque de Genie Logiciel, Nice*, 1984.
112. Maiocchi, M. and D. Pina, 'A framework for global software quality evaluation', *BICYPS 89—Beijing*, August 1989.
113. Maiocchi, M., B. Marchetti and D. Pina, 'Software quality, risks and costs: a proposed framework', *2nd European Conference on Software Quality Assurance, EOQC-SQA, Oslo*, June 1990.

114. Maiocchi, M. and E. Fagnoni, 'Argo: a software environment organising the software development process with compliance with international standards', *3rd European Conference on Software Quality, Madrid*, November 1992.

115. Marca, D. A. and C. L. McGowan, *SADT—Structured Analysis and Design Technique*, McGraw-Hill, New York, 1988.

116. Marks, D. M., *Testing Very Big Systems*, McGraw-Hill, New York, 1992.

117. von Maryhauser, A., *Software Engineering Methods and Management*, Academic Press, New York, 1990.

118. McCabe, T. J., 'A complexity measure', *IEEE Transactions on Software Engineering*, SE 2, pp. 308–320, 1976.

119. McCall, J. A., P. K. Richards and G. F. Walters, *Factors in Software Quality*, RADC-TR-77-363 Rome Air Development Center, Griffis Air Force, Rome, NY, 1977.

120. McGinley, J. and G. Hunter (eds), *Catalogue of Software Quality Assessment Procedures—Catalogue Guide*, SCOPE Consortium, 1992.

121. Möller K. H. and D. Paulish, *Software Metrics—A Practitioner's Guide to Improved Software Development*, Prentice-Hall, Englewood Cliffs, NJ, 1993.

122. Morgan, C., *Schemas in Z—A Preliminary Reference Manual*, Oxford University PRG, (Programming Research Group), 1984.

123. Musa, J. D. and A. F. Ackermann, 'Quantifying software validation: when to stop testing?', *IEEE Software*, May 1989.

124. Musa, J. D., A. Iannino and K. Okumoto, *Software Reliability—Measurement, Prediction and Application*, McGraw-Hill, New York, 1987.

125. Myers, G. J., *The Art of Software Testing*, Wiley, Milan, 1979.

126. Neil, M. D., 'Statistical modelling of software metrics', PhD Thesis, South Bank University, 1992.

127. Neil, M. D., 'Multivariate assessment of software products', *Journal of Software Testing, Verification and Reliability*, 1 (4), pp. 17–37, 1991.

128. NAMAS Information Sheet NIS35, *Interpretation of Accreditation Requirements for IT Test Laboratories for Software and Communication Testing Services*, NAMAS Executive, National Physics Laboratory, UK, November 1990.

129. de Neumann, B. and G. Bazzana, 'A methodology for the assessment/certification of software', *3rd European Conference on Software Quality, Madrid*, November 1992.

130. de Neumann, B., 'Software certification and a relativistic software reliability model', to appear in *Bulletin of the IMA*.

131. de Neumann, B., 'Application of mathematic axiomatics to software', *Bulletin of IMA*, March 1990.

132. Paulk, M. C., B. Curtis and M. B. Chrissis, *Capability Maturity Model for Software*, Techn. Report CMU/SEI-91-TR-24, Software Engineering Institute, Carnegie-Mellon University, Pittsburgh, 1991.

133. Peterson, J. L., *Petri Net Theory and Modelling of Systems*, Prentice-Hall, Englewood Cliffs, NJ, 1981.

134. Porteous, M. and J. Kirakowski, *Software Usability Measurement Inventory Handbook*, 3rd edition, MUSIC Project, 1992.

135. Program Validation Ltd., *SPADE Brochure*.

136. Pyramid Consortium, *Best Practices of Software Metrics*, Reference: Y91210-3, April 1991.

137. Pyramid Consortium, *Quantitative Management: Get a Grip on Software*, Reference: Y91100-4, December 1991.

138. Rex, Thompson and Partners Software Ltd., *MALPAS Executive Guide*, 1989.

139. Robert, P., *SCOPE, Achievements and Perspectives*, Commission of the European Communities, Proceedings of Esprit Week, 1991.

140. Robert, P. and F. Seigneur, 'A modular approach to software assessment: the brick concept', *Proceedings of Eurometrics*, March 1991.
141. Rumi, G. (ed.), *C Portability Brick*, SCOPE Consortium, 1992.
142. Salvaneschi, P., A. Boninsegna, D. Pina and R. Zambetti, 'Tailoring V&V plans through expert system technology', *3rd European Conference on Software Quality, Madrid*, 1992.
143. SCOPE Consortium, *Survey of European Certification Context*, September 1991.
144. SCOPE Consortium, *Technical Annexe*, Version 3, 1991.
145. Schneidewind, N. F., 'Methodology for validating software metrics', *IEEE Transactions on Software Engineering*, **18** (5), pp. 410–422, May 1992.
146. Schulmeyer, G. G. and J. J. McManus, *Total Quality Management for Software*, Van Nostrand Reinhold, New York, 1992.
147. Shepperd, M. and D. Ince, 'Algebraic validation of software metrics', *3rd European Software Engineering Conference, ESEC '91, Milano, Proceedings*, pp. 343–363, Springer, October 1991.
148. Silver, B., 'TQM vs the SEI capability maturity model', *Software Quality World*, **4** (2), 1992.
149. Souter, J. B. and D. P. Cheney, 'Information technology quality system certification in Europe', *Proceedings of the 3rd European Conference on Software Quality, Madrid*, 1992.
150. Sundman, S. and N. Bradburn, *Asking Questions: A Practical Guide to Questionnaire Design*, Jossey-Bass, San Francisco, 1985.
151. Troy, R. and R. Moawed, 'Assessment of software reliability models', *IEEE Transactions on Software Engineering*, **SE-11** (3), pp. 839–849, 1985.
152. Underwriters Laboratories Inc., *Proposed First Edition of the Standard for Safety-Related Software, UL 1992*, Underwriters Laboratories Inc, August 1992.
153. US Department of Commerce, *Malcolm Baldrige National Quality Award 1990 Application Guidelines*, 1990.
154. Verilog SA, *Logiscope—Technical Presentation*, 1992.
155. Woda, H. and W. Schynoll (eds), *IPSS—European International Conference on Lean Software Development*, Stuttgart, October 1992.
156. XIE, *Software Reliability Modelling*, World Scientific, Singapore, 1992.
157. X/OPEN, *X/OPEN Portability Guide*, July 1985.
158. Yourdon, E., *Structured Walkthroughs*, 2nd edition, Prentice-Hall, Englewood Cliffs, NJ, 1977.
159. Züse, H., *Software Complexity: Measures and Methods*, de Gruyter, Berlin, 1990.
160. Züse, H., 'Properties of software metrics,' *1st International Conference on Software Quality, Dayton*, October 1991.

All SCOPE deliverables can be requested from Etnoteam SpA, Via A. Bono Cairoli 34, Milan, Italy, the CEC, or the prime contractor, Verilog S.A., Toulouse, France (contact Philippe Robert, Project Manager). Pyramid and Bootstrap deliverables can be obtained from the CEC or Etnoteam.

INDEX

Anomaly checking, 60, 238
Argo, 194
Assessment, 50–52
  definition, of, 11, 238
  modules, 204

Batch mode, 133
Benchmarking, 21
Black-box:
  models, 110
  product assessment, 22
  testing, 75, 238
BOOTSTRAP project, 16
Bricks, 204, 227
BUILD tool, 192

Callgraph, 66, 68
Case studies, 149–182, 202–206
Certification:
  definition of, 11, 238
  from assessment, 216
Checklist manager, 83, 121–123, 239
Checklists, 82, 160–166, 239
Common metrics format (CMF),
  143–145, 239
Common pool, 96, 239
Compiler validation, 17
Component, 40, 239
Compound module, 42, 239
Configuration data, 141
Conformance Testing Services, 17
Control flowgraph, 66, 67
Cyclomatic number, 46, 50, 95, 148

Data collection, politics of, 215–216
Data transfer, 142–144
Database, 135–148, 175, 191–192
DDP coverage, 81, 93
Department of Defense (US), 17
Descriptive statistics, 89

Efficiency, 31, 75, 83
EN 45000 series standards, 4, 217–219
Encryption, 147
Evaluation, definition of, 11, 239
Event, 44
Execution analysis, 56, 239
External attributes, 49, 239

Failure data, 76
Fenton, Norman, 38, 49
Fenton-Whitty theory, 69
Flat file, 136, 239
Flint, 61
Formal methods, 110
Functionality, 29, 73, 75, 79, 83, 178

GGS scheme, 22, 60, 75, 205
Granularity, 48, 95, 239

Halstead's metrics, 64–65
Hewlett-Packard, 5, 24

IMQ, 224–227
Industrial domain, 175–182
Inspection, 58, 82, 239
Internal attributes, 49, 240

IQUAL, 197–198
ISO 9000, 3, 15
ISO 9126, 3, 13, 25, 27–35, 199, 210, 221

Kirkwood, Kenneth, 115

Lint, 61, 123–129, 196
Logiscope, 64, 69, 81, 100, 129–131, 196
  batch mode, 133
  flat files, 137, 142

Maintainability, 32, 63, 68, 83, 178
  spot-check, 175
Management by metrics, 12, 24
Measurement theory, 45–48
Metrics, 12, 240
  aggregating, 94
  collection, 36
  framework, 37
  standardization, 147
Metrics scheme, 5
Metropol, 69
MicroScope service, 180
Ministry of Defence (UK), 17
Modelling, 58, 85, 240
Models:
  data, 39
  evaluation process, 33
  product and process, 39–45
Module, 42, 240
Multicollinearity, 94

Naming conventions, 145–147, 240
Neil, Martin, 158
Non-operational testing, 56
Normal distribution, 90

Operational profile, 105
Operational testing, 56, 240
Outliers, 91, 96–98, 240

PCTE, 184
Portability, 32, 60, 83
Prediction, from metrics, 50–52, 166–171
Process assessment, 12
Process certification, 2, 226
  general, 15
  specific, 16
Process data, 86–87
Product Approval Scheme (PAS), 23
Product assessment, 12, 13

Product check-up scheme, 176

Qualigraph, 69
QUALMS, 69, 97, 100, 129
  batch mode, 134
  flat files, 137, 142
Quality, 1
  definition of, 3

Reliability, 29, 60, 77, 83, 105–111, 166–171, 178
Reliability models, 77, 107, 114, 240
Repository, 40, 135
REQUEST project, 5, 9, 40, 192
Right Writer tool, 64
Robust statistics, 91
RULER, 132, 154

Scales of measurement, 47, 92
SCOPE project, 7, 13, 40, 54, 112, 135, 149, 175, 183
  evaluation method, 219–224
Session data collection systems, 114–121, 142, 166, 240
SMARTIE project, 175
Source code, 42
SRM package, 116, 166, 170
Standardization, 216
Standards, 217–219
Static analysis, 55, 150
Structural analysis, 66, 171–173, 240
Structured programming, 154
Style tool, 64
Subsystem, 42, 240
Survey, of software assessment, 2, 207
SWDL project, 5, 9, 40, 192
System, 42, 240

Task, 44
TASQUE, 198
TEFAX, 73, 176, 196
Ten steps, 203
Test coverage, 79, 171–173
Test cross-referencing, 71–74
Testing, 56, 240
Textual measurement, 63, 240
Theories, 39, 50, 52
Threshold, 99, 240
Tick-IT, 15

Usability, 31, 64, 75, 83

Workbench, 183–200